Alex Protheroe

Embracing Italy

A Gunner's "Grand Tour" during Wartime

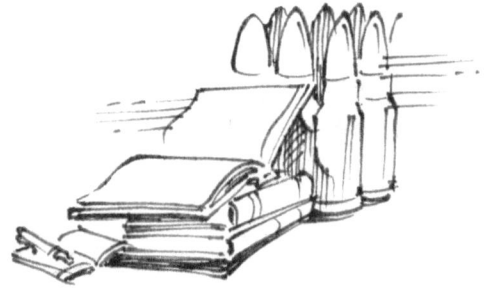

The diary and letters home
of a New Zealand artilleryman
in Italy, 1944-46

editor:
Simon Protheroe

ISBN 9798678438812

Also by Simon Protheroe
"Hullabaloo and Other Stories"

Open my heart and you will see
Graved inside of it, "Italy."
Robert Browning
(1812-89)
De Gustibus

Italia! oh Italia! thou who hast
The fatal gift of beauty.
Lord Byron
'Childe Harold's Pilgrimage'
(1812-18) canto 4, st. 42

There is a pleasure in the pathless woods
Childe Harold's Pilgrimage'
(1812-18) canto 4, st. 178

In memory of
our great uncle,
Murdoch Keith Macleod,
died of his wounds
Passchendaele, 1917

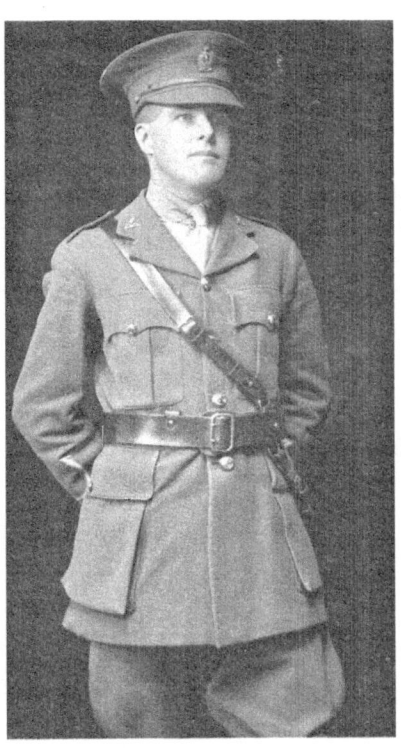

Table of Contents

The Little Red Book

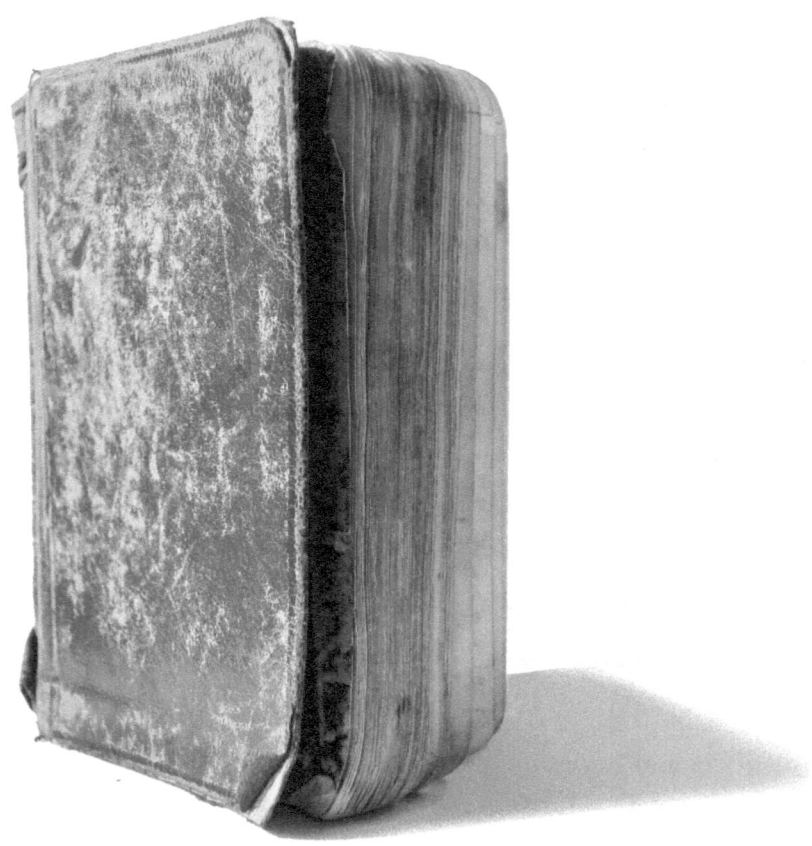

Alex's pocket diary (3"x 5") is the primary source for this book.

Foreword

I clearly remember the day we made our way through their assorted papers. Our parents Alex and Margaret Protheroe had just died leaving to us three sons Paul, Simon and Guy with a sensitive task —to take care of the last material vestiges of their once vibrant personalities. Despite our grief, this process proved to be surprising, bemusing, inspiring or bewildering in equal measure. Questions arose, such as: "Who is this person in this photograph?" or, "Where does this event fit into the overall picture?" It lead us down various byways. Mysteries were cleared up, but then new ones were created. And what a mess there was! Files, books and papers were strewn around the living room floor; documents exuded from old cardboard boxes. At first, the sorting seemed random—almost chaotic—with a lot of give and take being given over who got what, and what should be kept and what should be discarded, yet much of this stuff—the yellowing papers and the dogged-eared photos—turned out to be treasures in disguise.

The Little Red Book

By chance, Alex's wartime diary befell to me; Paul and Guy got the bulk of Alex's letters home. Sadly, Margaret's letters to Alex were nowhere to be found, probably because they could not be carried or were not shipped home. We shared out the photographs more equally. At first glance, the diary looked innocuous; it was small, red and sporting the Whitcombe's bookstore label. Perhaps because it was so worn and unworthy-looking it was overlooked in the rush. In hindsight, the state of it should have tipped us off. It suggested an item both treasured and kept close at hand.

It was not until I thought about it later that I realized the state of it spoke of his motivation. Living on the knife edge of life and death where each day could be his last must have focussed his mind on what is important. Yet his first efforts seem tentative at best. After landing in Taranto, was he too caught up in the moment to take the time to write?

But then, he began to elaborate. It must have been a conscious choice, like the decision he made in the early months of his deployment to learn Italian. And like learning Italian, taking up a diary would have required dedication—a routine. This would have required him setting aside a certain time each day, maybe at bedtime, to jot down a few recollections, and in times of crisis when keeping up was impossible, him making a concerted effort to catch up. The result of his efforts is a complete text, even when the entry is just one word or two; that is until a week before the end of the hostilities when mysteriously, he abruptly ended his entries in a moment of suspense as if he had deliberately torn out the last page of a mystery novel. My suspicion is that events overtook him, but this time, he never got back to recording the missing days. In fact, the diary was abandoned at this point.

The letters and other sources

Thankfully, many of his letters home were saved. To a degree, they fill in gaps in the narrative. As there were so many letters coming to him from New Zealand, responding must have occupied a considerable amount of his spare time. However, the letters in this book are exclusively to Margaret. All the others are lost to us. With his letters to Margaret, his primary concern seems to reassure her that he was safe, which he did while scrupulously complying with military censorship rules. Mentioning military planning of any sort was, as he said, "strictly verboten," but looking backward—letting Margaret know where he had just been, and not where he was going—was within the rules. Thus many of the letters have the quality of travelogues, which, in addition to making them safe for sending, gave him an opportunity to opine and describe. As such, the letters are useful in giving insight into his personality and attitudes—in what interested him. They are also educational; they give us a glimpse of an Italy that no longer exists, one more deeply rooted in tradition than now. Unlike the diary, the letters never deal with the actual war.

In addition to being a direct communication with Margaret—they show a real affection of a young husband for his wife and child—the letters serve a similar purpose to the diary. They keep track of events for his, as well as Margaret's, benefit. We know this because he numbered the letters so that they could be kept in chronological order. The numbering system showed how often he wrote, but the gaps in the numbering also point out how many letters have disappeared over the years. Still

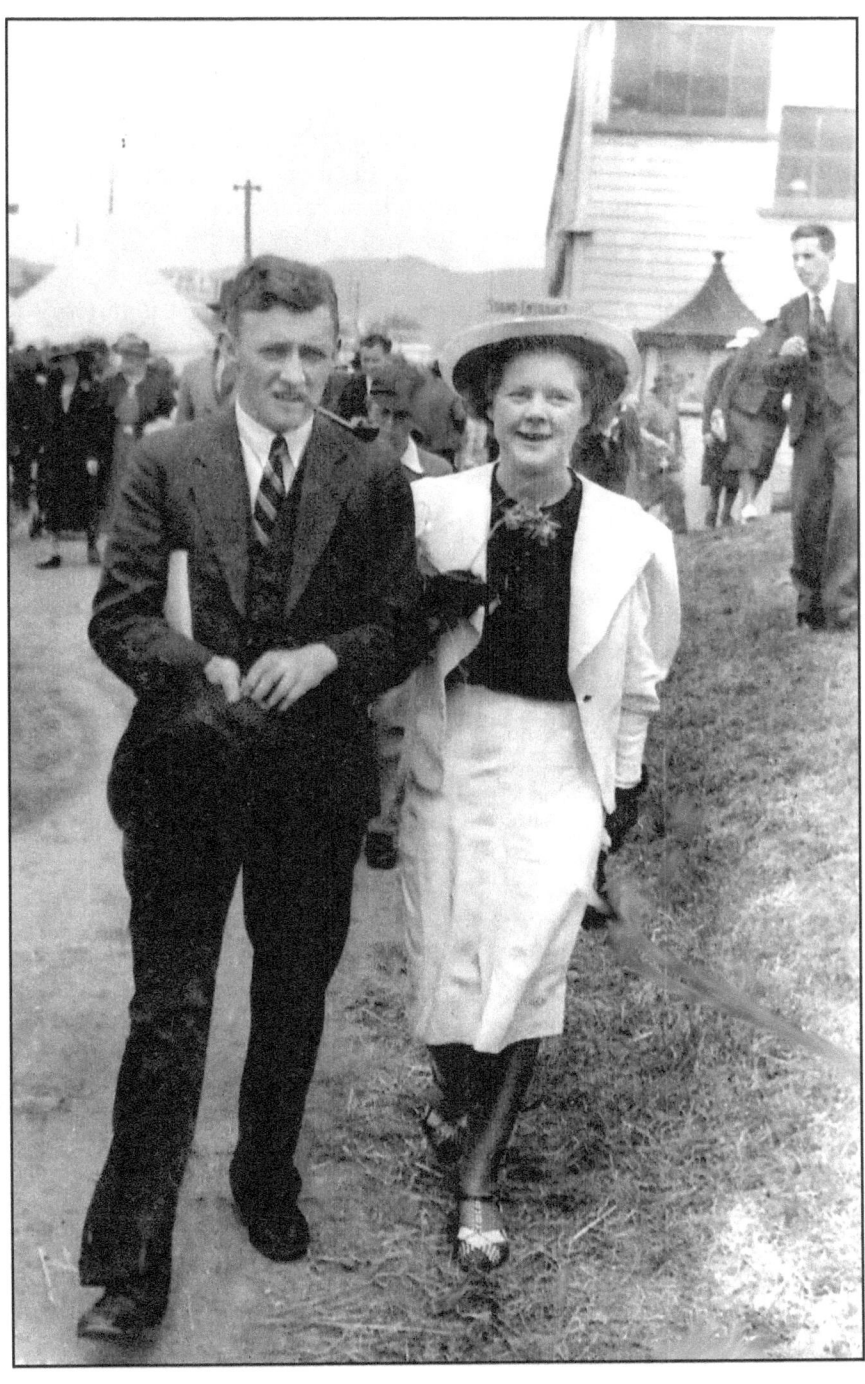

Alex and Margaret Protheroe

others appear uncannily similar to his diary entries, and so I suspect he used his diary as a template when he was churning them out. To avoid duplication, I have opted for the diary versions as they are more contemporaneous thus avoiding unnecessary breaks in forward momentum of the storyline. To paint a fuller picture of the course of events, lines from the letters not included in the diary have been added.

However, after May of 1945, we are left solely with his letters to advance the narrative. They cover the period of the occupation of Trieste by New Zealand forces and the subsequent standoff over the fate of the city with Tito's Yugoslavian forces after VE Day. They also deal with the concerns he had over potentially being deployed against Japan. The final draft of letters following VJ day deal with peacetime concerns. They deal with his job as an educator, his continuing University studies, and with how the shortage of ships was an impediment to him returning home. Apart from the diary and letters, anecdotes from our collective memories add to the mix. Another major source of information is his military and health records.

Acknowledgements

I want to thank my brother Paul for requesting them from the National Archives in Wellington. They were particularly useful in clarifying his army career in New Zealand before he left for Italy, which was more nuanced than we previously knew. Also, I need to thank Victoria University for permission to reproduce an article Alex wrote postwar while employed at the War History division of Internal Affairs, Wellington. Victoria University hold the rights to all those particular publications. To avoid the danger of duplication in the storyline, another much longer article that Alex wrote on the Italian campaign that could have been included has been left out although it is still on file at the Archives. I hope to read it someday.

And I must extend my thanks to my brothers Guy and Paul for assembling, editing, and typing up most of the letters. It was a big job. Thanks also go to Ashley Smith and Mary Clark for some choice anecdotes. Ashley Smith also created the maps and title page graphic. Anne-Marie Chisnall used her skills as a book editor to make a more professional product. I am deeply grateful for that help. Mary Clark also helped by providing the photograph of Second Lieutenant Murdoch Keith Macleod, born 6 October, 1890, who was our great uncle on our mother's side. Uncle Keith died of his wounds at Passchendaele on October 13, 1917 and was, before going overseas, one of the architects that worked on a Christchurch landmark, the Sign of the Kiwi in the Port Hills. And of course, we will have to belatedly thank Alex for his diary, letters, photos and for saving all the Italian wartime postcards he brought home.

A final piece of the puzzle needs to be acknowledged. It is a piece that was both mysterious and controversial. We grew up with the knowledge that Alex had a "friend" with whom he was corresponding for a time. "She" was a "widow," and later, after he died, we saw a picture of Alex standing beside a youngish Italian woman. Although he was adamant their relationship was purely platonic, we could not help but draw conclusions. When sorting through his stuff, her letters were found in an army kit bag stuffed on the top shelf of our storeroom. The fact that he kept them, even after forty-four years, meant they still held a special significance for him. We had them translated thanks to Paul's friend, Susan Jacobs of Auckland.

This is what we learned: Late in 1945, while on leave in Chianciano Terme, a spa town in southern Tuscany, (A location that brings to mind the spa scenes in Federico Fellini's "8½."), Alex met Celeste Cussoni. It was at one of the nightly dances held there. She was part of a group from the town of Grotte di Castro, near Viterbo in central Italy, presumably there to "take the waters." Despite the potential for scandal, it seems their friendship was short, only lasting a few days. The two letters left to us have been included unexpurgated. We don't know if any more letters exist, but if there were, they are gone, perhaps destroyed. Yet the letters we have, written with such simplicity and dignity, speak volumes. They might have cleared the air for us permanently as to the nature of their relationship.

Why the book?

This brings me to the impetus for writing the book. At first, I must confess I did not pay too much attention to the diary. I said that I will look at it in due course. Years passed, then for no apparent reason, I picked it up. Reluctantly, I thumbed through it, then I began read. While deciphering the microscopic handwriting and by checking on a map the places mentioned, I became engaged. This tiny book opened up a world that had always been a mystery. A picture of Alex's life in the army emerged.

All our lives, we had heard anecdotes from his time overseas—the one about killing a black snake with his shovel while digging a trench particularly comes to mind—but they were just anecdotes devoid of context. Yet there must have been reasons for our lack of knowledge. Perhaps it was because, like many of his generation, Alex was loathed to discuss his war experiences, or was it that we were too circumspect to ask?

I suspect it is more out of reluctance on his part, not so much because it was a big secret, but more because there appeared to be an ill-defined line that he chose not to cross. I wondered why this was so. Was it because he sensed it as unseemly to boast over his wartime exploits when so many had done—had given—so much more? Or was it because, like many of his fellow citizen/soldiers, he chose to look ahead, plowing his energies into his career and raising a family. Maybe that was it. Then again, another potential factor is at play: Paul said recently—and this surprised me—that Alex, during those early postwar years, still had nightmares from what he had seen in battle. Perhaps he was just wanting to forget.

One presumes, however, that on at least one day of the year memories of the war were aired more readily. That was on ANZAC Day, April 25th. It commemorates the day in 1915 when Australian and New Zealand troops landed at Anzac Cove in the Dardanelles of Turkey as a part of Churchill's plan to take Turkey out of the war. Despite the heroism of the troops, the campaign ended in withdrawal. Unquestionably, Gallipoli was a military fiasco, but it was also there, in the fulcrum of battle, that the identities of two newly-formed colonial nations were forged. For the first time, it seemed that men fought and died as Australians and New Zealanders, not as transposed Britishers. As a result, April 25th has become a day of remembrance. On that day veterans of World War II— those that once lived, and the very few that might remain—acknowledge their military service. With their medals pinned to the lapels of their suits, Alex and his fellow gunners would march at dawn and place wreaths at the Cenotaph before adjourning to a local pub and take a few drinks. (We assume) it was there, in that "sacred" space of the bar that they would spill the beans. With the alcohol flowing, they would put aside their self-imposed inhibitions and talk about the good times and those that never returned.

And so now, we the progeny of the World War II generation, particularly those of us that never served, have been given yet another opportunity to glimpse the universality of war through one man's eyes. We can pique our curiosity without the fear of touching upon the raw nerves of those who were there, for surely enough time has passed; at this point we will not be offending anybody's sensitivities.

As to the content of the diary itself as the book's primary source—it speaks for itself. Written with a reporter's eye—mostly, dispassionately and simply—the diary and letters have survived the test of time well, although by modern standards, Alex was not always "politically correct."

But should we judge Alex by our current mores? As to his character, the focus of his interests and his reactions to the pressures of army life create a cumulative impression. We derive further clues to his personality through what is left unsaid. We can read between the lines as one might do through reading the sparse prose of Ernest Hemingway.

Finally, a large part of this story is of one man's fascination with Italy, its people, language, geography and its ancient culture, even though it was an Italy diminished by war. The text shows that his knowledge of Italian history and art was substantial. It is for this reason that I have subtitled the book *A Gunner's "Grand Tour" during Wartime* in deference to the English aristocrats of the nineteenth century—Browning, Keats, Shelley and Byron in particular—who went to Italy to find themselves. Of course, for Alex, being in Italy was no lark, but it is easy to see that he knew how to take advantage of the situation while, at the same time, rueing the interruption made to his career and life at home. But how could he have been there under the extremest of circumstances and not want to see and do all he could. In a way, this quest interested him more than soldiering, so that after battle was done when his duties as a soldier were fulfilled and the needs for spit and polish met, that was when his story really began. It was during these times that he wrote most effusively; him seeing the sights, him exploring ideas with his cobbers; him cultivating his personal interests. These were the precious moments that helped him mollify the stresses of his life on the guns—the long hours spent in the field without sleep, handling heavy shells and equipment in difficult terrain, digging in and setting up, the dangers of explosions both accidental and from enemy fire, sleeping rough and being out in all weathers—and the prolonged effects from the din of battle on his hearing!

Finally, this story speaks to larger issues—the banality of violence, how killing at a distance becomes routinized, how soldiers become desensitized over time. Yet we are thankful that men like Alex were willing to take up the fight, although it was a tragedy that their service was necessary at all. And thank goodness that among countless millions that fought in the anti-Nazi cause, Alex was on the side that was able to wear down and ultimately thwart, once and for all, Hitler's warped ambitions.

Introduction

THE PERCEPTION THAT NEW ZEALAND'S role in both World Wars was minor is easily dispelled by the facts. For a small country located on the periphery of the world stage, its role was outsized both in terms of the overall role it played in the war effort, and the losses it endured. With a population of a mere 1.1 million, sixteen thousand died in the First World War; another twelve thousand died in the Second out of 1.6 million, yet throughout this entire period the relationship between Britain and its the ANZAC partners—New Zealand and Australia—remained steadfast. And such was the strength of the bond that when Britain declared war at 9:30 p.m. on 3 September, 1939, it took the then New Zealand Prime Minister, Michael Joseph Savage, just two hours to follow suit.

The mobilization that followed—slow at first in the wake of the Depression—was soon all-encompassing. By 1940, New Zealand troops of the 2nd NZEF (New Zealand Expeditionary Force) were already serving in the British 8th Army, both against Axis forces in the deserts of North Africa, and in the defense of Greece. Then in Crete, New Zealand infantrymen heroically faced down and were defeated at the airfields at Maleme by elite German paratroopers during the invasion of 1941. Many died on both sides, and in defeat many more were taken prisoner in that ill-fated campaign.

My father was not a part of that first wave. Objectively, he could have been. Born on 13 March, 1916, Alexander George Protheroe, being just twenty-three in 1939, was of a perfect age for conscription had there been any at that point. Ironically, an exemption from conscription might have already saved him from the outset since during the First World War, his father George was exempted because of his reserved occupation so that he neither went overseas nor saw battle.

As for Alex (or Alec) and his sister, Mona, having a father at home was undoubtedly a blessing they would have taken for granted, unaware

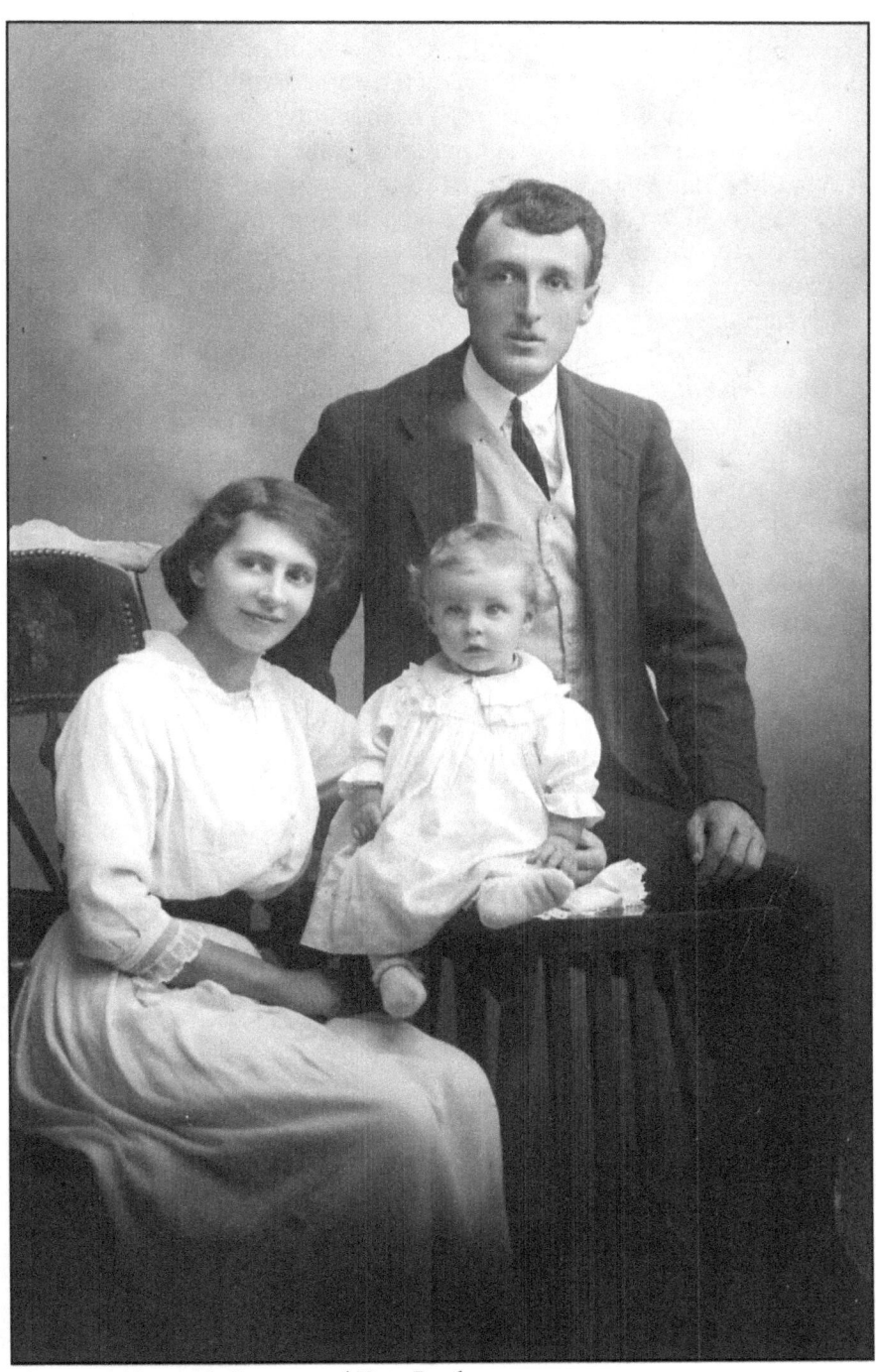

A young Alex with George and Kate Protheroe

as they would have been of the carnage happening far across the sea. What effect this seemingly normal thing had on them is impossible to judge for how could they have predicted the coming turmoil? Nor how will we ever know whether glimpses of the ambition, intellect and sense of duty, the hallmarks of his adult personality, were evident then?

What we know for sure is that Alex's mother, Katherine ("Kate") Broughton, who was born and grew up in England, emigrated to New Zealand partly due to her unhappiness over her widowed mother marrying a Frenchman she did not like. She left England in 1914 just as war was declared. Heading south to the underbelly of the world without knowing a soul was undoubtedly a gamble and an act of courage, but it paid off when she met her future husband George Protheroe at a dance.

They were soon married. Even in the darkest days of the war, the prospect for a happy family life for Kate and George seemed assured. George's work as a guard at the Paparoa Prison, near Christchurch, provided the stability and income they needed, and his reputed popularity with the inmates helped make a difficult job more palatable and their lives together easier, and so in a cottage close to the prison in semi-rural Templeton located on the main highway south, George, Kate, Alex, and Mona (born in 1917) settled down.

Yet tragically, the promise for a normal life was cut short. In 1918, the Spanish flu swept through the land, and George was laid low by it. Then, with his system severely compromised, a bout of pneumonia took him the following year. With no direct family roots in Christchurch, and with the prospect of only the Widow's and Orphan's Benefit to survive on, Kate was forced to manage as best she could. We were told that for a time the children were placed in an orphanage, although the evidence of this at this point is only anecdotal. So is the reason for their stay there; whether it was out of poverty, or whether it was due to Kate briefly returning to England to see her aging mother. Still, either way, the abandonment must have been a time of deep trauma and dislocation for such small children.

Eventually, George Protheroe's death led the family to move south to George's hometown, Ashburton, a place that is still essentially the same agricultural hub it was then. There, on the Canterbury plain amongst the waving grain and in the shadow of the Southern Alps, they started over, close by members of her late husband's family.

This was in the 1920s, and as the trauma of war and the fallout from the flu epidemic faded, life eventually assumed a semblance of normalcy. Kate found a cottage near the town Domain and the children attended

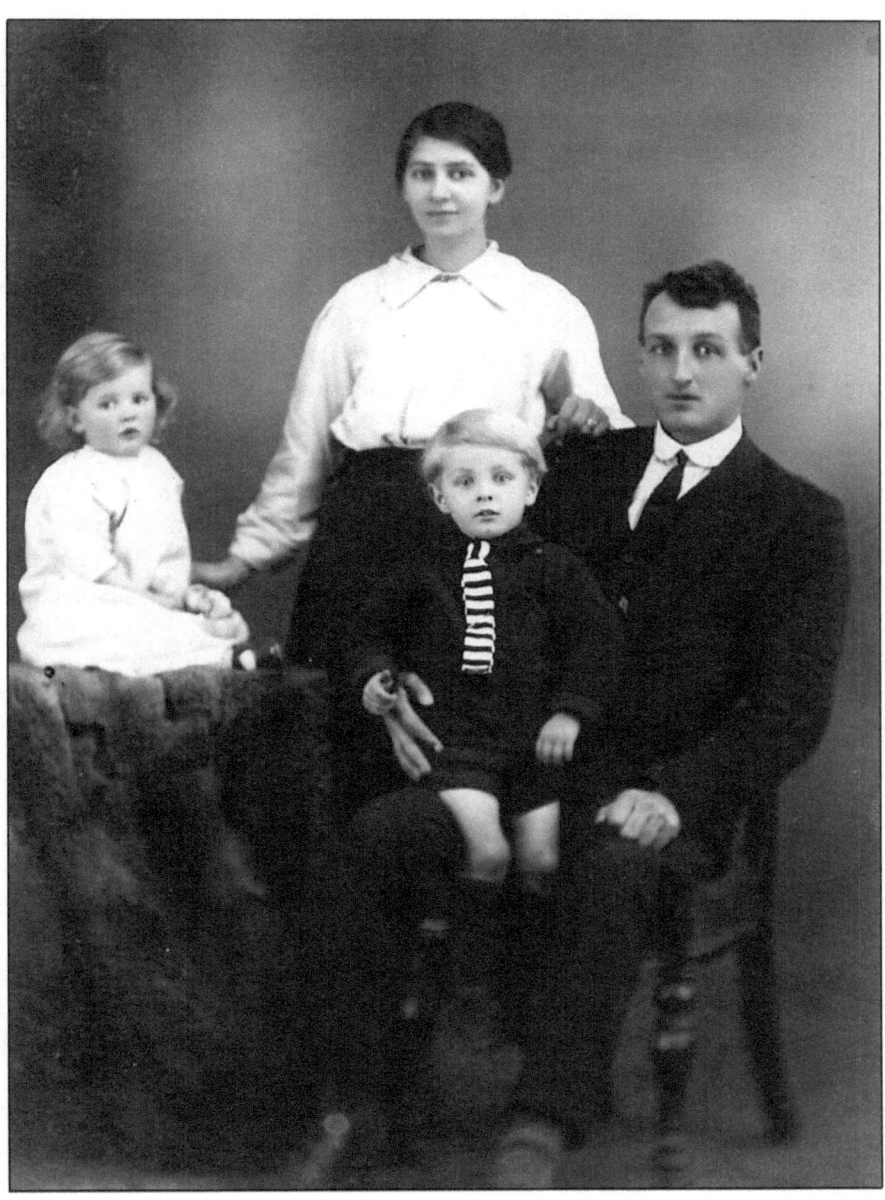

Mona, Katherine, Alex and George, circa 1918

local schools, first the local primary school, then in the case of Alex, Ash-burton High School in 1929. Testimonials from teachers produced later describe him as a dedicated and diligent student. Mona remembers him doing his schoolwork by candlelight. To survive, we believe Kate took in sewing, and returned to doing domestic work, and despite being only twenty-eight at the time of George's death, she appeared to have shown little interest in remarrying, despite being engaged for a time to a local landowner before breaking it off with him when she caught him in a lie. She would remain single until her death at age 102.

Alex himself had a different take on his childhood, particularly on his education. Growing up in a small town environment, he felt burdened by the low expectations of his teachers and school administrators towards him. In a letter written much later, he complained how he was actively discouraged from pursuing a classical education, specifically in the study of Latin.

I now understand more how these childhood experiences helped mold his adult personality. Throughout his life, Alex's politics and views on life were essentially conservative and traditional. Even in those years immediately before the war, when the left-leaning Labour Party totally dominated politics, he remained a stalwart for the conservative cause. His values were a reflection of his deep allegiance to social institutions of the time: school, the church, family, the British Empire. If you read Alex's schoolboy essays you get the picture of the way he saw the world. They were full of effusive patriotic sentiments, expressions of faith in the institutions of Empire, a belief that New Zealand was and should remain a part of the British family of nations indefinitely. In one school essay, he described how proud he was of all the red—the color of Empire—girding the globe, seeing it from the point of view of a loyal New Zealander looking north across the vastness of the Pacific at the nations united under the umbrella of King and Country.

Yet with the losses of war being so extreme, one might conclude that New Zealanders would have chosen a different path forward in the aftermath of so much suffering—that in disaster those left to pick up the pieces would become warier of further foreign entanglements. Yet the opposite occurred: New Zealand cleaved tighter to the concept of Empire as the best way of ensuring survival, this despite losing a generation of young men—a loss expressed through the proliferation of war memorials in every small town, losses that helped reinforce prevailing attitudes to stay the course.

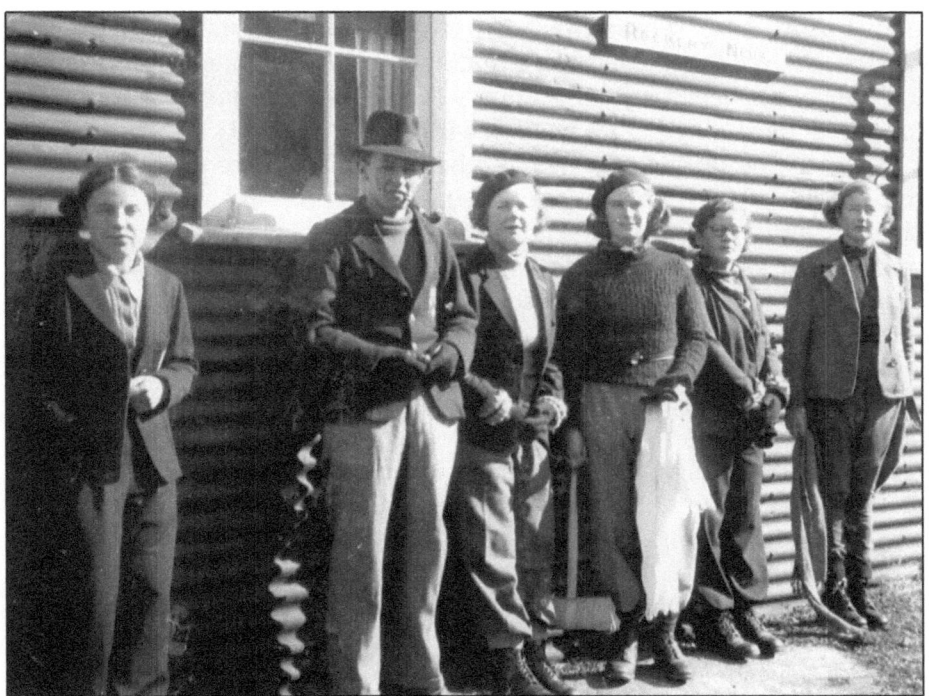

With future in-laws at Arthur's Pass, August 21st, 1938, with Margaret, Margaret's sisters, Jean and Hilary (far right) and Joyce Kidd, (far left).

And with the slow healing, along with a steady, if unspectacular growth in prosperity boosted by incremental improvements in New Zealand agricultural productivity, the prospects for a better future seem assured. So with Britain still willing to absorb the bulk of New Zealand exports and provide almost all of its imported manufactured goods, the thought of changing economic horses midstream was neither contemplated nor needed. The relationship with Britain was therefore thought of only in positive terms. It was hardly surprising, therefore, that even up until the 1960s, such were the strength of these ties that many New Zealanders still talked of Britain as "home," even when they were not born there. This was the environment that nurtured Alex as a boy.

But then, the decade of the twenties ended abruptly; so did the good times. In Alex's early teen years, the Depression hit hard. He was forced to leave high school after just three years when he was fifteen. He found work in a foundational New Zealand industry, a wool store. It would have been warehouse work then with a young and slightly built Alex helping a sorter move around hundredweight bales of wool to the various staging points. How long he was there is a mystery, yet of this I am sure, the dreams he had for himself were undimmed. He remained committed to his education, rejecting his mother's Depression-era inspired ambition for him of becoming a railway clerk with steady pay and a pension.

Instead he put his energies into being a cub reporter to the Ashburton branch of the Christchurch paper, *"The Press,"* and while attending classes at the Ashburton Technical High School, joined various groups, notably the St. Stephen's Literary and Social Club where he was secretary, the Ashburton Sports Association where he took up competitive cross-country running, and, in 1934, the Territorials as a volunteer reservist.

Yet before long, the inevitable happened. Ashburton would be just a stepping stone for him; his cub reporting a springboard to the Christchurch office of *"The Press,"* and his education his ticket to the Canterbury University College. He began taking classes in 1938, and in 1939 was awarded the undergraduate Emsom Essay Prize, then in the following year, the Arnold Atkinson Memorial Prize. As a junior employee at *"The Press,"* he switched between assisting the literary staff, working on the agriculture desk and as a sub. Surprisingly, with the world tipping towards war, the dream of grander things refused to budge. In 1939, he garnered a testimonial from his employer—we still have that testimonial—for a gambit on Fleet Street, one that was, sadly, never to be as war intervened.

Those early years in Christchurch showed him as a young man on the move. He lived a life filled with activity, close friends and an active social life. This led, in May 1938, to romance when he met at a dance a young Margaret Macleod, a Christchurch girl and primary school teacher from an academic family of teachers and doctors. She was second of four children of Donald, a Doctor of Physics at Canterbury University College, and Nellie, a poet and writer. They lived in the Cashmere Hills in a house that looked out over the city.

But then war was declared on 3 September, 1939. This did not put a stop to everyday life, at the beginning anyway. It took three months before there was change when, in early December, Alex's association with the Press came to an abrupt end. We have correspondence to that effect. At this point, the cause for his rift with the editor is unknown, but it appears to be related to a breach of journalistic ethics. Then external events eclipsed this temporary setback.

By 1 April, 1940, the need for war readiness offered him an opportunity. He was transferred to Army Headquarters in the rank of sergeant

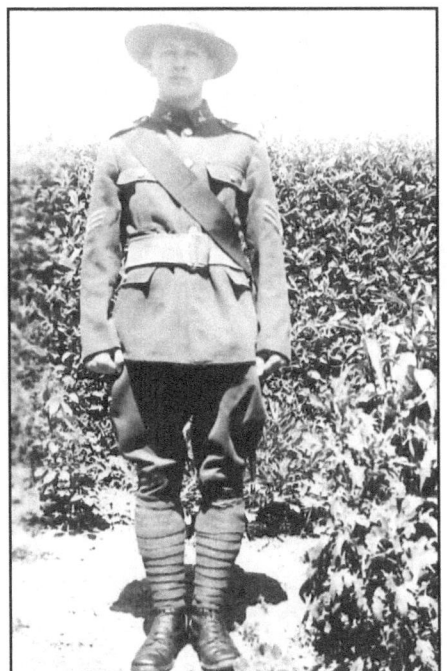

As a territorial

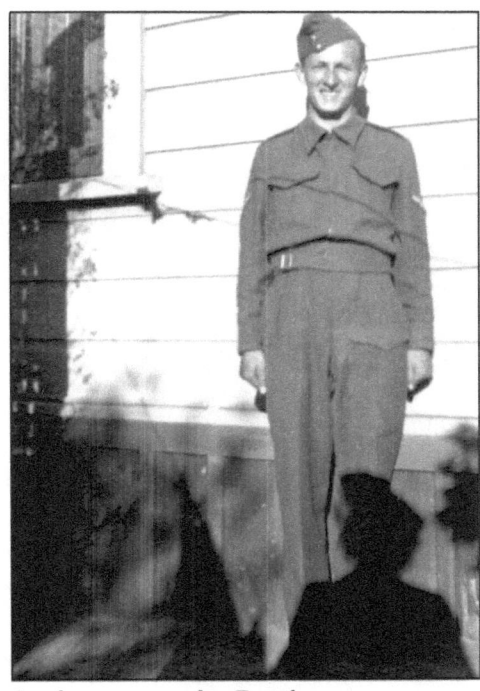

As a lance corporal at Trentham camp

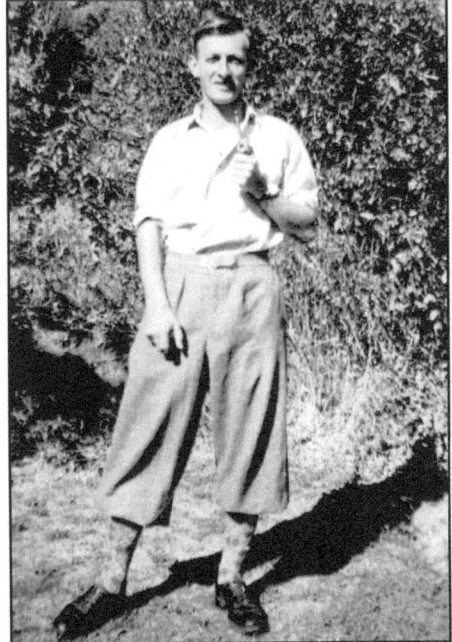

On civvy street

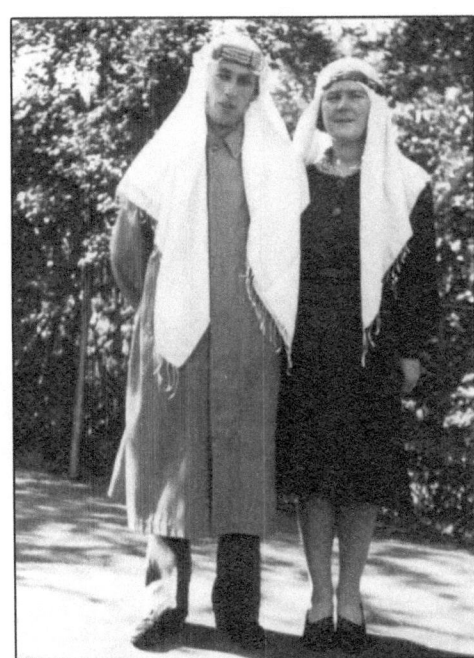

April 8, 1941

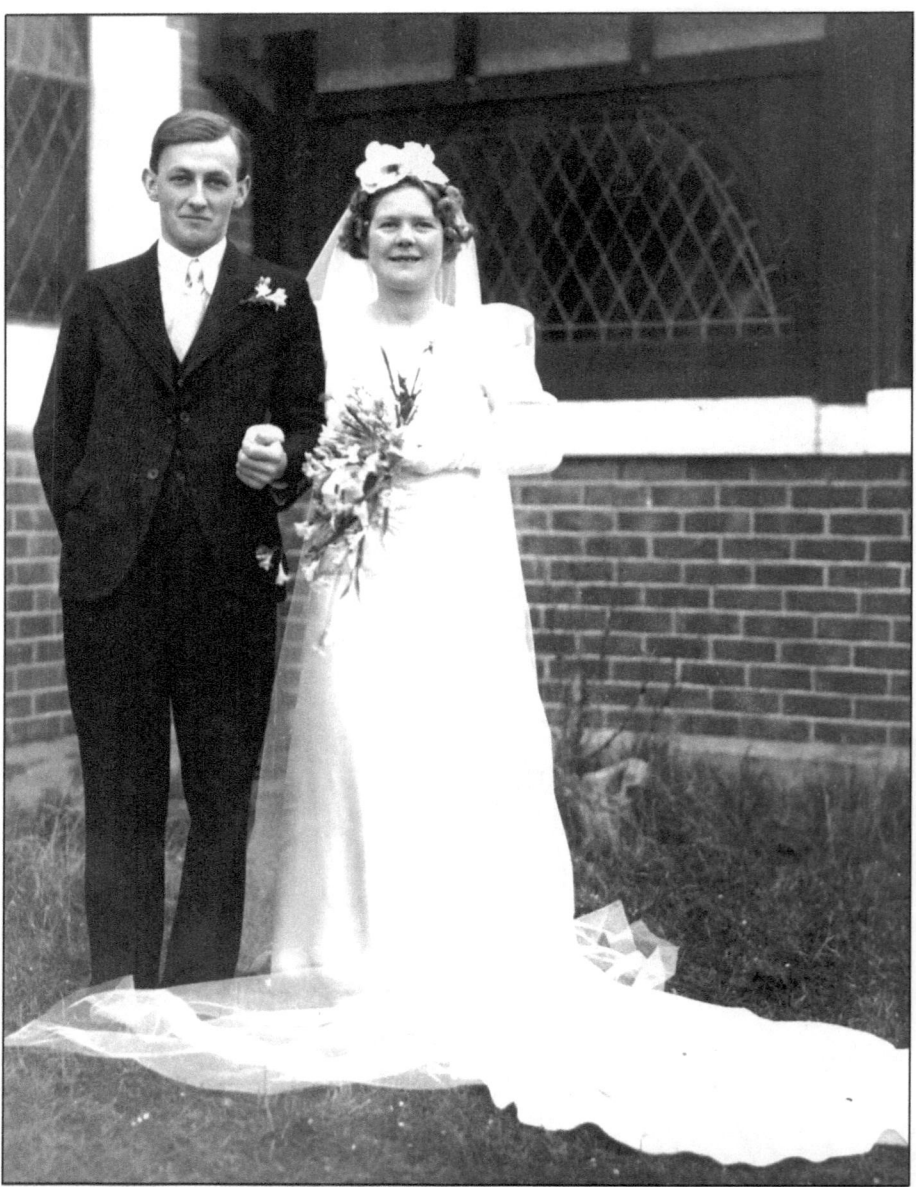

July 6, 1940: St. James's Methodist Church, Cashmere Hills, Christchurch

with "special duties," presumably while still a territorial. How long he was there, or in what these special duties were is also unknown, but it cannot have been long—a matter of months—so that by the time he volunteered both he and Margaret had already relocated to Wellington where he was employed by radio station 2YA in their news department.

That year proved to be a difficult one in New Zealand. With military recruitment levels failing to keep pace with need, the government was forced to reintroduce conscription in June. In light of this, volunteering must have been tough decision, yet perhaps because of his age and military status as a territorial, he knew that, although his time would come, he might not be amongst the first to go, and that while there was still time, he could control his military destiny, at least to a degree. Thus on 30 July, shortly after Margaret and Alex had their wedding of 6 July at St. James's Methodist Church in the Cashmere Hills, he made the leap. Alex put his name in for the 5th Reinforcements.

He did not go immediately into training. It was not until 7 January, 1941 that he entered the Trentham Camp, located just north of Wellington. At first, he was given the rank of temporary lance corporal. But soon health issues intervened. On 31 January, he was hospitalized for the first time with asthma, although the X-rays showed nothing significant. Meantime, plans for the 5th Reinforcements were moving forward with alacrity. It was the rapidity of these plans that alarmed Margaret, who with Alex in camp, was living alone in a small flat in the Wellington hills, at 18 Central Terrace, Kelburn. It soon became clear that her anxieties warranted a medical intervention, and she was given a diagnosis of "neurasthenia." The prospect of having Alex sent away was causing her to show classic signs of nervous exhaustion associated with the condition. It was recommended that Alex's mobilization be delayed. But then Alex reenrolled later through the 6th Reinforcements.

And then his old medical issues reasserted themselves. In March while in camp, the asthma flared up again, and, once more, he was briefly hospitalized, and so, on medical grounds, he was discharged from 2 NZEF—the active duty part of the army serving in Europe and North Africa—on 18 April, 1941. At this point, his military career seems to have become peripatetic. At first, he was given training at the School of Artillery at Fort Dorset, Wellington. Then there are letters that asked him to return to his duties in radio news that came to nought. Finally, he was given a trial for the Secret Intelligence Service, but was told afterwards that no position was available.

From there, he applied for and was accepted into the OCTU (Officer Cadet Training Unit.) In March, 1942 we find him back at Fort Dorset as a temporary 2nd Lieutenant, then in May, we learn of his experiences at the OCTU as described in his diary—how he looked forward to becoming an officer in the field, having already passed the requisite exams and received training on 25-pounders with live fire. It was not until 6 August, 1942, however, that his commission as a temporary 2nd Lieutenant was formally gazetted.

Ironically, during his officer training days, he was not directly involved in field artillery as you would expect, but was on a 74 H (Heavy) Antiaircraft Battery on Mt Victoria, then soon after at the 16th AA Regiment, then on 16 June, 1942, the 23rd Light AA Regiment. But then the record gets hazy. Later, in his diary, he harks back to 4 July, 1942 when as officer in charge on the Wellington docks, he remembers waiting at the Wellington Post Office with his sister-in-law, Hilary, for word of the birth in Christchurch of his first born, Judith. Was it possible that he was serving on the docks and with his AA unit simultaneously?

However, in one respect, the official records do confirm what we know from what we were told growing up, that at one stage he was involved with the Royal NZ Air Force. They show he was initially attached to RNZAF station Rongotai as a liaison officer with No 2 AA Coop Flight. From 26 October, 1942, his liaison work involved him coordinating with the Army and the Navy, and with U.S. military units in the area. For this he was highly commended by his superior officer, yet he was not officially transferred to the Air Force until 7 July, 1943. As a child, I remember being told how he missed getting his wings as a pilot after failing the physical, specifically the test in which a candidate had to hold his breath under duress. Had he succeeded, our family history might have been significantly different as the casualty rate with pilots was among the highest in the war.

But then, just as he was settling into the Air Force life, we suddenly find him on 10 September, 1943 at Burnham Army Camp, near Christchurch, serving as a private, although by 13 October, he had already been moved up to temporary sergeant. What explains this precipitous transition?

What we were told is he and a group of his cohorts—some of them must have been the recent graduates of the OCTU—were passed over on their commissions in favor of men with direct wartime experience. Thus when he was finally shipped out on 12 January 1944, he was not with the Artillery, or the Air Force, but with the 33rd Battalion of the 2nd New Zealand Expeditionary Force as an infantryman. In a letter written later he described the bittersweet nature of his departure, how as he stood on the deck of his troopship, he felt torn about doing his duty, while he watched first his family, then the shores of New Zealand slipping out of

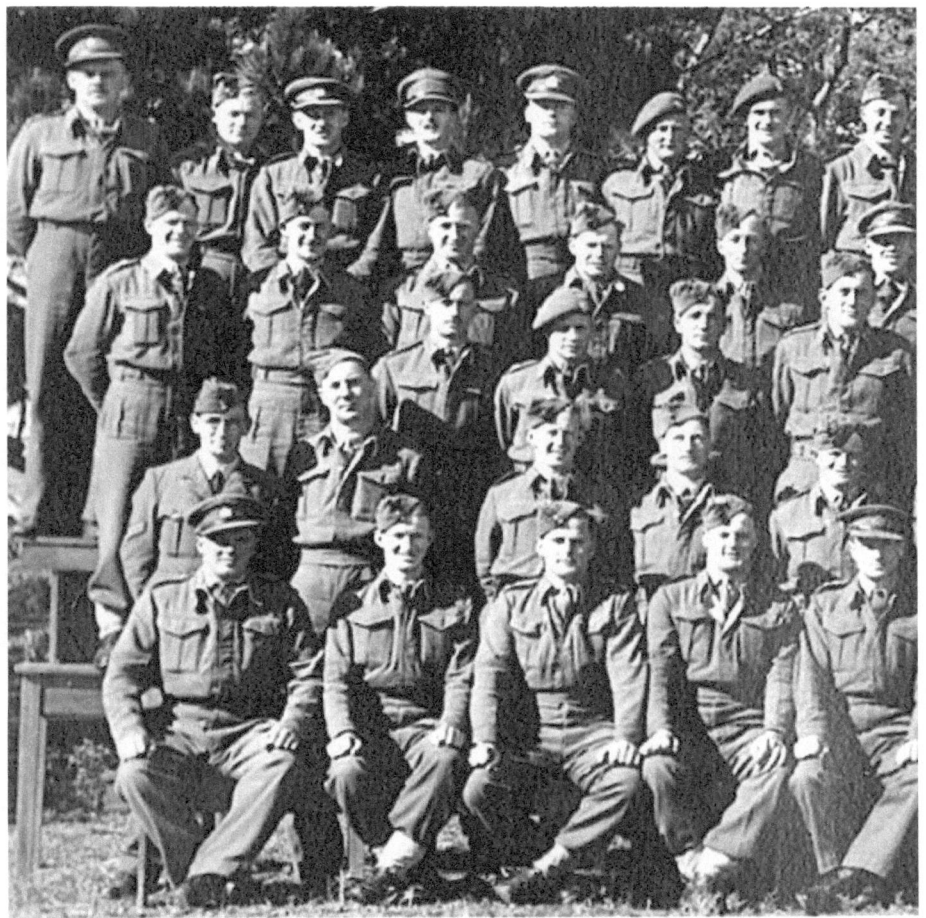

As part of an Air Force officer's training course in Tauranga, August, 1943. Alex is the back row third from the left.

sight, leaving behind one child, Judith, then just nineteen months, and Margaret, expecting another.

What rank was he then? All we can say is that in an early letter from Egypt, his rank on the letterhead shows him as a T (for "Temporary"?) Sergeant. It was not the rank he expected or wanted, although undoubtedly he understood the need for the demotion. Still, he and the other ex-officers in his position did what all good soldiers do: they followed orders, hoping that in due course, the promotions they had been stripped of would be duly reinstated.

How does all this relate to what we knew growing up? In retrospect, we three Protheroe brothers, Paul, Simon and Guy, and our first cousin,

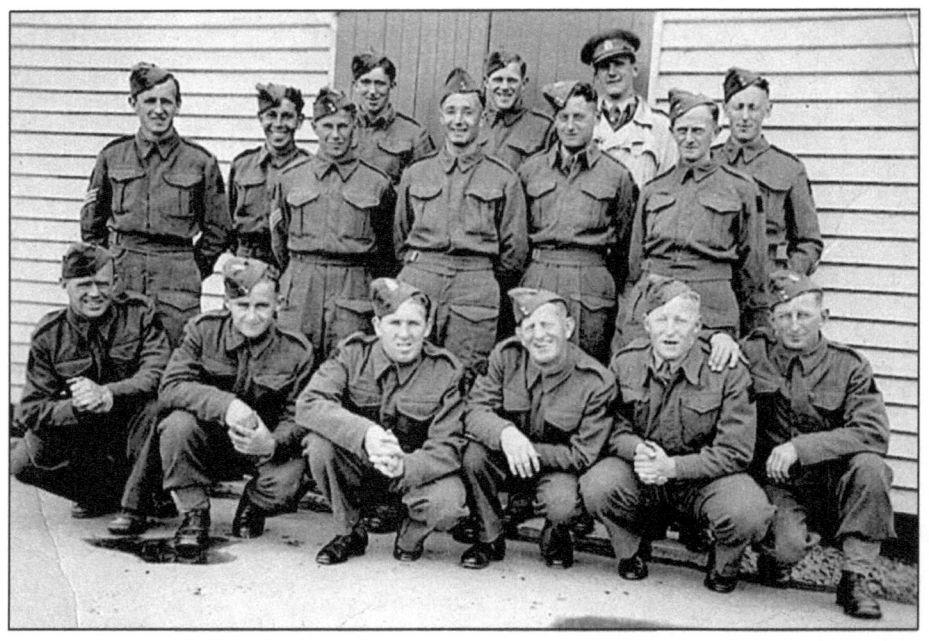

At Burnham military camp, near Christchurch. Alex, top left.

Ashley Smith, son of his sister Mona, knew relatively little. What we gathered from the various anecdotes was essentially a romantic inter-pretation of the truth. Now, through having access to his military records, and through his diary and his letters we have learned that the progress of his military career was more complicated than we supposed.

First, the story of him being on guns protecting Wellington harbor turned out to be incorrect; not as we thought. That he worked on AA bat-teries, not on the big guns, was unknown to us, yet our mistaken notion of him assigned to the concrete emplacements that lie about the city was understandable in the circumstances.

As early as the Russian scare of the 1880s, gun emplacements had been built at various strategic points around the coast. Hostilities after 1939 made the strengthening of these defenses more imperative, espe-cially after the Japanese began expanding to the west and south follow-ing Pearl Harbor. In Wellington's case, a massive new underground forti-fication was built overlooking the city on Wright's Hill to protect against invasion and incursions by German or Japanese surface raiders. In fact, German surface ships did lay mines and attack local shipping around the New Zealand and Australian coasts resulting in ships being sunk and lives lost. One notable case was that of the 16,712-ton New Zealand

Shipping Company liner, M.V. Rangitane, sunk by two German auxiliary cruisers (armed merchant raiders), Orion and Komet, in November, 1940, far out to sea off East Cape. But despite the real concerns for the security of shipping, in the end, the big guns were never fired in anger, especially after the successful Guadalcanal campaign by the U.S. Marine Corps between August, 1942 and January, 1943 brought Japan's southward expansion to an end.

The second story is more mysterious, but may also be grounded in fact. In the Wellington suburb of Island Bay lived a community of Italian fishermen—some trace their ancestry back to the island of Stromboli. These men plied their trade on the choppy waters of Cook Strait, and although they had long been integrated seamlessly into New Zealand society, this held little sway in New Zealand's intelligence gathering circles, specifically the Secret Intelligence Service (SIS). With Italy at war with New Zealand, suspicions over the loyalties of the fishermen arose. Whether this fear was well founded, or was done out of an abundance of caution is impossible to say. The question for us was whether it was true that Alex was ordered to join the crew of an Italian fishing vessel to see if there was any contact between local Italians and an enemy shipping, particularly submarines. Could it be that our father was involved in espionage? We know he was given a trial by the SIS that was not accepted, but whether it related to spying on Italian fishermen is still moot. Still, what we heard was mysterious and intriguing.

Our cousin Ashley Smith came to hear this story through our mutual grandmother, Kate, and we three brothers through our mother. It goes as such. One day, we were told, Alex returned home wet and smelling of fish, and without a rational explanation for his absence and condition. We can only presume he leaked the story at some point, but long after the supposed "event," as obviously, at the time, he was in no position to confirm or deny it. The fact is we never heard the truth directly from him. Obviously, no clandestine contact was made by the Italians, and in retrospect, despite the justified paranoia of the time, this action was a long shot at best. Yet in the end, we are left with a question unanswered. Did it even happen?

Simon Protheroe

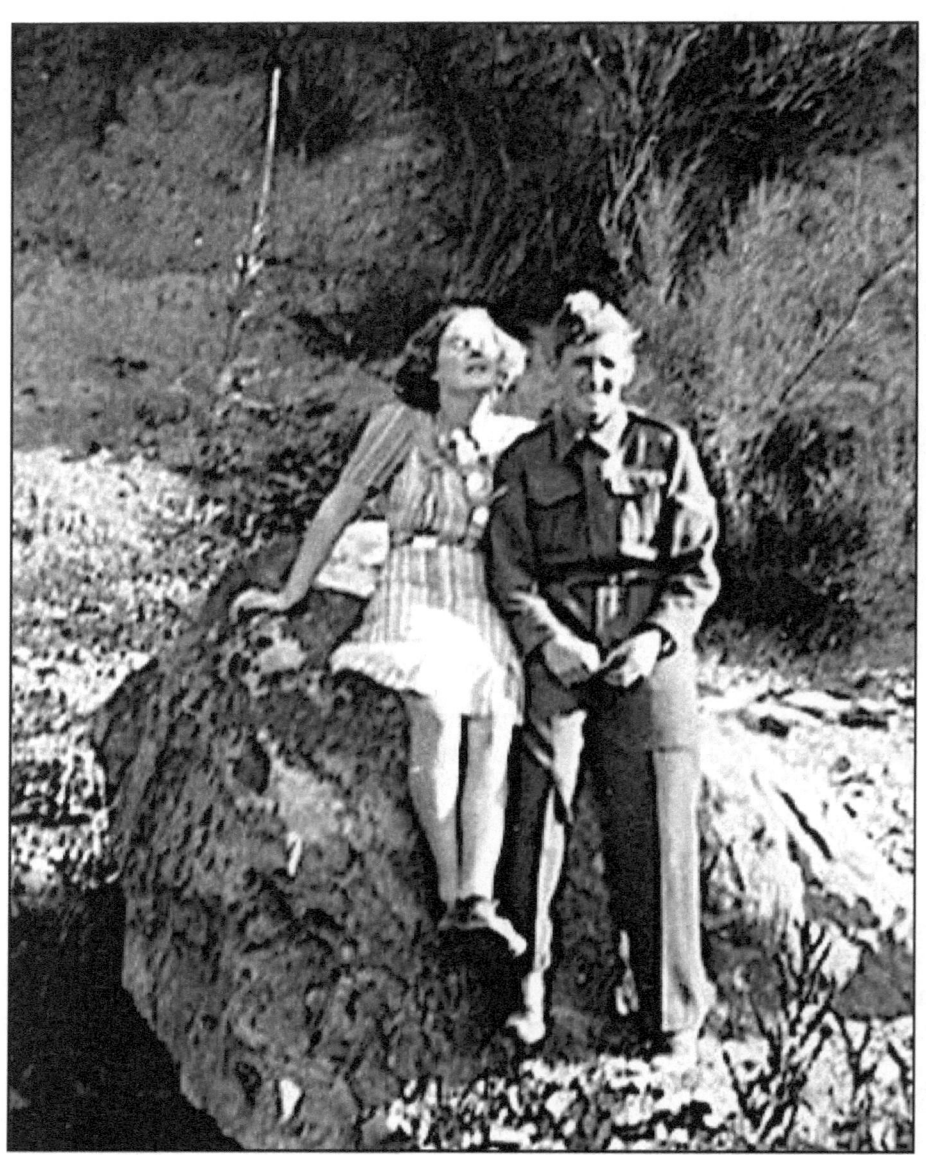

The young couple soon to be separated

OFFICERS' TRAINING

NEW ZEALAND
MAY, 1942
Wellington

DIARY ENTRY
In Officer Cadet Training Unit (OCTU)
8 Friday: The final examination was held today concurrent with the examination for members of the Officers' Refresher Course. The exam came as a great surprise to us: we were under the impression that we would be finally examined just prior to the termination of the course on the scheduled date, May 25th. We were given about twenty minutes notice that the exam would be held at 9 a.m. Five questions, including a compulsory one on a meteor telegram, had to be answered. I found the paper interesting and was still writing when time was called by Sergeant W. Cox, the supervisor, about midday. In the evening, we celebrated with a dinner at the St. George. The dinner and the celebrations afterwards were highly successful and most enjoyable.

9 Saturday: Everyone was keyed up this morning from the interview by Lt. Col. F. L. Hunt, G.S.O I, Training. The worthy Colonel did not arrive however. About 2:30 p.m. we were interviewed in turn in the order of our places in the first exam by Lt. Col. Brooke, who was supported by Major Chappell of AHD, and by Major Anson, the Chief Instructor. The Colonel asked me what position I held in civic life, what school I had attended and then referred to "Anses's" report on me and told me a few "home truths." I assured him that I would bear them steadily in mind. He wound up by congratulating me. We all passed. Leaving in the evening, I returned to camp fairly early as I had not recovered from the previous night's celebrations.

10 Sunday: The day of the shoot at S.Q. The drogue was shot down. It was found, however, after firing about two hundred and seventy rounds that the two guns would not fire. Arrangements were made for the OCTU to act as a picquet overnight until the arrival of the ordinance men the

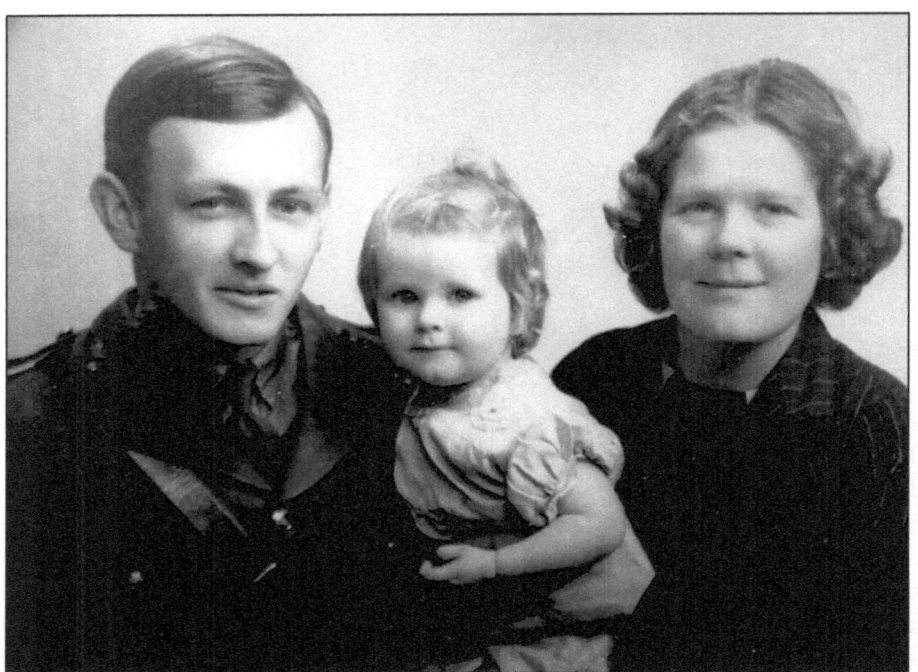

2nd Lieutenant Alex Protheroe, Margaret and Judy

following day. Captain Packard and "Hilly" (Officer Cadet H. S. Hill) rectified the trouble. I later ascertained from Ron Davies that the trouble was due to the almost complete removal of white lubricant from the working parts of the guns. When we cleaned the guns in preparation for the shoot we were told (I don't know by whom) to remove the white lubricant. The guns, because of the removal of the white lubricant, seized up and their breeches could not be opened.

11 Monday: I spent the night with Gus (A.T. Gault) at Jock Macleod's. We returned to camp early about 9 a.m. With the other officer cadets, we were given a "pep" talk with "Ans," who stressed the duties of an officer to his men. Although quite informal, the talk could not have been bettered. In his quiet way, "Ans" impressed. He is a man of character with a deep and penetrating understanding of his fellow man, although on the face of things this does not appear to be the case. We were then given leave, and were told to be back by 2 p.m. We all went to the Winter Show, where five or six of the boys purchased fan books. "Gus," Bob Sims, and I had lunch at the National Club, and then returned to camp. The Auckland boys were told to be ready to leave for home at 2 p.m. They were "Gus," Bob Sims, Don McKenzie, H.S. Hill, McCoy, and R. J. Ross. In the afternoon,

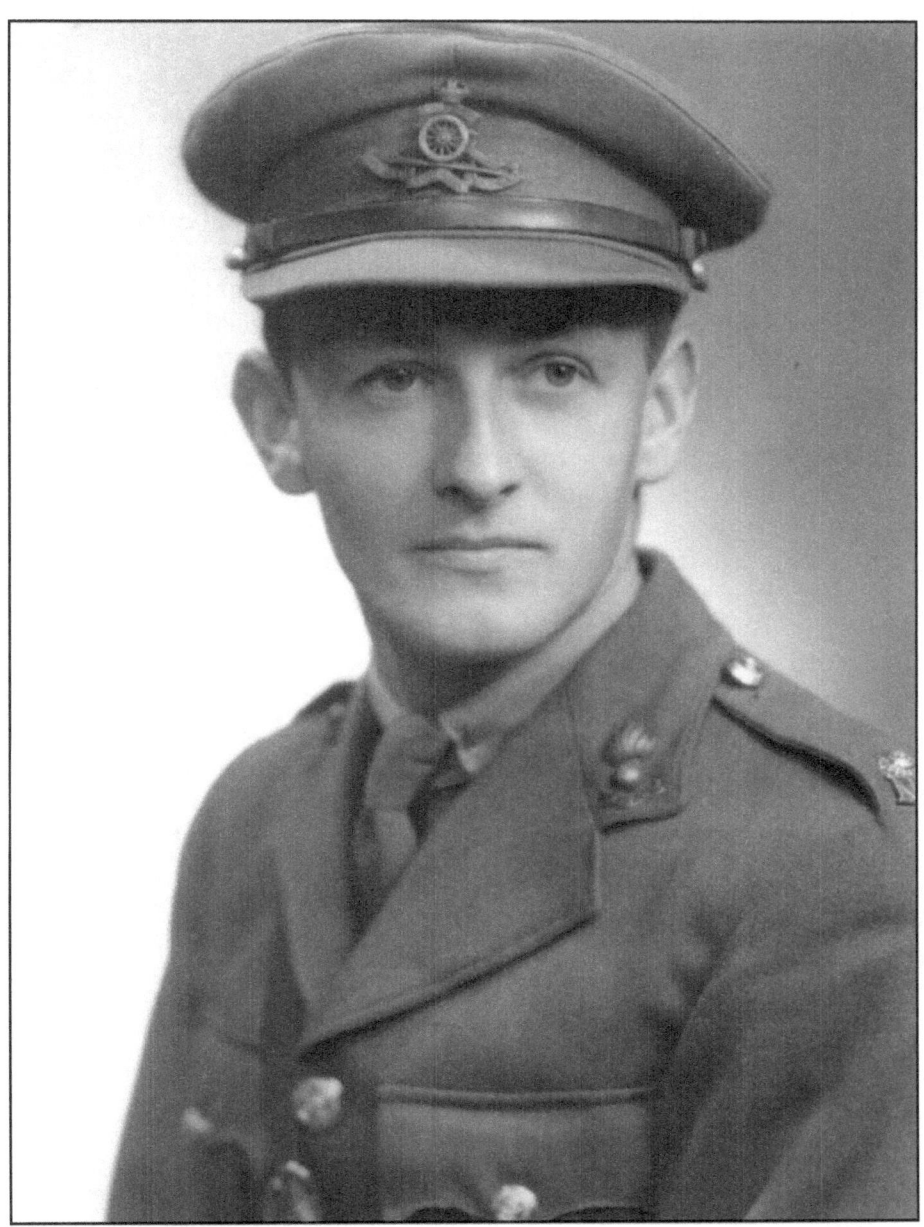

2nd Lieutenant Alex Protheroe

we cleaned the guns and ammo cartridges. The weather was shocking. Jack Balharry and I went into town in the evening and were told to be back by 8:30 the following morning.

12 Tuesday: Jack and I were marched out to our new batteries—Jack to the "heavies" at Mt. Victoria and I to the "Lights" at C.I. I was pleased to find that "Silver" (A.N. King), who left the Army School of Artillery about three weeks ago, was on the 3/4 LA A Battery also. I met the B.C., Major Lindsay-Gardiner, later in the day and took a liking to him immediately. Because of the lack of accommodation, I slept in town that night.

13 Wednesday: Marched out with two NCO's and eighteen men to Q.I. for a week's instruction under Lt. Ron Davies, just back from Egypt. Ron is a first-class chap. He has a very fine and taking personality, and is first-class at instruction. Other officers there are George Richards, the B.C., Ken Thompson, Earl Adams, Ron Graham, Harry Askew, and Tom Rowell. A fine lot of chaps, and a home away from home. I know I will be happy at Q.I. Ray Overton is also here, a contemporary of Keith (*Macleod, broth-er-in-law*) at Otago University. My duties as a subaltern really began to-day. I have much to do, but experience much pleasure in doing it.

14 Thursday: On the guns. A lecture by Ron.

15 Friday: The same again today

16 Saturday: And again today.

17 Sunday: I intended to go to the Church Parade being taken by the Padre, Lt. Col. Hayes, a real gentleman and man. But, somehow, my working of notes, etcetera, precluded my doing so. To town in the afternoon to Saint Andrew's Church with Joyce, Jock, John Burgess, and Bee. The minister, the Reverent Brian Kilroy, preached on the dangers of self-satisfaction in religion. We should even aim higher and higher, and strive to rise to the level set by Christ Jesus

18 Monday. A very fine day for Q.I. But the shoot was not held. Gun drill for the sections during the day.

Leaving for Egypt

DEPARTURE: Wednesday, 12th January, 1944
Letter No. 1

40455
Sgt. A. G. Protheroe
33 (NZ) Battalion
2nd NZEF   MEF
14th January, 1944

My sweetest beloved little girl,
Written at Sea.

The censorship regulations preclude my telling you anything of any great interest. I can't tell you the name of the ship, our possible first port of call, the number of troops onboard, add infinitum. I think I am right in saying that any man on this ship who keeps his health and good spirits could live anywhere! There is plenty of good natured banter and fun and that helps a great deal, and enables one to overlook the monster rats and cockroaches. It is renowned that the cats go around in pairs for the sake of mutual protection from the rodents! And not knowing where we are going makes the sea all the more fascinating. One looks south and conjures up thoughts of icebergs and the intense cold; one looks north and thinks of withering sun and warm and shark-infested seas.

We rise at six, roll up our hammocks, wash and breakfast, have company parade later in the morning, do boat drill at any time, which is an ordeal, and apart from the two other meals, and a cup of tea in the afternoon, that is the sum total of our daily routine. At the moment one can only read, write, sleep, walk or play games, because the weather is too cold and unreliable for sunbathing.....there are numerous chaps I know here.

I will say this for the ship, there's little vibration and she travels very smoothly. It is very hot down below....but because of the smooth traveling of the ships not many chaps have been seasick.

We will really appreciate *terra firma* when that occurs.

Alex

Letter No. 2
Saturday, 15th January, 1944
My sweetest beloved little girl,

We buy tinned fruit and biscuits at the canteen, but little reading matter is to be had. A padre handed out a few American magazines yesterday afternoon, but they were, as was to be expected, insufficient for all.

It is a foregone conclusion that the chaps will get in supplies of cakes, books, magazines, etc. when we get our first leave.

I don't think there is any prospect of seeing my cousin, Margaret, or Max Grey and Margaret. I might, of course, but I think that the odds are very much against it.

I can't close, little girl, without making reference to the sendoff at Lyttelton last Tuesday night. I must count myself very fortunate in having the luck to see my wife, my mother and sister, my father-in-law in such an occasion. And more so in that I was able to kiss you before I left, dearest. I saw you at the end of the wharf until we passed out of view.

Alex

Letter No 3.

T/Sgt. A.G. Protheroe
33 (NZ) Battalion
2 NZEF   MEF
23 February, 1944

My sweetest beloved little girl,

Here I am at last, dearest, at or destination. We set foot on this distant land on *(censored date)*, then set off by train at 6 o'clock that night, and arrived at camp in the early hours of yesterday morning. A meal was waiting for us, and we tired mortals were then sent off to our quarters—fine roomy tents. As was to be expected there was some sorting out yesterday. I asked the Adjutant of the Battalion about a transfer to the Artillery, and he told me it was almost impossible to transfer from one arm of the service to another. Meantime I am remaining where I am and with with Eric Greenall, Chappie, Bob Hawkins, and Roy Johnston. I hope to get some interesting training in the intelligence section in the near future. I haven't seen anything of Vic. The climate here at the moment is

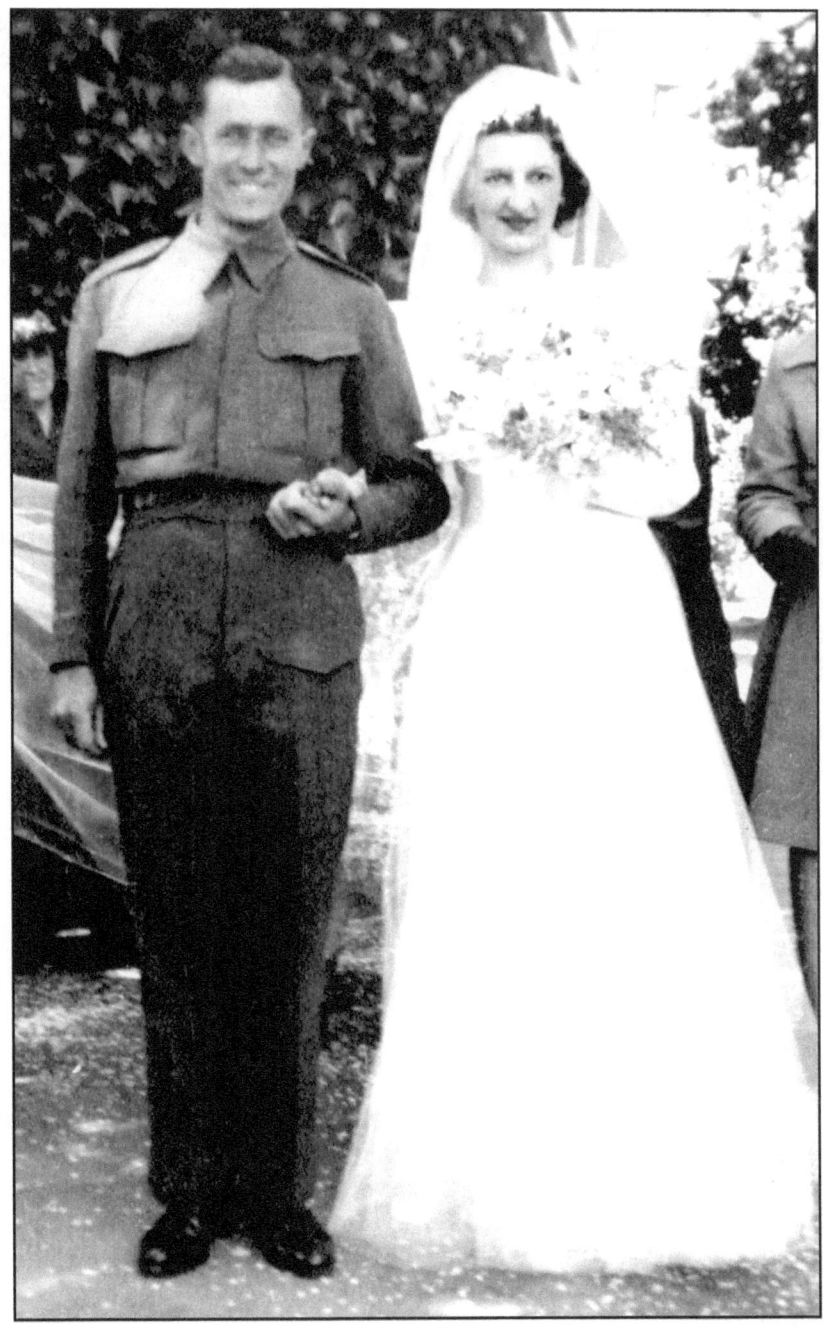

Alex's sister, Mona's wartime wedding to Vic Smith

good. It is not hot during the day, but the night is very cold. I have never experienced a colder journey than that in the open baggage van overnight on Monday. We ex-officers will probably go on a course within a few days, and if we qualify will be given a substantive rank—sergeant or corporal—I don't know which. However, we are currently in the Sergeants' Mess. The meals are a great change from the poor and tasteless food we received during the voyage. It is good to get an orange, a good cup of tea and tasty meals once again. Three or four of the chaps received airgraph letters today. Some were of a comparatively recent vintage. Perhaps I will get one or two from you in a day or two, dearest?

I'm afraid, because of security reasons, that I can't say more in this letter dearest. I won't be able to post *Down the Hatch*, our ship's newspaper, until permission is granted to do so.

I have just met Vic. I'm looking forward to going out with him. I saw him coming through the tent opening while I was typing a letter. He is still in the same job. I am looking forward to going out with him, perhaps during the weekend. He is keeping good health, he tells me. I showed the photo of the three of us, and he thought Judy a wonderful little girl. I can't say how much I miss you, but let's hope it won't be long to the day of our reunion. My best regards to the rest of your family. My deepest love and affection to you and Judy.

Alex

MARCH, 1944
Letter No. 10

40455
Sgt. A. G. Protheroe
33 (NZ) Btn.
2 NZEF   MEF
Thursday, 2 March, 1944

My sweetest beloved little girl,

As promised, I'll now give you details of some of the interesting trips I have made. As I have a lot to write, I'll start straight away.

Saturday 26th February: The afternoon was devoted to a trip around the sights. One of the ladies was our guide. First, through the Dead City area. Here is the graveyard of Cairo. But unlike our burial grounds, the Dead City has inhabitants. As we drove through, the Arab children chased the truck crying "Baksheesh!" Further on, towards the Citadel, is to be found a large area of what appears to be half-finished buildings with no roofs. They are utterly desolate. Just why they were never completed I could not ascertain. There was much life to be seen as we neared

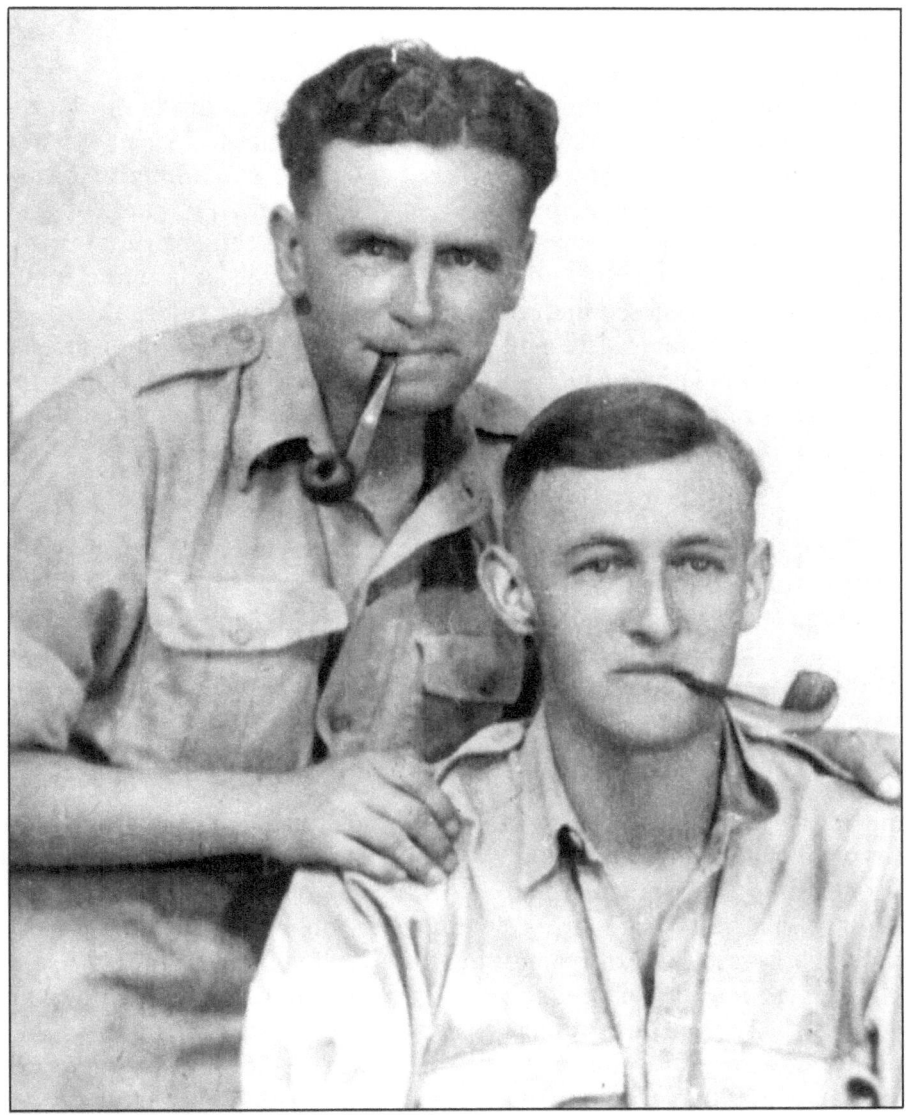

In sunnier climes, perhaps with Jack Mercer

the Citadel. The Citadel and its mosque dominate the city. As we drove through the arched gateway I couldn't help but think of the strength of this castle in the olden times. We drove to an open courtyard near the mosque (Mohamed Ali) and after walking through an arched gateway reached the mosque courtyard, and put on the slippers provided for visitors. Our Arab guide told us all about the place as we went around. Mohamed Ali, the great, great-grandfather of King Farouk, began the erection of the mosque in 1824, and had it modeled on that of San Sofia in Constantinople. The architect was a Greek. The building was finished in 1857. The main courtyard, which we visited first, has a floor of Saharan marble. In the centre is a magnificent fountain, containing alabaster stone said to have been stripped from the faces of the Pyramids of Giza. Here the faithful wash before entering the Mosque to perform their devotions. The water for the fountain comes from a well sunk in the courtyard to a depth of three hundred feet. The echo of one's voice takes quite a long time to come up. The main minaret is 290 feet high. When entered the mosque we were struck with awe and amazement. The place is truly magnificent and any description I can give would not do it justice. The magnificent central dome is literally covered with gold leaf. Then there is the floor with eighty-five pieces of Persian carpet, red in color with a central pattern of yellow in each piece.

The reader's box was pointed out to us, and our guide emphasized that the reader recited the Koran, reading by heart! (A nasty dig at readers of the Bible in Christian churches.) There are two staircases, i.e. pulpits; one being presented to King Farouk and costing twenty-eight thousand guineas, and the other being the Staircase of the Rising Sun. The Rising Sun points at the altar, which is a plain semi-circular recess in the wall. To the left is a revolving pillar of marble, which indicates to a blind man who touches it that he is at the altar. We passed under the Staircase and as each of us filed through our guide asked us to make a wish. Need I say what the wish of all would probably be? Above the staircase is the Arabic motto, "God is generous." Beneath the great dome hangs a chandelier, beautifully wrought, weighing two tons, presented by Louise Philippe of France. Words cannot describe it adequately. It must be seen to be appreciated. We passed outside to a courtyard from which we could view Cairo. To the south could be seen an ancient Roman aqueduct; directly below to old mosques; next to the Citadel (which is itself the fort of Saladin, redoubtable opponent of Richard Coeur-de-Lion) stands a ruined mosque built in 1317; and across the valley is a fort built by Napoleon in 1898; and a quarry from which the stone of the Pyramids was hewn. We left the Citadel with reluctance because we realized that our visit had been all too short.

The padre wanted us to see the Obelisk, near Heliopolis, and our journey there took us through suburbs of contrast, some ancient, dirty, and squalid, and others containing modern flats and shops. The Obelisk is one of three—one of the remaining two (Cleopatra's Needle) being on the Embankment of the Thames, and the third is in New York. According to the Padre, Biblical evidence in Genesis 41, the hieroglyphics and the fact that the Nile has built up the surrounding ground a half inch a century, all together date the Obelisk back about 4500 years. The Obelisk appears to be of brown granite, and seems to be about fifty to sixty feet high.

We then went to the Club. With two other chaps, I took a gharry to the King Fuad Museum of Hygiene, but it so turned out that I no sooner got inside the door than I met my old Wellington boss, who is attached to the British Army in these parts. We walked back to town together and over a cup of tea we had a great chat. He told me about his activities since I last saw him, and I tried to give him as much information as possible about people mutually known to us. In passing I mentioned that I was keen to see "The Merry Widow," which was to conclude a most successful season that night. He told me that he knew Madge Elliott, and would see what he could do for me. The upshot was that Vic and I were later able to get seats. But before I tell you about the show, I'd better describe what Vic and I did beforehand. We did some shopping in El Muski, the bazaar area. El Muski is a long, narrow street packed with small shops selling almost anything under the sun. After nightfall, it is a good place to keep away from, because it is very badly lighted, and one is thus likely to be had over the quality of purchases. If you want to get anything at what you would consider a fair price, you've got to be prepared to bargain perhaps for an hour or so. The price asked at the start is usually about double that what the article is worth. If you finally offer a certain price, you've got to stick to it, and can't go any lower.

When we arrived at the side street of the Opera House, we noted it was guarded by the red tarboosh and blue-uniformed Egyptian police. This indicated that some Royal personage was going to attend, and on questioning one of the policemen, I found that it was Queen Farida. Vic and I were allocated a box high up in the theater, but looking down on the stage I saw that the Opera House was fairly small. I should say it holds no more that twelve hundred persons. Just before 9:15 (the time the shows commence here), Farida, the Queen Mother and two young women (probably princesses) arrived. Farida, I could see clearly. She was dressed in white with a solitary diamond-encrusted necklace, and is a beautiful young woman. Her attention was riveted on the performance right throughout. Franz Lahar's music, Andrian Bolt's lyrics, the acting, and costuming, color, humor, and the rest were all that could be desired.

A show turned on by a West End company is something not to be forgotten, and we were indeed very lucky to have had the opportunity to see it.

More diary extracts in letter No. 11, dearest. I have posted a dozen snaps home—of the Pyramids, the Mohamed Ali Mosque, and of Memphis and Sakkara. Please keep them safe, dearest. God Bless you, and sweet little Judy, so very, very much. I'm always thinking of you both, and longing for the day of our reunion,

Deepest love, devotion and many kisses from your loving,

Alex

Letter No. 11: Friday, 3 March, 1944

My sweetest beloved little girl,

This is a continuation of my trip to places of interest, and I'll get on with the job straight away.

Sunday 27 February, 1944: Our first halting place was to be Memphis, the ancient capital of Egypt, some twenty-five miles from the city. Our circuitous route enabled us to see at close hand the ancient but effective methods of cultivation used by the natives. We saw the methods used to raise water, blindfolded bullocks walking round and round for hours on end drawing water from the wells; men drawing water up from the canal through spirals; and even cupping it out with their hands. Then there were the yoked oxen pulling the ploughs, cultivation by hand and so on. There was the modern touch too. A large excavator was scooping out huge quantities of soil from the canal sides and bottoms. The soil was rich and the growth excellent. The Nile is indeed the lifeblood of Egypt for without her waters all would be barren.

Memphis at last. I have never seen a more persistent baksheesh-seeking crowd of children at any other place. Although we were fairly rapidly along the road, the children followed us with much tenacity, and for their pains one or two of them got some cigarette butts. We visited a building containing a large sandstone figure of Ramses II (circa. 1300 B.C.). Ramses II was apparently a very egotistical Pharaoh because he is reported to have had several hundreds of these statues of himself executed. In the left thigh of his statue we inspected is a carving of old Ramses's favorite wife!

A drive along a dusty, palm-flanked road brought us to the water-covered ruins of the Temple of the Sacred Bulls. The stone pillars are lying about in all sorts of positions, and the place cannot be recognized as a one-time temple. This temple has a sequel at Sakkara, some miles away, and to that place we were soon on our way. When the sacred bulls died, their bodies were preserved at the temple at Memphis and then taken to the tombs at Sakkara for burial. We had to walk down a long sloping tunnel to reach the tombs, which are all located in recesses hewn out of the rock on either side. With the aid of torches and burners carried by native guides, we made our way through the inky blackness. The tombs, I understand, are all empty. The jewels and other offerings placed in the tombs were stolen by the Romans who cut a hole through to the tunnel. After leaving the tombs, we inspected the Step Pyramid built by Zasser (*Djoser, ed.*) of the 3rd Dynasty. This is said to be the first of the stone pyramids, all previous ones erected being made of baked bricks. We went down into the Temple of Offering of Ptakoteh (?), high priest and Prime Minister under Zasser. (*The vizier, Imhotep, maybe! ed.*) The walls are covered with brown and red-colored murals of the life of the times. The work has been excellently executed, and the figures of men, women, geese, boats and so on are very lifelike. In one mural, Ptakoteh is shown having his face and feet washed, and his fingernails cut. Much excavation is being carried out at Zasser's magnificent temple, which covers a large area. Here the while pillars have been (and are being) raised and a table-like roof has been built on top of them.

We then took the road to Mena, where the famous Pyramids of Giza are located. Just before the Pyramids are reached we passed the Mena Guest House, a fine hotel built for the best tourist traffic, which goes through this part of the world in peacetime. The Pyramids of Giza comprise nine in all—three large and six small. The latter are the tombs of the children of the pharaohs who erected the Pyramids. We only had time to look at Cheops, which is the largest—451 feet high and covering an area of thirteen acres. The huge blocks of stone appear to be about three feet high, and it was amusing to watch the efforts of many would-be climbers. There is a deep pit in the shape of a boat nearby, and here the remains of the boat used to transport the stone from the quarries across the river where found. The Sphinx has been carved from one piece of stone, but I forget the measurements. It has the head of a man, the face of a woman, and the body of a lion. The front has been protected with sandbags and concrete against bomb blasts. The Sphinx and its temple were built by Khafre whose pyramid (behind Cheops) still has its alabaster top. We went into the temple with the tombs of the high priests. The huge blocks of Assoman marble have been pulled together so well that one cannot place a knife between the blocks. The steps are of alabaster which glows when when a light is placed near it. On the way back to the Club we drove through the beautiful, wooded suburb of Giza, where many of the rich live.

I have sent have some snaps (Eleven in all, I think!) of the places mentioned in this letter.

Please let me know, dearest, what parcels and letters you have received, and then I'll know of anything that might have gone astray.

I haven't done any trips since. There are still many places to be seen, and I hope I'll have an opportunity of visiting them.

Will you please pass on all these news letters to Mother, sweetheart! It will save my writing them again.

Deepest and enduring love for you and our sweet little girl, and my kind regards to the family from your loving and devoted,

Alex

Kisses for wee Judy

from her Daddy!

DIARY ENTRY

4 Saturday: Our little girl Judy is 20 months old today. I can hardly realize that she will be two years old on American Independence Day—July 4. May God bless her! I saw the adjutant this morning about my application for a transfer back to Artillery. He told me that would have to wait until I reached advanced base. In honor of the pledge I made to my dearest Margie and Mother, I must strive my utmost to get back to Artillery. Those of us who didn't go on leave spent a quiet time in camp. I saw the Russian film "Natascha" in the evening; what courage, what sacrifice! War is horrid and loathsome; and I pray the words, *"Pax in terris in hominibus bonae voluntatis,"* (*"Peace on Earth, Goodwill toward Men"*) will soon echo right round the world.

5 Sunday: On leave this afternoon and evening. Took tram to the Pyramids. At Giza, I found that center section of the bridge had been secured. I had to leave the tram and so I rowed across Nile and then took the tram again. Bill Lone (?) and I visited the King's chamber, then we revisited the temple, the Sphinx and the tomb of Cheops' daughter and son of daughter. (Ventilation!). We climbed to the top (View!), before heading back to town via the club, then went shopping and home. (Les Taylor.)

6 Monday: Cable of loving greetings from dearest Margie. Issued with gear. To the pictures with Jack Mercer.

7 Tuesday: No entry

8 Wednesday: Up at 4:45 a.m., breakfast at 5, waiting around and finally departing by train from Maadi at 7:35. Closely packed in old carriage—gear everywhere—long stops at several stations. We reached Ismailia with its tree-lined streets, seeing the first ship masts and funnels just protruding above sandbank on our side of the canal. Other ships were proceeding through canal at the crossing point to Palestine. Finally at 7 p.m.—nearly 12 hours—we took lighters to other side of the canal, to a transit camp with troops from every part of the Empire—Indian tents, and flags on route.

9 Thursday: Sergeants' mess. Early afternoon, (at 3:45), we took the lighters and boarded the ship—with Cliff, John Rogers. Sgt.'s Ward and Blakey. With the gangway secured, I went shopping for paintings.

10 Friday: Embassy entertainment trio, piano-accordion.

11 Saturday: With fruit in a basket tied to porthole, we embarked at 3:45 p.m. and passed the town with its fine buildings, statue, and break-water. We sailed past small boats, bathing sheds, and out to sea into the evening.

12 Sunday: E78 (?)—Bible reading—PP for crew (?)—dancing—costumes—band songs.

13 Monday: My (*28th*) birthday—(*warnings over*) typhus—off Derna, (*a port in Libya*)—rough seas (*In a later letter, he acknowledged the troop-ship was MS "Batory."*)

Letter No. 14: Monday 13th March

My sweetest beloved little girl,

I am writing this at sea on my birthday.....I am trying to recall what I was doing this time last year, but all I can remember is that I was very happily settled in my job as liaison officer with the Air Force...I recall I was on a course at Palmerston North for the whole of January '43. Two years ago I was in O.C.T.U.

It is now more than two months since I left home. The distance I have travelled and the varied experiences I have had during that time unfortunately makes it seem longer. About a week ago I wrote a letter giving my name suggestions for the 'little stranger:'

Boy: Roger Broughton, or David Broughton
Girl: Geraldine Broughton, or Alice Broughton

Alex

DIARY ENTRY

14 Tuesday: Rough

15 Wednesday: Cold wind—Sicily hills—snow-capped—convoy—Italy

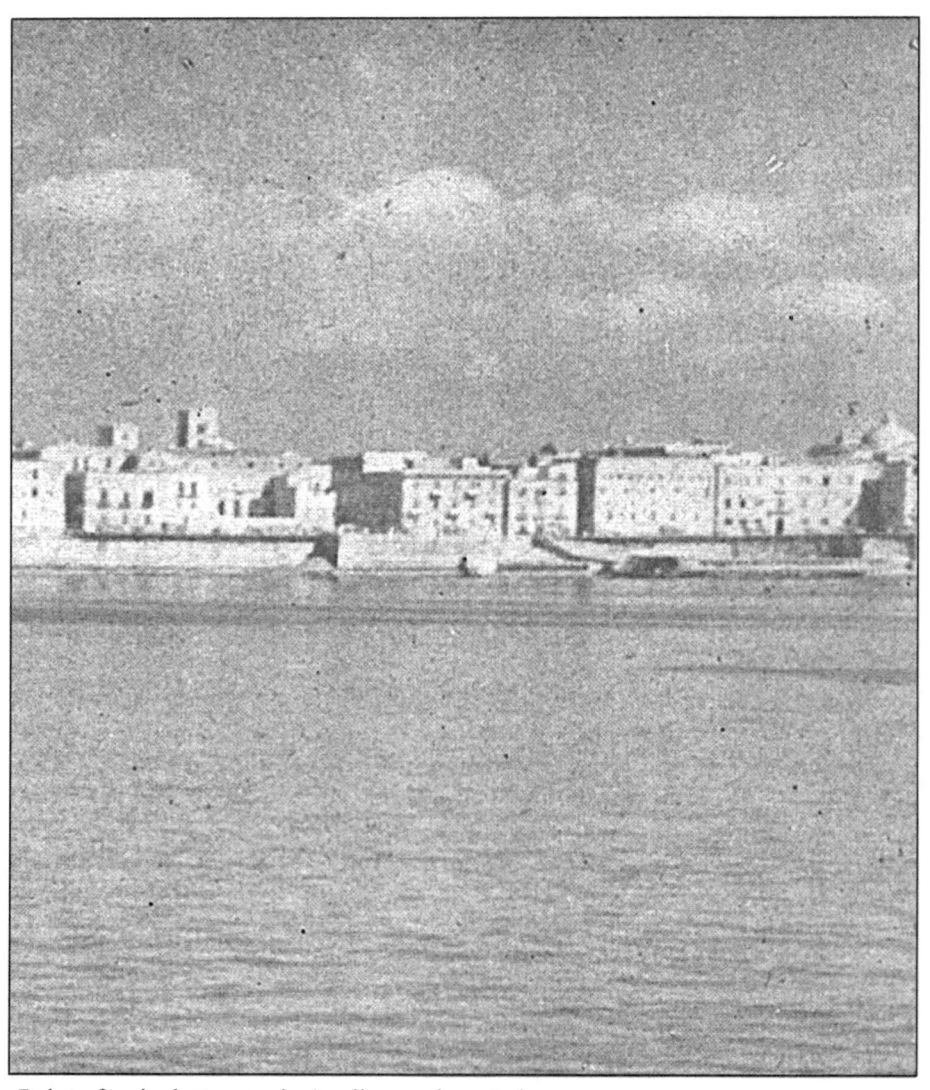

Point of arrival: Taranto, in Apulia, southern Italy.

Arrival in Italy

16 Thursday, March, 1944: Arrived (*in Taranto*)—Bitterly cold—first impressions—(*disembarked at)* 0830 hrs—olives—villages—monasteries—cobbled streets—bombs—dirt—castle (*Castello Aragonese*)—meeting tent "cobbers" *(buddies)*—gear, isolation.

17 Friday: Colonel Mair—"Ities" *(Italians)*—mail—route marches—O.C. *(Officer-in-Charge)*—Trees—fuel, plonk (*cheap wine*)—quarantine.

18 Saturday: O.C.—q (*quarantine?*)—100 (*?*)—EMc (*?*)—pay—inspection—St. Basilio, near Taranto—baptism.

19 Sunday: Visited Padre.

20 Monday: Route march—Walked over hill—witnessed charcoal monger—donkeys and pigs—well—George=community settlement (?) — Mottola—moles.

21 Tuesday: Colonel Boyd—observation

22 Wednesday: Captain Hodge—discussion of religion

23 Thursday: Hail, snow, rain—went to an ENSA (*Entertainments National Service Association*) show, Fred Bryant—Peggy.

24 Friday: Excursion for wine, change in hat, coffee (*?*)

25 Saturday: Today to Gioia, then Casamassima, then Bari.

26 Sunday: Rough weather—lecture.

Letter No. 17: Sunday, 26th March, 1944

My sweetest beloved little girl

I went to Bari yesterday.

History Bari dates back to a period even prior to the foundation of Rome, and it has had uninterrupted relations with its neighbors in the

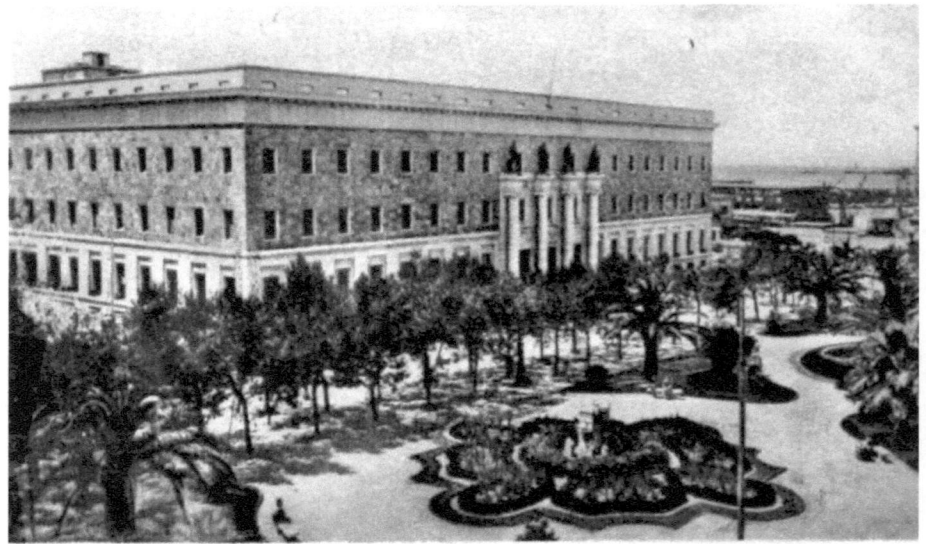

Bari - Palazzo delle Finanze

Far and Middle East since the most remote times. Phoenicians, Greeks and Romans have all left traces of their domination in the city. During the middle ages, when the lower Adriatic was known as 'Mare Apulicum' (the Apulian Sea), Bari was the stepping stone between the Latin World and the Levant, and in the course of time, it acquired considerable influence. The Norman-Swabian rule brought great splendor to the whole province and magnificent churches and castles were built in an architectural style of showing signs of the Renaissance, which took place elsewhere centuries later.

Bari Today: The city has (or had) a population of two hundred thousand, and developed much during the twenty years of Fascist rule. The modern part of Bari contains many imposing buildings, but many of these lack finish. Some of the main streets are tree-lined, but when one gets off the main thoroughfares one finds dirty and fairly narrow, cobbled streets.

From the appearance of the place, the war has ruined Bari. Only a relatively small number of shops are open, and these have very little to offer. There is no haggling over prices as one finds in Cairo. If you won't buy at the price asked, that's the end of it. It seems to me that all that was worth buying has disappeared a long time ago. Of course, there are the usual street stalls selling junk from Birmingham and other such places.

It is pretty much impossible to get a meal other than at the club. We went to the Warrant Officers and Sergeants Club, where we had tea and

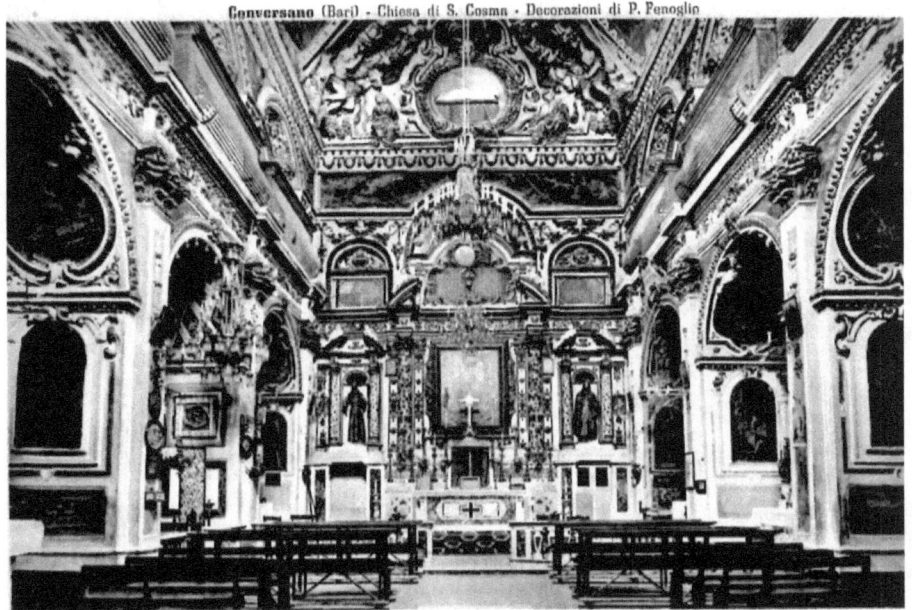

Conversano (Bari) - Chiesa di S. Cosma - Decorazioni di P. Fenoglio

'cakes' the later turned out to be nothing but stale fig scones. The usual drink is wine, of which there are several varieties, and cognac, Vermouth and brandy are also in demand.

People: No one appears to have much to do. Business must almost be at a standstill. We saw a few very well dressed men and women, but the majority of people are poorly clad, particularly the children, who wear worn out clothes, long stockings and dilapidated shoes. Many of these little ones were barefoot and walked nonchalantly through the water and mud of the dirty cobbled sheets. They called soldiers "Johnny," and are continually pestering us for cigarettes and chocolate. Incidentally, we saw many of these youngsters of eight to twelve years smoking. The children appear to have a better knowledge of English than their seniors, and "okay" figures much in their speech.

The women wear high-healed shoes with no instep. Many of them go hatless, as do many of the men.

Traffic: Few private cars are to be seen, but those few that are about are very good ones. There are a number of four-wheel carts pulled by a single horse. Traffic proceeds on the right, like Egypt. There are also a few dilapidated tramcars, not quite as bad as those in Cairo, but nearly so.

Old Bari: We wended our way to the old city, which is really fascinating. This area is separated from the newer city by a highway. It is here

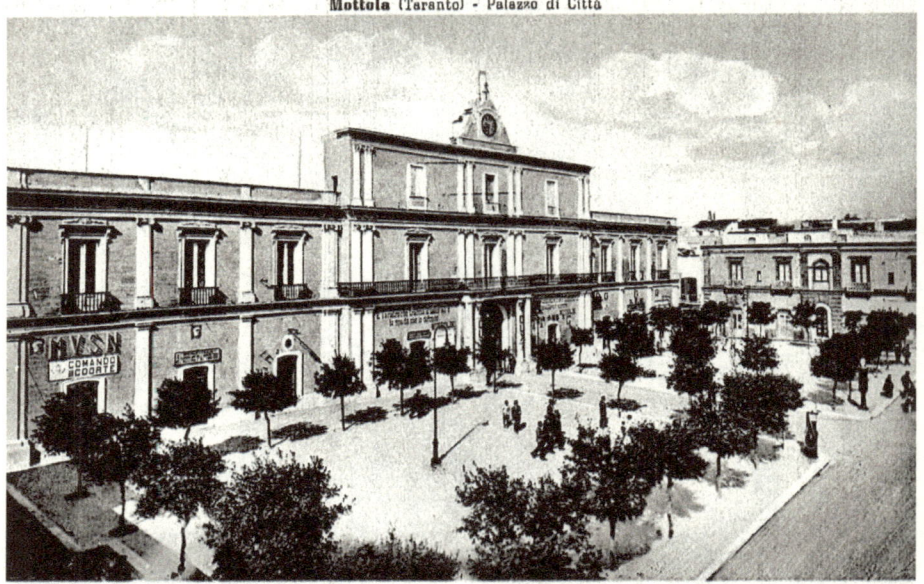

Mottola (Taranto) - Palazzo di Città

that the lower classes live in conditions which we would scarcely consider fit for a pet dog or cat. Thousands of men, women and children sleep, eat and carry out their lives in this labyrinth of lanes and alleyways. We walked along the worn, cobbled streets and could not help but observe through the windows, the Italian at home with his wife and family in a pokey little room opening onto the street. Some of the alleyways off the lanes lead to enclosed courtyards. Here staircases lead up to dozens of rooms, which these people call 'home.' In the midst of this labyrinth was the ancient church and shrine of St. Nicholas, Patron Saint of Bari. I have sent a postcard, which gives a somewhat erroneous impression of the building. It is not isolated as one would gather from the postcard, but is surrounded on all sides by tenements, which have probably grown up around it. We went inside, then down some steps into the crypt to the tomb of St. Nicholas. It is metal and has been adorned with carvings dealing with various aspects of the Saint's life. Behind the tomb is a fine mosaic floor, which was covered with water when we were there due to the fact that the crypt is below sea level. We were taken into the room where a priest sat at a table and we were given a souvenir of our visit. All of us gave a donation of seven to ten lire each.

One of the church attendants then took us in hand and led us to the chapel where there was a plaster effigy of the Saint in a large glass case. It was somewhat similar to the picture above the Basilica in the photo I

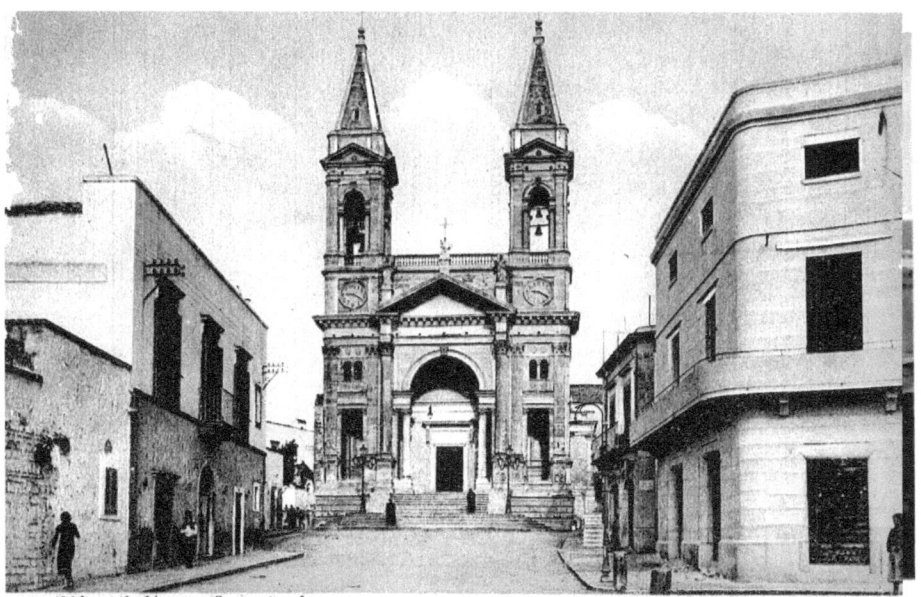

Alberobello - Cattedrale

have sent you. The Romanesque architecture of the Basilica is rather fine but, of course, the ages have had their effect on the building.

Not far from the Basilica is the ancient castle of Frederick II of Suevia (Swabia). It is surrounded by a moat today.

The postcard showing the 'Nuovo Fontana di Piazza' also gives a wrong impression of what it looks like today. The water is not bubbling up, and the fountain itself has been defaced with slogans, 'W Stalin,' 'W Lenin' 'W Il Communismo,' and so on. The 'W' stands for 'Long Live.' In fact, hundreds of buildings in Bari have slogans like the above on their walls. If the slogans indicate anything, Communism has a big hold in Bari. The town is alive with wayward women, but every effort is made by the Red Caps (Military Police) to keep the troops away from them. The haunts of these people are marked by 'Out of Bounds' signs, and anyone caught in such places goes for a skate.

'The Merry Widow,' which we saw in Cairo, is now being presented in Bari.

This will give you a rough idea of what we thought of Bari. To see it at its best one would need to visit in peacetime.

I will write again in a day or two giving more impressions of the countryside.

Alex

DIARY ENTRY
27 Monday: Met Captain Kinder—the move to artillery—Went to the pictures.
28 Tuesday: Col Boyd—Alan and John in tent, new chaps.
29 Wednesday: Settling in. Joined with John and Allen in the evening.
30 Thursday: With John & Allen to Mottola.
31 Friday: To Noca, Alberdello, Putignano with Jack, then to the Castellana Grotto.
APRIL 1944
1 Saturday: Went to Mottola. I bought ribbon, elastic; language difficulties.
2 Sunday: Stayed at the Depot—I was O (*Orderly?*) Sgt. on Palm Sunday
Letter No. 20: Sunday, April 2nd, 1944
My sweetest beloved little girl,

In this letter I will give you a description of the places I visited in the course of a tour arranged by the Depot. I made a trip the other day with twenty chaps on the 'caves trip' with the chief point of interest being the caves of Castellana. We walked down several flights of steps to an immense limestone cavern with an opening to the sky above. The cavern was not rich in stalagmites and stalactites, but, all the same, one was struck by its size and its fascination.

Our Italian guide led us on further down into the bowels of the earth —to the Black Cavern, to the Monumental Cavern, the Cavern of the Owl, through the narrow Organ Cavern to the twisting Cavern of the Cobra, and on through other caverns until we reached the end of the pathway, but by no means the end of the system of caverns. The work of cutting the paths through these caverns is still going on, and I gathered that there are numerous caverns below us which had scarcely—if ever—been explored. One of our party who had been to the Waitomo Caves said they were not as extensive but more beautiful, because the stalagmites and stalactites were white rather than yellow-orange as at Castellana. There is a small statue of the Madonna in a dim recess. When light is held to the limestone it glows considerably. We were met by the inevitable seller of postcards of the Grottoes.

Another place we visited was a small town called Putignano—really an excellent little place according to Italian standards. The beauty of Putignano lies in the fact that from the point of view of the buyer of things to be sent home, the town has not been bought out. We also went to a smaller place called Alberobello, in a locality where there are a large number of '*trulli*,' or quaint conical roofed houses. The '*trulli*' remind one

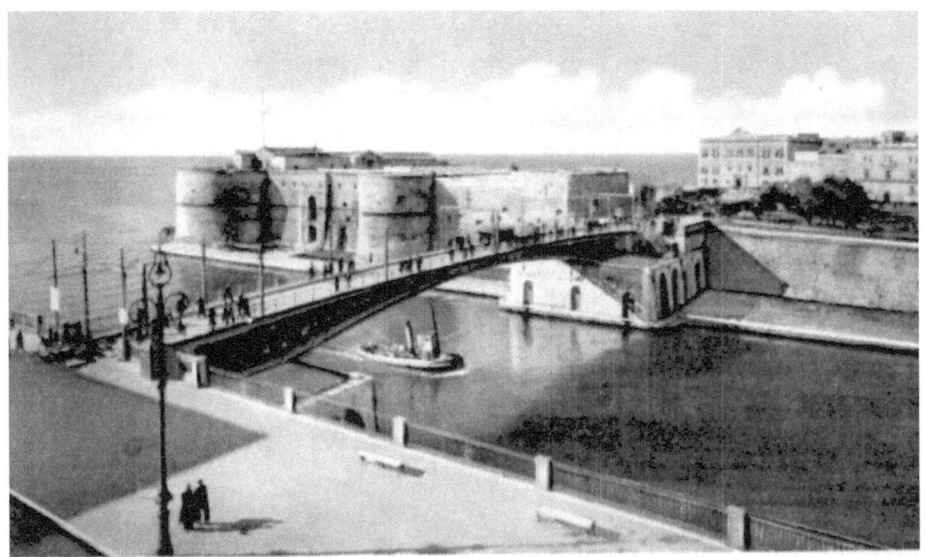

Taranto - Ponte girevole e Castello Aragonese.

of the homes of knaves and gnomes in the fairy stories of one's child-hood. The walls are of whitewashed stone and roofs of small slabs of stone with the chimney protruding through the apex. We met an English-speaking shopkeeper here. This man told us he had served in the U.S. Army during the last war, and he proudly pointed to a picture of himself in the uniform of an American soldier.

Alex

DIARY ENTRY
3 Monday: Airgraph—Drs. discovery of "classic equation"(?)—draft—lectures on security and chemical warfare issues.
4 Tuesday: To Taranto
5 Wednesday: Off with D. and McI (?), ex-officers—medical clearance—thunder, rain and lightning
Letter No. 21: Wednesday, April 5th, 1944
My sweetest beloved little girl,

I decided to have a look at Taranto, the scene of the Royal Navy's bril-liant action against the Italian Fleet. We struck the best day during sev-eral weeks I've been in Southern Italy. The principal part of the city has the Gulf on one side and the Inner Harbor on the other. One enters the city across a swing bridge, which joins the northern quarter of the city proper. The castle is called Castello Aragonese. We walked around the waterfront where, in my opinion, the many fine buildings were of a bet-ter design and finish than those in Bari. The shops were open and people

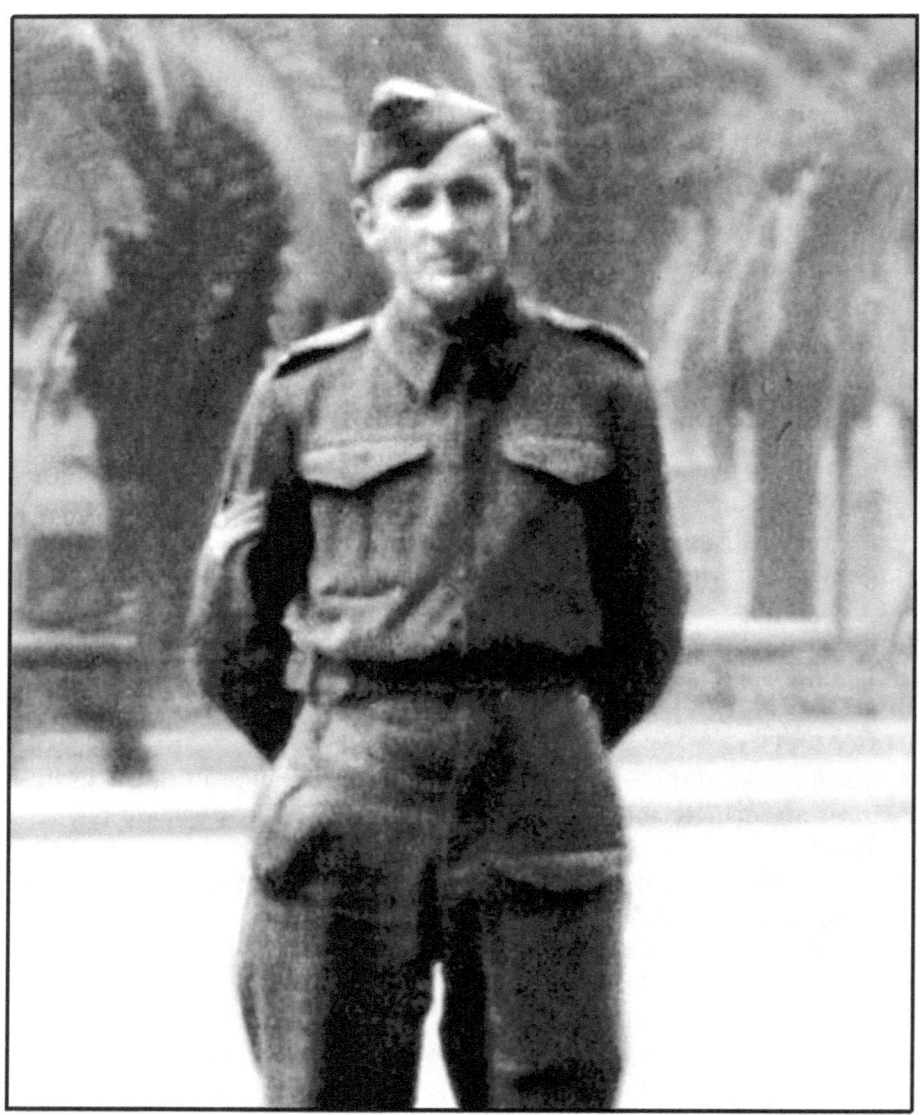

Sergeant Alex Protheroe in Taranto, early April, 1944

were going about their business. Unlike in Bari, the shops had something to sell, although the prices were slightly higher. The poor soldier is being frightfully exploited in Southern Italy. The £1 or so he draws on payday goes nowhere.

In Taranto, there is no building that you could call a skyscraper. Instead, Taranto business streets are long and broad, and several are tree-lined. The main ones run into squares (*piazzas*) in which one sees some very fine North African palms and other trees. The Italian is keen on tree-lined streets; I think the trees improve their appearance very much. In the centre of the piazza is usually a statue or memorial.

In all Italian towns are numerous lanes and alleyways leading to the dingy homes of the poorer classes. In Taranto, as in other towns, the main streets have alleyways off them, which are extremely dirty and are in many cases partly under water. The shops, of course, cater for the 'soldier tourists.' There are numerous postcards of places of interest in the city; thousands of hastily prepared books on 'English-Italian Conversations,' cameos for the wife, mother or girlfriend, crudely-made fountain pens, cheap jewelry, and so on. These are all expensive, at prices that no Italian would pay.

The '*vino*' shops and bars are many. Nearly all are extremely dirty and I can't understand anyone drinking in them.

Then there are the numerous shops selling babies goods. I think Italy must be in the forefront for shops selling such goods. I think this is largely due to the fact that the female members of the family help to augment the family's income by making baby clothes, which are displayed in a window of a home and not in proper shops. This struck me very much yesterday when we entered premises, which were half-home, half-shop to find several girls working on materials with their skillful and nimble fingers. Unlike us, the Italians like very bright colors and much of their work in clothing could not possibly be worn by womenfolk and children. Also the quality of many of the articles is very poor and a large number are dirty to boot.

The Italian infant of the poorer classes is carried in a peculiar sheath-like arrangement. The infants arms, body and feet are inside.

In the poorer areas, we found the street sellers with stalls laden with oranges, almonds and other nuts, fish and other foodstuffs. We soldiers have been advised to touch nothing that does not have a protective covering, for example, orange skins. And when one sees the dirtiness of the persons who sell foodstuffs in the street one realizes what good advice this is. Apart from infections in the foodstuffs themselves, many of the hawkers are not only dirty, but have nasty-looking sores on their hands and legs.

We did a little shopping for lace and ribbons.

In this quarter of the town we found prices weren't as high.

Afterwards we went to the YMCA—a well run show with a happy atmosphere of laughter, music and talk—for a cup of tea, a bully beef sandwich and bun. It really is a home away from home. One rejoices to see the YMCA triangle above the doorway. The same applies to NAAFI (*Navy, Army and Air Force Institute*) and other service institutes in these Italian towns.

We decided to see the part of Taranto over the swing bridge, next to the Castello Aragonese. Here we found a long winding, rather narrow cobbled street, which reminded me of El Muski, the bazaar street in Cairo. This street and its environs were very Italian, where we Europeans of other nationalities were decidedly in a minority. We heard shopkeepers engaged in loud and voluble conversations, saw children playing in the street, and gazed up at the women and children hanging at the windows above. In lowly dwellings the people were dancing, listening to singing, and involved in conversation in the numerous vino shops.

The people in this quarter appeared to be extremely poor, and the conditions in which they live are appalling. The filth, defective drainage and cramped living rooms must make disease rife in summer.

One of the most interesting sights was a procession of small boys and girls in the church. Both sexes were dressed in white, but the boys had blue collars and the girls pink. Easter is almost here and naturally there is much activity in the religious world at this time. At the top of the steps at the main door of the Church stood the village priest blessing his flock, who stood below with branches in their hands. Religion is deeply rooted in this land and the church undoubtedly has an all-powerful influence in the lives of its adherents.

We decided to go to Gioia del Colle (pronounced "Joya"). This is a fair sized town with many shops. We were hungry and thirsty and made for the YMCA. What a pleasure it was to see the face of an Englishwoman here, and that we could have one sausage roll each! After so much bully beef and dry buns the sight of sausage rolls was like an oasis in the desert. So was the sound of an Englishwoman's voice after the endless Italiano.

We found that there were some really good articles to purchase in Gioia, but the prices were preposterous. For instance one shop wanted £25 for a camera, which would cost at most £7 in New Zealand, and £1

15 shillings for an umbrella which I got for 14 shillings in Putignano. Gioio also has tree-lined streets.

It is great the way the Italians misuse the English language. An example "Military Reparations" (*instead of repairs*) printed on board outside a tailor's. But we, of course, murder their language in return, and the state of affairs has arisen where the Italian peasant even mispronounces his own words.

The dress of Italian women. Some wear long coarse woolen stockings, some silk, and most half-hose of wool like the stockings of a schoolboy. You ought to see their dirty knees!

Italian is a musical language, good to listen to and not difficult to pronounce provided one concentrates on pure vowels. Somehow I have not brought myself to the stage of making up my mind to learn it. The other night I went along to a class with Jack Mercer and got a fair idea of its elements. I know only too well how much trouble I would save myself in the shops if I settled down and learned a few phrases. Incidentally, the peasants in Southern Italy don't speak pure Italian, but dialect. They know pure Italian, however, and if one spoke to them in it they would respond in it.

Alex

DIARY ENTRY
6 Thursday: Departure of *Ruapehu*—perimeter picquet.
7 Friday: GOOD FRIDAY. On perimeter picquet, between 3 to 6 a.m. I heard owls. Caves' leave.
8 Saturday: Colonel's parade—lost mail—visit to Communal Farm—Allan

Letter No 22: Saturday April 8th, 1944
My sweetest beloved little girl,

We had the impression that business would be at a standstill in Italy on Good Friday—like it is in New Zealand, and that only religious services and processions would be held. However, we saw some Italian workmen on the job yesterday morning, and this sight convinced us that business would probably go on as usual in the villages. This turned out to be the case. In the first village, we passed through the shops were open and the people going about their business in the free and easy Italian way. Later we visited Alberobello. I tried out my little Italian in the shops. The natives of this country are pleased when they see soldiers are making an effort to learn their language. I asked: "Oggi è il Venerdì Santo!" ("Today is Good Friday!") When speaking English, the Italian find 'Fr' difficult to say; he also stresses the vowels in the word 'good.'

Alberobello is the site of the *trulli*, the quaint conical-shaped slate roofed houses. It is quite a good little place by Italian standards.

I priced some silk stockings and nearly collapsed when the woman asked £2 for them. It is better I don't buy stockings at such a price in case they don't turn out to be any good. The Italians are always on the cadge. Things, particularly food and tobacco are scarce. I am approached for cigarettes—often the locals want them to resell at a very high price. The 'Ities' are very slick in business, and are up to all sorts of tricks.

We eventually arrived at Putignano—the site of one of the famous series of grottos. Before visiting the grotto we spend some considerable time watching the town's Good Friday procession. At the head of the procession was a youth of about sixteen beating a kettledrum. Behind him were four or five small children carrying wooden crosses with wreaths of thorns on them. Then came two lines of black clad women and girls. They proceeded into the church for their observance and came out, some carrying candles and others chanting quietly. Another group proceeded onto the Basilica with the procession comprising boys in black velvet capes with gold border; men with the same types of capes who carried crosses; priests who chanted in Latin and an effigy of the Virgin Mary, dressed in black. Attendants collected money from the villagers. The returning women and girls bowed low before the effigy. Many were tearful. Some of the spectators removed their hats and others just stared and watched. Behind was the village band and, although dressed in dirty uniforms, were a surprisingly good combination. Business went on as usual in the street as the procession proceeded. Many of the fat shopkeepers just sat and didn't appear to take much interest in the procession. This surprised me much.

As we walked out of the town and along the quiet country road, I couldn't but comment on the perfect day, the quiet countryside and absence of anything military, which made me think that all was at peace. Our senior guide's promise that it was only one kilometer to the grotto seemed to be wrong, but it turned out that it wasn't much beyond that distance. A *trulli* stands at the entrance to the grotto. We had to pay 5 lire to enter. A small boy—presumably a son of the woman attendant—acted as our guide. We walked down a sloping tunnel to the spiral staircase, which leads to the bottom of the cavern. The Grotto was lighted by electricity and reminded us of the fairy palaces of our childhood stories. The formations were much better than those at Castellano. Like the latter, there were figures bearing a striking resemblance of persons and things: the Madonna, buffalo, grapes and so on. The Town Council of Putignano is justly proud of its little grotto. We walked back to town with two youths who had brought us to the grotto. We had an amusing discussion on smoking with these lads. They claimed to be fifteen. I gave them some cigarettes each. They went on to tell me that in Italy children of *"quindici anni"* (fifteen) smoke. (*Dad had mistakenly put "cinque anni," which is five.* Ed). I found out later that this appears to be a town and village where children have not much parental control. Those children that are well controlled by their parents do not smoke at so young an age.

Back in town few shops were open because of the siesta between 1 and 3 p.m. In one shop we found that the woman behind the counter was an American by birth. She said her father was Italian and her mother Irish, and rejoiced in the Christian name of Kelly. Kelly told us she had lived in Italy for twenty years and had eight children. In America, she said, most couples contented themselves with two children. From her we gathered the sorry state of affairs in this country. Her children she said lived almost entirely on greens. They had no meat and flour. It was her intention to take herself and her eight children to America after the war. We passed an interesting hour or so in that shop.

When it was time to leave in the truck, crowds of children flocked around us pestering for cigarettes and chocolate. So ended our Good Friday tour.

My collection of interesting insights is growing considerably. Please look after them and we'll sort them out and arrange them in the correct order when we are reunited.   Alex

DIARY ENTRY

9 Sunday: EASTER SUNDAY

H. C. (*Holy Communion*) with Jack. Visit to Gioia.

Letter No. 25: (*written on Tuesday, April 18th, 1944.*)

My sweetest beloved little girl:

On Easter Day, called *"Pasqua,"* I went to Gioia del Colle. I found things very quiet. I passed an interesting hour or so with a woman who had lived in America. Here with her and her relations we 'got on famously' They were very proud to hear us speak a little Italian. One of those present, a girl of about sixteen from Bari, told me she was learning French and German. Although I speak French appallingly, she was able to understand me. My German, however, was too rapid for her.

One always knows when one is getting near a village as one sees the domes and towers of churches jutting into the sky. I noticed this particularly during a train journey recently. It is surprising the number of churches some villages possess. In one, there were no less than eight.

Some contained some very good oil paintings, which must have considerable monetary value. On any available ground around here you see crops of wheat, beans and grape vines. Even in the mountains among the rocks and the scrub are small terraced strips of soil. The Italian peasant of the mountains must be a dogged, determined individual to persevere with his labour, which must give only a small return for his efforts.

The roads built under the regime are really very good considering some of the country they go through. Some people must have worked very hard to have accomplished what there is in the way of mountain roads. But I can't understand why some villages have been built where they are—away up in the mountains with no signs of land worth cultivating.

A custom here is the tendency for villagers to foregather for a chat in the principal square at eventide. A short time ago I watched with fascination the nightly scene at the village fountain. Here I watched women up to sixty years of age, and girls as young as twelve carrying 4-gallon tins filled with water on their heads. Their arms were free and they relied on their excellent sense of balance. Their only head protection was a rag turned into a circle. They must start doing this at a very young age to acquire the skill they display. One woman was a cripple and carried one basket contained a live fowl, a large bottle of water and a small bag of flour. In hanging out the washing the woman just reached up and took one article after another from the bucket or basket. The washing is then hung out on the upstairs balconies of most of the houses.

Alex

DIARY ENTRY
10 Monday: Ordinance instruction—on draft—Synchronization (*of watches, etc?*)
11 Tuesday: Lecture on security, the risks of malaria and VD—played bridge with Geoff Phelan.

Moving North

12 Wednesday April, 1944: Up since 3 a.m. yesterday.—Parade 9 a.m. There was an inspection and a talk. We left at 1300 hrs arriving at Bari at 4:30 with Barry Ogilvie—past villages and towns—A large donor gave us wheat, beans, almonds, olives.

13 Thursday: Up about 4:15 a.m. to board the goods trucks—we wanted tea, but there was no wood. We passed the damaged Station Palace— from the transit camp, we got trucks to the towns of Riardo, Pietramelara, *(then we crossed)* the Piedmonte Mountains, heading north and west *(towards Cassino)*. We took on water, met a Canadian doctor, and saw war-torn buildings. We visited a village and saw a father in the square—multi-"bambini" in Italy. We walked home with Don and Allan— war arms, lightning and thunder, heavy rain—saw a castle, dated 1422.

14 Friday: We were up at 7 a.m.—packing to move, setting off at 10 a.m. for Venafro *(in Molise province.)* We dropped off some chaps, then arrived there about midday. We drove over a mountain road, saw blown up culverts, passing down into a depression with a village—interviews with a CNA *(nursing assistant?)* We were posted following tea and bully *(tinned beef)*—To units 12 here?—Bed in a nunnery tiled with a red and white floor—damaged roof. We could hear gunfire.

15 Saturday: Woke to the pealing of bells in the nunnery—tiled floor— locality under the shadow of a rocky peak—olives were on the side of the hill—a rich, grassy valley—patches of snow to east. I walked to a village

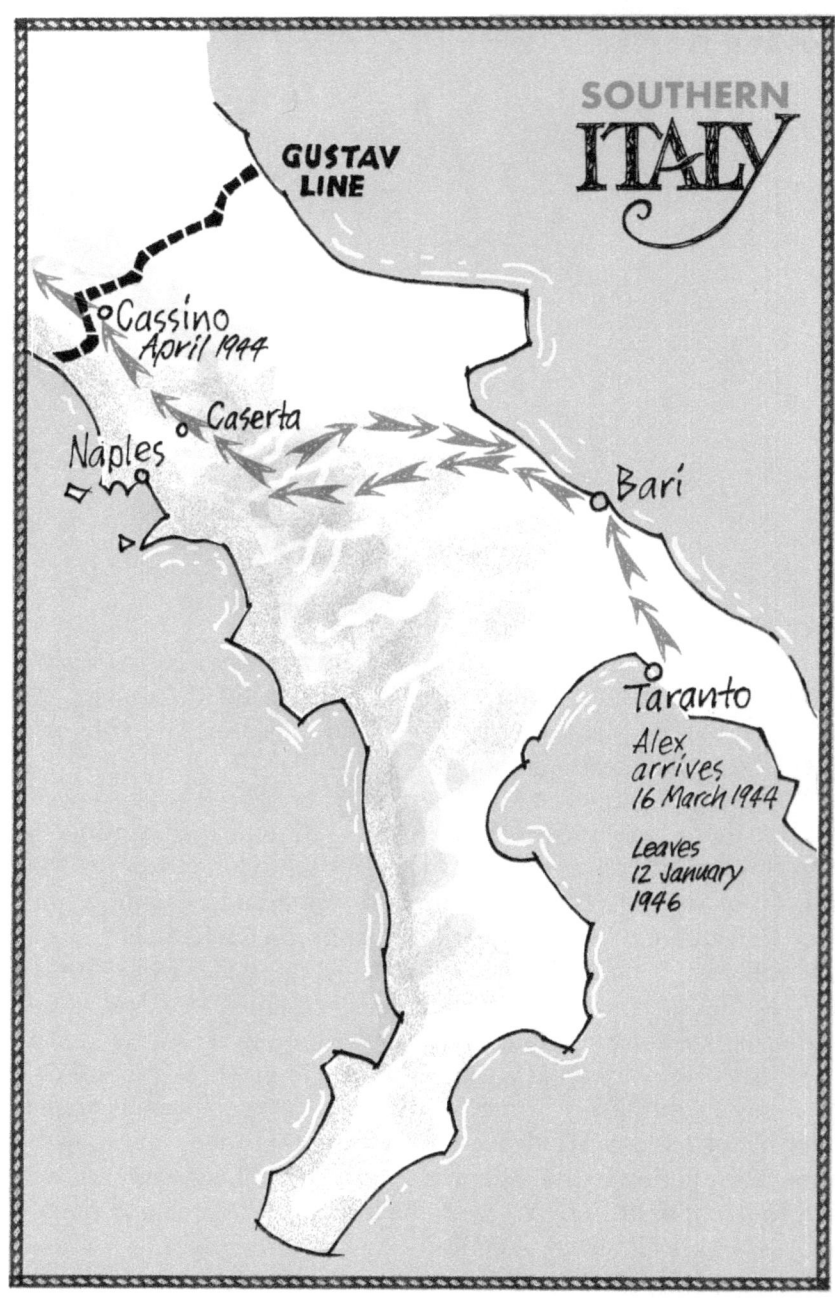

where there was an agricultural institute next to a spring—I counted eight churches, including the Chiesa Annunciazione, which we visited. I saw paintings, one dated 1088, and an organ in the chapel. To the village again in evening seeing people carrying water from a fountain—children, young and old women with 4-gallon bottles—wonderful balance, suppleness. With the washing done, they brought baskets from their flower gardens with their washing to hang out. There was a congregation at cookhouses for scraps. We saw "Gentleman Jim," with Errol Flynn.

16 Sunday: Another perfect day—took washing to village about 11, but as we were ready to move at 1230 hrs, I rushed back, picked up washing—lunch—left 1250 hrs, and arrived Echelon 'B' at 1340 hrs. About 7.15, at the last light—we left for the starting point at village, and reached RHQ 9:30 p.m. Talk to twelve of us by C.O. (L/Col Stewart). He laid out a plan for us. A few weeks will be spent on guns, then possibly gunnery school and recommissioning, with four to each Battalion. A struggle in dark for gear. We were told the road was shelled behind us on the way to the Regiment. Heard 88 mm guns and air bursts. Charlie Williams and I had to stay in hole in cliff at the cookhouse for the night. Some shelling.

17 Monday: Breakfast. Then interview by Battalion Commander, Major Spring, very decent. Reported to Bob Baker at the CPO (*Command Post Office*)—Posted to No. 2 Gun—Sgt. Harris. Shelling of road due to presence of a working party, eleven wounded—all spent day in dugouts—more shelling at night.

18 Tuesday: Fired five rounds in the morning. Jerry replied—rain in afternoon, later sunshine. A few rounds fired. (Airgraph from Mona). Rained some more. Wrote a letter to Margaret on Easter in Gioia.

19 Wednesday: More rain and intermittent sunshine. quiet in morning. Fired 3 rounds—preparing positions. (HS and M)

20 Thursday: A day of extremely hard work. To new position to prepare gun pits. Gil Patchett and I spent morning demolishing dugout and mending with sandbags and logs. Moved in during evening. Road shelled half an hour before Quad. We needed a winch and manpower to get guns in position. Retired about midnight.

21 Friday: A hard day in the dugouts. Felt exhausted, went to the doctor. Away all morning and the best part of afternoon. To come off guns. Worked till darkness on hole in ground. Lofty slept in dugout with me. Trees down.

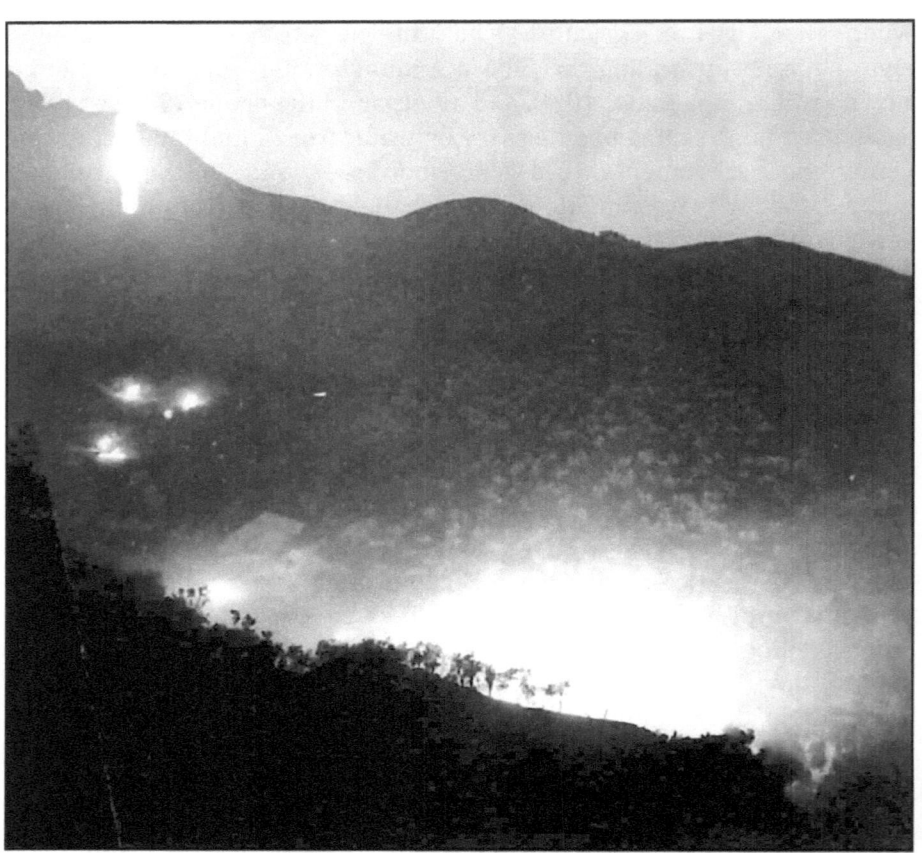

At the Cassino front

22 Saturday: How it blows here! Dust and stones whirl around the area. Smothered in it. In dugout all day. Played cards with Wally, Stan and Hugh. Bob Baker yarned with us for an hour or so at night.

23 Sunday: Another fine but windy day. Raising guns. Helped Bill, Patch and Lofty on dugout. Dust everywhere. A ME (*Messerschmitt 109*) was over our position. Dropped bomb on gully when chased by Spitfire. The AA opened up. Four guns, settled in new dugout. Frayed nerves through most trying weather conditions. Harassing and DF (*defensive fire*) during night.

24 Monday: Still blowing hard. Sandbagging to keep wind out of dugout. DF early morning. Heard enemy air cover overhead and AA opened up on them about 6 a.m. Did some more work on dugout. Played 500 with Wally, Stan, and Hugh at night. Jerry put airbursts over Tommy positions on the other side of hill.

Letter No. 26: Monday, April 24th, 1944

My sweetest beloved little girl,

Mostly recollections of times in NZ.

The Adam and Bruce cakes which I received (from New Zealand), although the lid was only sealed with sticking paper, was in excellent condition. A good fruit cake, or anything tasty like that would be most welcome now.

The question of a name is a big one. By the time you get this, you will have received my suggestions. I quite like Geraldine Broughton Protheroe and Richard Broughton Protheroe. I leave you to choose from Richard, Paul, Roger, David or Geraldine, Alison. Any of the above will please me.

Alex

DIARY ENTRY

25 Tuesday: ANZAC Day. People at home will be holding services of remembrance. Thank goodness the wind has blown itself out—at least temporarily. Fine, sunny and warm. Cleaning up area. Lt. Black, CPO, had a talk with me about my army service. (Letters 6th and 9th from Margie, 4th from Hilary. and photos of little Judy) A day of letter writing. Many took opportunity to take a good wash.

26 Wednesday: Wet and very cold today. Confined to dugouts. CDF (*concentrated defensive firing?*) tasks and harassing fire carried out overnight.

27 Thursday: Much firing by the crews in early hours—up to about 4.30 a.m. A little rain this morning. Very cold, but remained fine. Played bridge in evening with Bob Baker. Lt. Norman and Jim Rennie. Beer issued. Got bottle of gin and bottle of squash for 163 lire. Also issue of chocolate, cigarettes, and matches. Firing by D troop extinguished hurricane lamp, but candle still kept burning.

28 Friday: A really beautiful day. Crew fired a few rounds about 5:30 a.m. Gun maintenance. Read and rested in afternoon. Had a few drinks with Barry and others in honor of his 22nd birthday. Malarial prescription tablets, ointment and nets.

29 Saturday: Dull yet warm. Jerry shelled the road near old position during morning. I was told by Bob Baker that I would see M.O. at Battalion tomorrow. Spent the afternoon and evening reading "To Sing with the

Angels," by Maurice Hindus—a story of the struggle of the Czechs under their German masters. An able, well-constructed book.

30 Sunday: Packed my gear, shook hands with the boys, and left in the Jeep at 9 a.m. for RAP (*Regimental Aid Post*) at RHQ. Brief examination by doctor of abdominal trouble, then in ambulance along the "Inferno Track" to ADS (*Advanced Dressing Station*) at San Elia. All was quiet on the Cassino Flat below the monastery when we drove to Sant'Elia. The ADS is located in a large concrete stone building among the ruins of this village, and one looks across at Mount Cairo from the entrance. Saw doctor and stayed for lunch. The village buildings have been reduced, with few exceptions, to rubble—apparently by bombs. In places that once were offices and shops lie broken furniture, twisted metal, and so on, plus paper is scattered over many floors. A driver of the American Field Service drove another chap and myself to the C.C.S. (*Casualty Clearing Station*) How he sped along the road cut through the trees on the flat below the Monastery! His handling of the ambulance along a road pitted with holes, with bumps and sharp turns, was superb. What a position Jerry has—he can see everything from Monastery Hill! The fields around us were green and fresh. The cultivation of grape vines was going on. We sped past two fields of red poppies—and headed along Route 6 at between 40 and 50 m.p.h. to C.C.S. at last—I suppose its about 25 miles from Cassino. Given a bed in a tent. About an hour later 2 S.C. and four others of us were taken in a Tommy ambulance to Capua. There we changed ambulances and were whisked to 2 GH (*General Hospital*) where we arrived about 5.30. After the usual red tape, we were sent to the wards. Tea, chicken and lettuce were given us, then a basin of water for a wash. Then to bed.

MAY, 1944

1 Monday: Thorough medical examination by doctor. Told organically sound. Read, and played bridge at night.

2 Tuesday: Spent morning reading. Got up after lunch. Blue pants from QM (*Quartermaster's*) store. Walked around grounds. Former Italian barracks. Italian plaques still in buildings. Played bridge afternoon and evening. A beautiful sunny day.

3 Wednesday: Examined by Col. Coker just before lunch. Told nothing grossly wrong with me. In afternoon visited other wards and talked with Bas Sanders, Alan Black, Erne Blakey and Jack King. Heard details of poor Mark's death...Played bridge in evening.

4 Thursday: Our little Judy is 22 months old today, also it is six years since I met my beloved Margie for the first time. Walked around grounds with George Donnelly. Played bridge at night.

5 Friday: Another fine sunny day. Bridge this morning and again in the afternoon, and the evening. George Donnelly and I turned a score of 1000 behind from the night before into a win by 400 odd points.

Recuperation in the South

6 Saturday, May, 1944: A hot day. Left hospital in troop formation at 5 p.m. for Caserta Station. Drove through town. At the eastern end of what appears to be the main street is a very fine war memorial of marble with a bronze figure on top. I was able to see the King's palace. It and the flanking buildings are fine examples of architecture. The front face of the palace is rectangular wall on each side is an identical building curving in towards the corners of the palace. I was told that the grounds extended to a distance of four miles behind the building. The square in front of the palace—now a shambles—was probably a very fine one in peacetime. To the west of the square, across the railway line is a magnificent highway to Naples flanked either side by a line of majestic trees, which looked like elms to me. We boarded the hospital train about 5:30 p.m., and the carriage doors were locked. We walking cases were accommodated in six to eight-seat compartments. About 8 p.m., we left. I was disappointed that I couldn't see much of the countryside because night was coming. We went by way of Solomento. The grade was fairly steep. Below us to the southwest lay a magnificent highly cultivated plain of rich soil, with a generous number of trees as well. It was disappointing that I couldn't see it properly. This large area of land was indeed a contrast to the extensive stony areas I have seen further south. About 10:45, we reached Benevento, and here the diesel engine was replaced with an electric one.

7 Sunday: When we awoke in the morning, we were nearing Bari, having passed Barletta, Trani, Disceglie, Molfetta, and one or two other places on the Adriatic. We reached Bari just before 8 a.m. Our journey across the peninsula (for Caserta is no distance from the west coast) had occupied about eight hours. To "3" G.H., and after lunch we convalescent camp men were taken to Santo Spirito. Each of us was given a grading, and allotted a tent. We were soon in the process of settling in. (Bill Broad, Bill Marriott, Arch Bradford.)

8 Monday: A very hot day. We noticed it particularly at lunchtime in the mess when we were sweating profusely. I was examined by Major Blake Parker, 2 I.C. and was told I would be given two weeks' remedial treatment before reassessment. With two other chaps, I walked to Santo Spirito, which is on the calm and blue Adriatic. Here we saw adults and children swimming in the tiny harbor. Santo Spirito is much like other Italian villages, but is cleaner than most and looks more attractive as it lies on the coast. Some miles further north built on a stretch of land jutting out to the sea is Giovinazzo. Things were very quiet in Santo Spirito today due I suppose to the fact it was the festival of St. Nicholas in Bari. A truckload of chaps went to town to see the procession but they did not see too much owing to the denseness of the crowd. Relics and other emblems of the city's patron saint were carried through the streets. In the evening I walked through the olive grove to the nearby village of Palese to see "Mary Ann," an American air film at the cinema. Recce plane over at 1 a.m.

9 Tuesday: This morning I was transferred to "A" Company. We went on a route march to Palese and back. Although it was short, I found the going tough. In the afternoon, I walked to Santo Spirito, and then across paddocks to Palese. B. W-Williams, and another chap who came across from New Zealand with me, called at the camp. They told me they had been in Italy for six days. The greater part of the regiment had arrived here about a month earlier. B. W-W thought that the next regiment had arrived in Egypt. To Palese again tonight to see, "One Dangerous Night"—a really good murder mystery.

10 Wednesday: Much cooler today. This morning, we received our summer issue. In the evening I played several interesting rubbers of bridge. Taking the tattoo report here is a big job. With the aid of a hurricane lamp, I inspected the tents to see if each occupant was beneath his mosquito net!

11 Thursday: The weather is still fine and sunny. I gave a hand in the orderly room in the morning and afternoon. We had an identification parade this afternoon. Apparently, one of our number was suspected of committing a serious offense. The "small" Italian boy who looked us over did not pick out any of our number. In the evening, I went to a lecture by

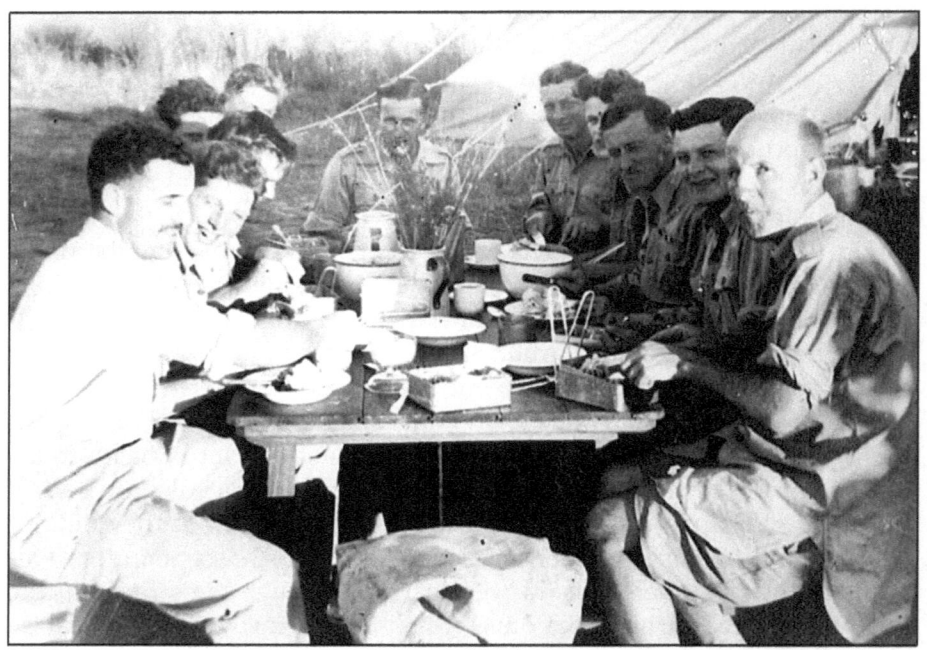

Dining *al fresco*. Alex is third from the right

R.A. Scobie of the Auckland Museum on the origin and migration of the Maoris. Fancy my coming all the way to Italy to improve my scanty knowledge of our Maori people! Scobie spoke from memory and presented a mass of argument to support the modern view that the Maori came from India, down through the chain of islands to Polynesia, then sailed from Tahiti to New Zealand. I learned a lot and am pleased that I know something about that fine race. (Letters 12, Margie, 1 from NM, one JR)

12 Friday: The weather in the early morning was fine, sunny and hot, but towards midday it cooled considerably. M.I. (*Medical Inspection?*) by Major Palmer in afternoon. Began fortnight's remedial abdominal exercises. Went for walk to Palese in evening, later played bridge.

13 Saturday: A really perfect day. Not a cloud in the sky; delicious sunshine and the slightest of breezes. I spent the afternoon and early evening answering letters, then I went to a private screening of pictures of Egypt, Palestine, Syria, and Italy taken by Bill Broad and S/Sgt. A Channing. They were very interesting, and some were really artistic.

14 Sunday: Today I revisited Bari. I spent the morning in a fruitless search for a good Italian grammar, and a good book on Southern Italy. I was not successful. Many grammars have been brought out for the English-speaking soldiers, but it is a waste of time buying this trash. However I met with some success in the after lunch when with Jack Mercer, (who is still at Advance Base) we came across a good grammar by an Italian scholar. The villagers understand me when I speak to them even having not studied the grammar, and with my vocabulary limited and my phraseology and grammar faulty.

The day was perfect and the sunlit Marine Parade looked wonderful. Later, I attended the presentation of Lorenzo Perosi's, "The Resurrection of Christ," at the famous Teatro Piccinni. This is an oratorio in two parts for soloists and orchestra. The choir was that of the Academia Polifonica Barese. The soloists were Giovanni Assante (Narrator), Jenano Godoy (Christ), Rosa Pazienza (Mary Magdelene), and Linda Scalera (Mary). The two parts of the oratorio were "From Death to the Tomb," and "The Resurrection." The symphony orchestra and the choir played and sang beautifully, but the work did not appeal to me the same as some of our fine English religious oratorios. I suppose my lack of appreciation was due to my lack of knowledge of Italian music. The conductor, Biagi Grimaldi, was most vigorous and tempestuous in his conducting. He was very amusing to watch.

There was an unfortunate incident during the performance. Someone sitting in the box above the Royal Box inadvertently dropped a cigarette butt on a cloth crown. It burnt through into the material below. Attendants rushed back and forth with water, which they poured on the crown. The water poured down on the box below and the occupants had to move back in haste. It also went down onto the floor below causing a tremendous commotion. However the choir kept singing and the orchestra playing. We returned to the Club and when Jack left for San Basilio, I went to the Garrison Theatre to see, "A Girl in Trouble"—amusing, but rather silly. The Marine Drive was thronged with people out for a walk before retiring. The sea was perfectly calm and the evening was perfect. (Airgraphs from Margie, Mother, Mona, Hilary; Letters Margie, Mona)

15 Monday: A medical inspection this morning with Major Knight. I am to stay here another week. I hitchhiked to Giovinazzo and Molfetta, a village and town respectively on the deep blue calm waters of the Adriatic. Giovinazzo is a fishing village largely built on a headland on the coast. Its chief interest for me was its collection of fishing boats on the calm blue Adriatic and on the beach. The village itself contained the inevitable square and *chiesa*. From the coast looking south this village looks magnificent. Distance lends enchantment to the view, but when I got there it seemed to be much the same as other Italian villages—several churches, the tree-lined village square, the dirty closely-inhabited tenements and other typical features.

Molfetta is one of the best towns I have visited in this land. It has a large fishing industry, which is natural, of course, for a seacoast town. There are many fine ancient and modern buildings and some show of life. The shops are open and have something to sell. I bought some post-cards with the intention of seeing some of the places pictured. First, I walked around the boat harbor to the twin-towered church of San Cor-rado through which I was conducted by a priest. In addition to the two twin towers, the church has three fine cupolas, the later being supported entirely by four stone pillars. Against the wall lean marble slabs on which there are etched figures of bishops and other persons. This place was a treasure of the period which later blossomed into the Renaissance when men turned to nature for inspiration in art and in all ways of life. The priest was filled with enthusiasm for his church and kept stressing 'anti-co,' disparaging other modern churches in the town. When I saw the oth-ers, I heartily agreed with him. There was the Church of the Heart of Je-sus, for example—a modern edifice made largely of marble. The interior, with its marble columns, looks very fine, but this and the other churches were showy and did not possess the quiet beauty of the ancient edifice. There are two fine memorials in the principal square. I spent the re-mainder of my time there in shopping. (Mother 18/4. Ash.)

Letter No. 30: Monday, May 15th, 1944

My sweetest beloved little girl,

I am looking forward very much to receipt of the snaps of Roger and our little Judy.

I received your No.1 Parcel. Everything was in excellent condition in spite of the fact that the (*biscuit*) tin had been bashed about....

Stan Bowker was the M.O.(*Medical Officer*) at Advance Camp about my asthma.

Alex

DIARY ENTRY

16 Tuesday: A conducted tour was made today. At 11 a.m., we went to the Castel del Monte, the hunting lodge of Frederick II. This is a superb example of Gothic architecture. There is a magnificent Gothic arch at the doorway; in the courtyard is an octagon; in fact, the whole building is an octagon. There are eight sides, eight rooms on the first floor, which is reached by a spiral staircase, and eight O-shaped towers. The beautiful Gothic arches and pillars, and the windows were things not to be forgotten. The spiral staircase leads to a vaulted roof. It is said that it is dangerous to go near the sides on a windy day because of the strength of the wind. I must consult the works of experts on this building. I know that the Castle was completed in 1240. The site is the key position to the whole of Apulia. It commands an approach from the Ofanto river to the north, is situated on the top of a rib of hills. I only wish I could draw. What excellent material for sketches—the symmetry of the building, its position the beautiful windows and arches, the quaint cone-like fireplaces. It is believed that a balcony once ran round the walls of the courtyard. All the rooms—with the exception of two private rooms which are walled up—are connected by doorways. I shall never forget the beauty of the blocks used. They are a natural conglomerate of marble, flint, pebbles and a ferrous material. And then there are the triple marble pillars in the rooms, which are broken at their tops by a simple, yet beautiful, leaf design. There is so much I could write about this castle if I had the architectural knowledge. We went there by bus, passing through Bitonto, Terlizzi, and Ruvo en route. We returned the same way.

In the evening, George Donnelly and I walked to Palese, where we had a few drinks and then went to the cinema. The film was a stupid American comedy, and we did not see it out. However, I didn't regret walking out as I had a chat with several Palestinians. Zionism is welding the Jews with a unity and giving them a national consciousness. These young men, alert, intelligent and keen were good examples of the young Jewish men who are bringing Palestine back to its former glory. Two were born in Berlin and the others in Palestine. Yet they all had something in common. They spoke to one another in Hebrew. The two former Germans spoke very good English; one had begun to learn it when he went to Palestine seven years ago and the other had learned it since he joined the army. He spoke with a German accent but said that was one thing the Army had done for him was to help him learn English! I must learn more about these interesting people.

More anon about this fascinating country. (Watch and birthday cake.)

17 Wednesday: The weather continues to be beautiful. The official photographer arrived this morning and took a photo of us doing remedial exercises. I spent the afternoon trying to get my mail up to date. The mess entertained the officers of the staff to dinner. The meal was good. There was the usual amount of drinking, songs and stories afterwards.

18 Thursday: Nothing of interest to record until the evening, when George Donnelly and I visited the home of an Italian in Santo Spirito. Two Mauritanians (*Mauritians*, Ed.) were also there—in a mixture of French,

N.Z. CONVALESCENT DEPOT IN ITALY

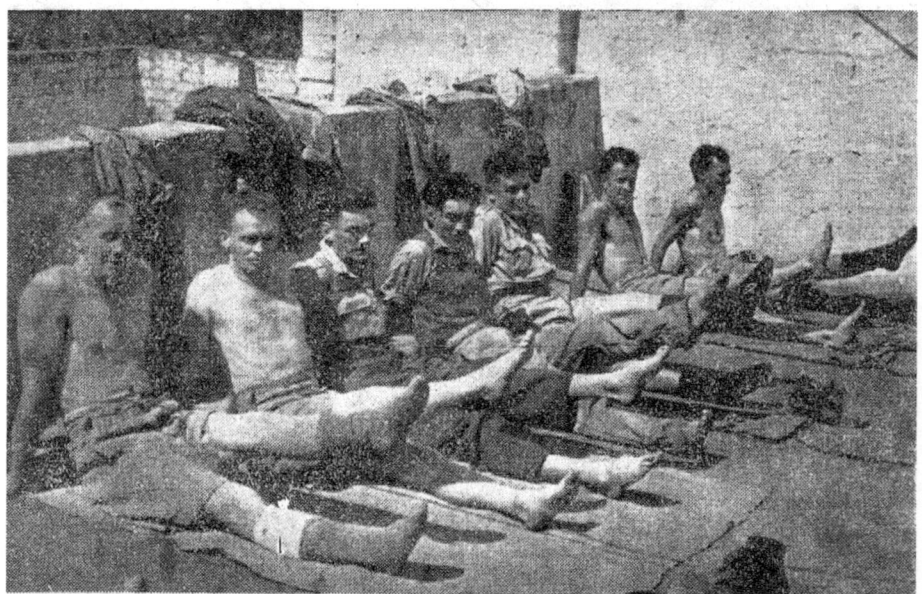

PATIENTS EXERCISING THEIR LEGS at the No. 1 New Zealand Convalescent Depot in Italy. From left: P. Morrison (Christchurch), I. F. Aitken (Hunterville), R. S. Downs (Shannon), H. L. Bright (Coromandel), D. F. Hiatt (Christchurch), Q. R. Purser (Pahiatua), A. G. Protheroe (Christchurch).

English and Italian we got on famously. The two natives were of Indian origin and one of them told me he could speak Hindustani. They gave us a colorful description of life on the island, of living conditions, climate and social life. I later took part in a Quiz session in the Welfare Centre. (Airgraph from Margie)

19 Friday: This evening I went to the opera—Puccini's "Madame Butterfly" at the Petruzzelli Theatre. It was the first Opera I had seen. What music, singing and excitement! No wonder the opera is regarded as the acme of musical expression. I particularly think that one must see the opera two or three times to enter properly into the spirit of it.

20 Saturday: A day in town with George Donnelly. It rained fairly heavily during the morning. We spent the day in walking around, chatting to Italian families, and on drinking *spumante*. It is a great custom of the natives to "air" themselves at night. There they were—in every street—chatting to one another outside their shops and homes.

21 Sunday: A perfect day. With Alf Canning and George Donnelly, I hitchhiked to Barletta. We were fortunate enough to ride on open trucks all the way. We passed through Giovinazzo and Molfetta to Trani. Here we walked the filthy cobbled streets. We visited the ancient church of

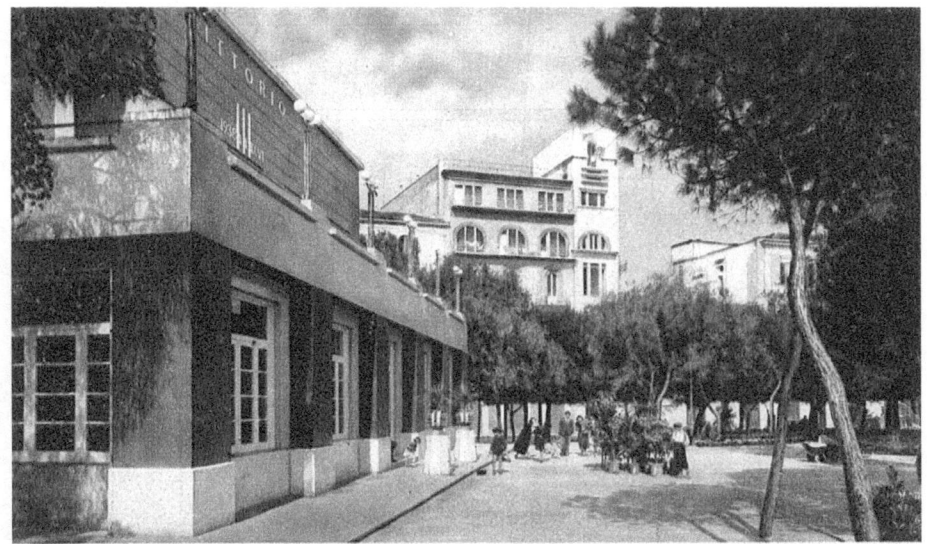

Barletta - Casa del Littorio.

Saint Francis (circa 1200), the interior of which was restored towards the end of the last century. The interior architecture—four columns supporting three cupolas—was reminiscent of that of the Church of San Corrado at Molfetta. We carried on to Barletta, a seaport town of forty-six thousand persons. The harbor is small—just an area between the land and a breakwater. In the backstreets, pea pods were being dried on the pavements prior to collection of the seed. Barletta is much the same as other Italian towns of its size—with good and poor buildings, a large tree and palm-lined square, and many churches, some old, some modern. We found a very good South African Services Club. We returned by ambulance and stopped at the YMCA in Molfetta for a cup of tea. George and I later visited an old cobbler in Santo Spirito, a village near to which were camped. The old fellow, although he makes you welcome with a bottle of *vino rosa*, will persist in speaking English of sorts, instead of giving us an opportunity to learn Italian. At some time, he had resided in America. He thought he knew English well, but personally I have never heard it spoken worse. He was illiterate in Italian also. We left early.

22 Monday: George and I went for a walk to Palese in the late afternoon, and along the Marine Drive, and through the streets of Santo Spirito in the evening. (An ammo explosion about 8:30 a.m. Blast broke many windows, some killed.)

Massafra (Taranto) - Santuario M. SS. della Scala Protettrice della città di Massafra

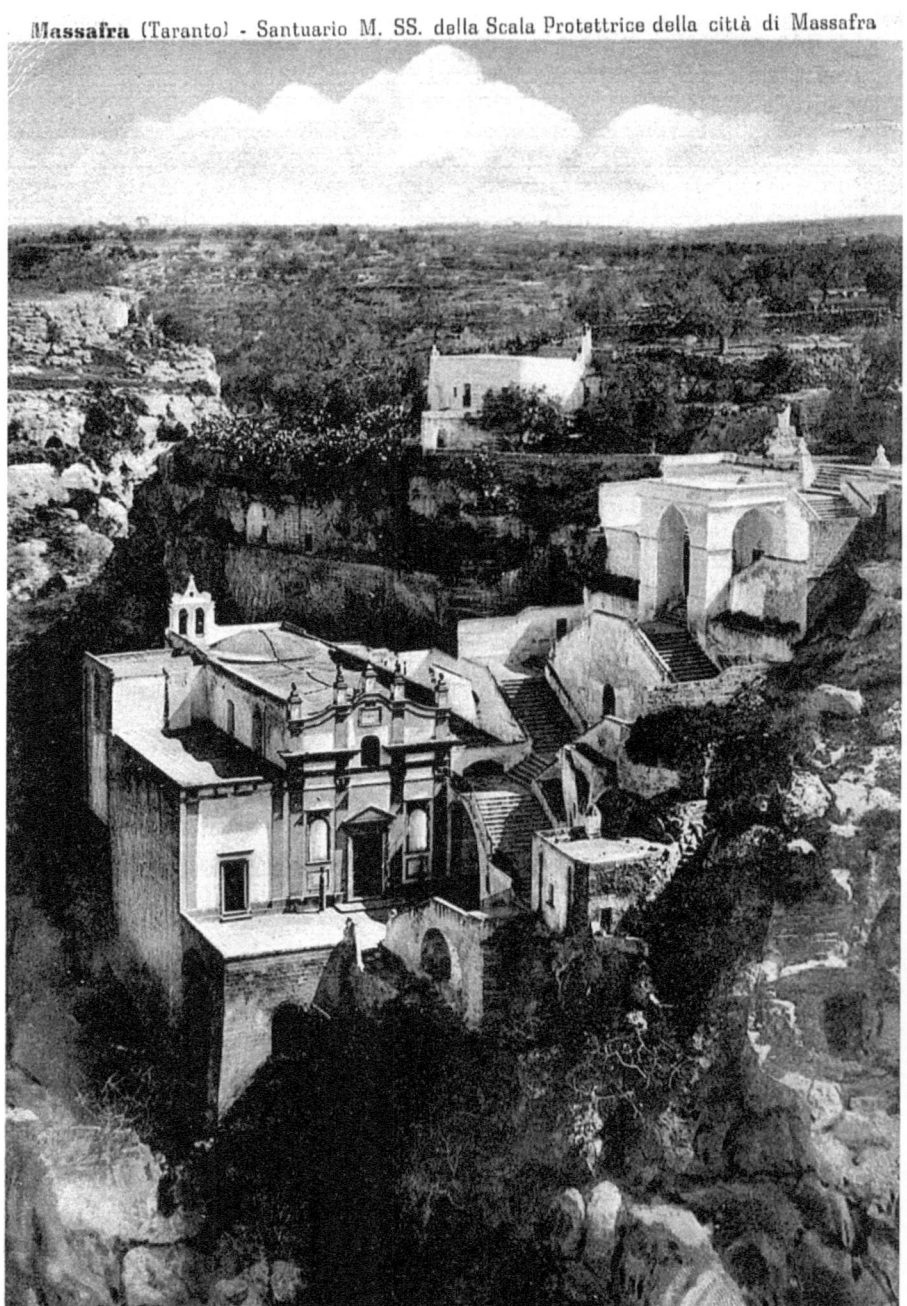

Foto Cav. V. Simone

23 Tuesday: Made A Grade this morning. I don't know why. After lunch, Alf, George and I resolved to visit Altamura, an inland town 30 miles from Bari. We were lucky. Two trucks took us to Bari and we set off along Route 96 to Altamura. We passed through Modugno, Biletto, Binelto, and Grumo, ordinary Italian villages and towns, to Toritto from which one gets a magnificent view of the Apulia plain, its towns and villages. After Toritto, the country became more open—reminiscent of much of New Zealand—green fields and a few trees. In most localities I have visited, there have been never-ending olives. Altamura is an old walled town. It is famous for its cathedral, which has been visited by Kaiser Wilhelm ("Kaiser Bill,") Victor Emmanuel and other celebrities. We reached the town during a storm and had to take shelter. When the rain ceased, we inspected the beautiful cathedral, of which the town is justly proud. I bought a book about it. It was by far the best church I have seen to date. When my Italian is better, I'll be able to enjoy the descriptions in the book, and learn something about the architecture. We climbed the belfry. What a panorama! The new and old buildings of the town and the rolling green land. We returned to town before dark.

24 Wednesday: C.O.'s parade this morning. Before lunch, Alf and I left on yet another trip—our principal objectives being the tombs at Andria and Canosa. Our first stop was Trani—there we spent a short time pricing goods in the shops, and then we visited *"l'antica cattedrale"* on the waterfront. As yet, I do not know the history of this ancient building, but what I saw of it convinced me of its antiquity—and of its importance in bygone days. There is a single tower—about a hundred and fifty feet high to the right of the entrance—the beauty of whose great bronze door we couldn't inspect because it was bricked up. The building is undergoing a thorough restoration. If repair work was not now being carried out there would be a strong possibility of the building collapsing. The interior has been stripped but there were signs of glory that once was there—traces of veneer of pink marble on the columns,'freckled marble' on the high altar, wooden stalls behind the altar and a few oils and monuments. The magnificent columns no longer have their veneer of pink marble, but traces of it indicated the former beauty of the pillars. We climbed the rotting wooden ladders to a point just below the steeple. What a show! To the east across the deep blue and calm Adriatic is part of the mainland—or an island near the coast of Albania; to the southeast are the headlands on which stand the towns of Biscoglie, Molfetta and Grannazzo; to the northwest is Barletta; and to the southwest the undulating landscape is capped by the Castel del Monte. An American Air Force officer, who had

Mottola (Taranto) - Corso Vittorio Emanuele

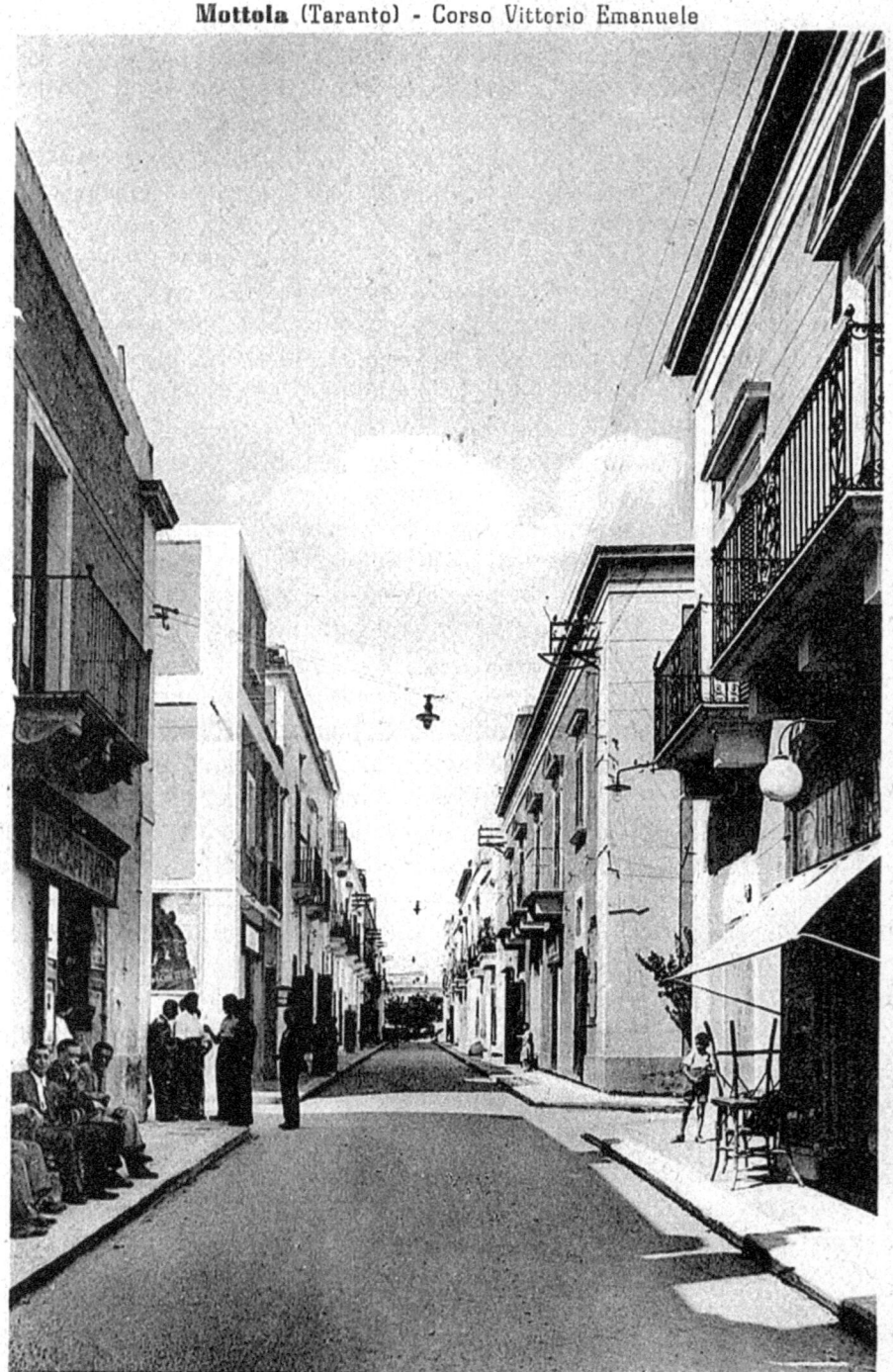

Foto Cav. V. Simone

nothing to do, gave us a lift in the jeep. First to Andria—a dirty old town with a famous antique—the tombs of the wives of the conqueror, Frederick II—Iolanda de Brienno, (died 1228) and Isabella of England, (died 1240). What a job we had to do to find their resting places. The natives were ignorant to an appalling degree of the most famous sight of their own town. The Cathedral turned out to be the correct place. The custodian was our guide. It was a very fine building with some particularly fine altars; notably the marble high altar of St. Richard. To the side of the latter are studies in stone of his life. Part of the roof is covered with excellent murals in oil. We went down to the crypt—what was formerly the ancient Royal Church. In fact, the Cathedral has been erected over it. The columns are of corona (*Coreno, ed.*) marble, and some of the tops are of Byzantine origin. The two queens are buried beneath slabs on the floor. The arches are Norman, i.e. circular. We then carried on to Canosa to see the lamb of King Boemondo at the Cathedral. This tomb is off the Cathedral. The doors of bronze have some medieval carvings and lettering. Inside are tablets relating to the life of this redoubtable warrior—conqueror of the Greeks and a Crusader. He died in 1111. Around the wall of the tomb are prayer boards in English, German and Italian and there is a slab on the wall with inscription in Italian. I must find out more about him. Our return trip—made at great speed in a bitterly cold wind—took us through Andria, Corato, Terlizzi, and Bitonto to Santo Spirito. We arrived back about 6 p.m.

25 Thursday: I left Santo Spirito at 8:45 a.m., and passed along the old familiar route—Bari, Casamassima, and Gioia to San Basilio. What was different from when I went along this road last time was the trees. They are now rich in flower and leaf, and looked very beautiful. The camp itself was improved—better roads and more buildings. I was very pleased to find that Jack is still here. At night, Jack and I revisited Mottola where we spent an interesting few hours drinking wine and chatting with a family we met there on a previous visit. A nephew was present. This young fellow spoke dialect, which I found impossible to understand. Many words were spelled differently from pure Italian, and those much the same are pronounced differently. The family had a young rooster tied by the leg. In vivid language, the *signora* described how enjoyable it would be for a meal when it was grown. We got a ride back to camp on a Polish truck.

26 Friday: M.I. (*Medical Inspection?*) Posted to "A" Depot. Early this afternoon, I revisited shop in Mottola with a Maori officer. Arrived during siesta period. Given three nips of fine rum and spent afternoon in improving my Italian. I learned a lot. Returned to camp for mess. Spent the evening at a Quiz and Brains Trust session in Lowry Hut.

27 Saturday: A day of activity. Transferred from Base Reception "A" Depot in morning. After lunch, Jack and I went to Massafra, the village on the Taranto road below Mottola. We arrived when all the shops were shut. Massafra has little of interest for the visitor—the chief exception being a deep valley where numerous little houses (now in disuse) have been built in caves in the valley's sides. An Italian truck took us to Taranto. The Italian soldiers who traveled with us were elated with the return that day of numerous P.O.W.s from North Africa. At a road junction on the island—i.e. old Taranto—a notice warned us that the area was out of bounds for health reasons. No wonder. When I last visited the area two months ago smallpox was then beginning to rear its ugly head. We spent the day searching bookshops as I am very keen to get a guidebook to Apulia. I half expected none (or not a comprehensive one) was to be had. Unlike Bari, the city was alive with activity: the shops had plenty to sell, and the natives looked as if they had something to do. I could not help but notice the better class of people compared with Bari and other places I have visited. In the business area, the men and women were fairly well dressed and most of them looked clean. We caught a RAF truck proceeding to Bari. The driver took the wrong road. We went to Martina Franca and had to come back to the main road through Massafra, where the streets were crowded with the natives and the Italian troops stationed there were taking their evening walk and having their nightly chat.

We caught a truck, and a passenger was a Dr. Heinrich Erlich, a physician with the Polish Medical Corps—a Polish physician holding the rank of private—and a sometime Lt. Col. in the R.A.M.C., Professor of Psychiatry at the Universities of Warsaw and Vienna, and a linguist to boot speaking Polish, German, Russian, French, Hungarian, English, Arabic, and Hebrew. He asked me to see him again. (M and M—airgraphs)

28 Sunday: This afternoon I went to Gioia del Colle with Jack. We obtained a ride on the back of a Polish ATS (*Women's Auxiliary Territorial Service*). I could not help but notice how neat, clean and fresh they looked compared with the *signorine*. The pride of Gioia is the Norman castle we visited—a very fine building. We climbed the tower from which we got a fine view of Gioia and the surrounding country. We, (or at least I,) visited the shop of (*Kelly*), the Italian woman who had resided in America. We practiced our Italian and her family tried English pronunciations. They found them very difficult. We later went to where our Italian

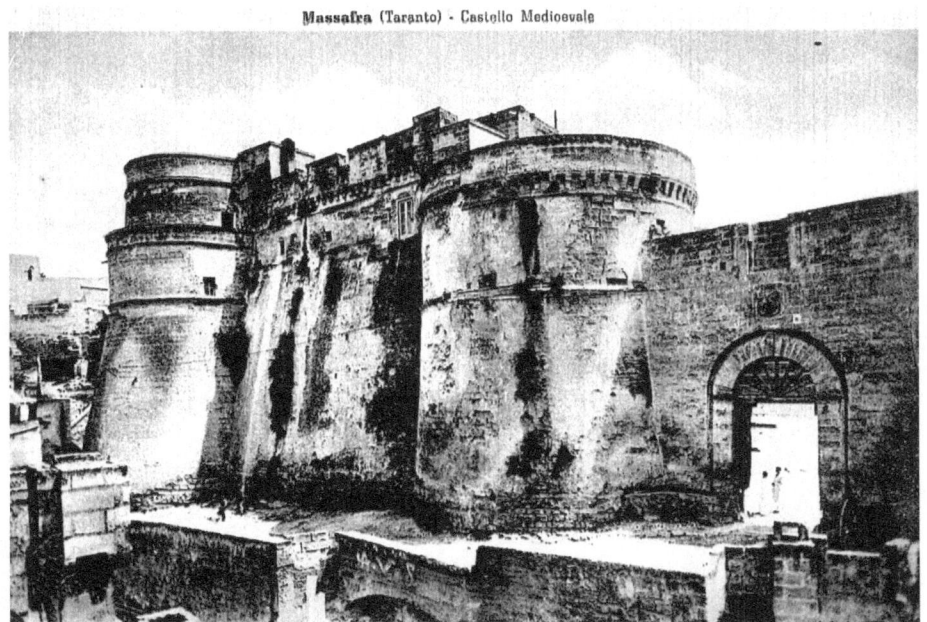

Massafra (Taranto) - Castello Medioevale

friends were getting ready to attend the Trinity Sunday procession. The procession consisted of children, church elders, priests, and an effigy of the Virgin Mary and Child borne on the shoulders of several sturdy men. The village band proceeded along the principal streets, with the priests chanting and the band playing suitable music. It was like other religious processions we have seen here.

29 Monday: Soon after 9 this morning John Drayton and I resolved to visit Brindisi, some 65 miles from the camp. We got a ride to Taranto, then walked through the city to the Brindisi road, and, in a series of rides, reached Brindisi about 1 p.m. En route, we passed through the hill town of Grottaglie, then Francavilla Fontana, Latiano and Mesagne. The Brindisi highway looked beautiful with its rows of cypresses and pines alternating in some places. The countryside nearer Brindisi is more open than that further back. On our journey we noted the fine fig trees and the healthy grape vines. Brindisi, a very ancient town, is the southern terminal of the Appian Way. This most famous of roads was begun by Appius Claudius in 312 B.C. It is about 350 miles long and it is paved with hard stones in irregular blocks fitted closely together. We unfortunately arrived during the siesta period, but we were not deterred. We made our way to the waterfront where we inspected what is left of the two pillars of the Appian Way. We learned that the greater pillar had been destroyed by bombs. Its base has been bricked up. Nearby is the site of the villa of Virgil. We then went to the Church of San Benedetto, renowned for its famous ninth century cloisters. These, we found, were bricked up against possible bombing, but we were still able to appreciate the beauty of the Roman architecture. A snack at "The Club" followed, and we set off to get back to Taranto. We stopped on route at Francavilla Fontana, where we inspected the chief church. The stone used has been painted to give the appearance of marble. A pity as the interior architecture is rather good. In Taranto, today an American and I were able to get some of the beautiful volumes of the Italian Touring Club. A great find and a great bargain.

The Italian peasants, and in particular, the womenfolk work very hard. About 7 o'clock at night they return home from the fields for the village packed like sardines in horse drawn carts, or on foot. Many of them have to walk several miles, carrying tools as well and end their walk with a steep climb. This is their life day in, day out, year in, year out. Then, of course, there is the matter of how 'ironing' is done here. As electricity is unknown to many of the peasants, the interior of any iron is filled with charcoal, and the iron is then whirled around until the red hot charcoal heats the metal.

Also, the locals do not show much respect for animals. In fact many are excessively cruel on them, particularly horses. Carts are overburdened. The poor beasts often collapse under the weight. When this happens several Italians will lift and shafts and horse to its feet. But none of the load will be removed.

Camp was reached again just after 8 p.m., and the two of us saw the first film to be shown at the open-air theatre, "For Ever and a Day," a tribute to London and its people. AA Guns at Taranto opened up during the picture. Was it a raid? (Jack)

30 Tuesday: A really hot day. After mess, Pat Bowes and I went to Mottola, but were ordered out by a provost at 7:30 curfew time, when the local Ities were returning from their labors. We returned to San Basilio, and visited my Polish friend, Dr. Heinrich Erlich. He welcomed us with a feed of scrambled eggs. Later in the evening some other Polish medical officers came into the tent. We had a lively conversation—on Russia, the war, and English speech idioms.

31 Wednesday: Again a very hot day. I went to Mottola in the late afternoon to collect the snaps. The Italians do make a poor job of photography. Perhaps the poor quality paper is partly the reason. Pat and I revisited Dr. Erlich, who returned with us to our camp. We put him on the Chess Club.

JUNE, 1944

1 Thursday: A sweltering day. On duty all day as Depot Orderly Ser-geant. In view of this, there is little, if anything, to record, as I was tied up in the Orderly Room at the time. (Airgraphs M and M)

2 Friday: I rose early and reported to the RAP (*Regimental Aid Post*) at 6:45. The M.O. (*Medical Officer*), a major, arrived about 7:30 and I saw him about 8 a.m. He told me if the pain got worse to take aspirin! Don't worry about it, he said!! There are some remarkable medical men in this army of ours!!! In the early afternoon, I went to Gioia with Mac. The American with the jeep took us out to Putignano. We passed the best part of the afternoon in a restaurant, Mac talking with four Americans, and I with the family. A Tommy ran us back to Gioia. As is the custom in this country, the streets were thronged with people making their nightly chat with the neighbors. (In Italian, the *passeggiata*, Ed.) We returned to camp about 9:30 in the Provost Truck. Jerry was over Taranto about 11 p.m. He dropped flares. The AA opened up vigorously. (2 Margie, 1 from Mother).

3 Saturday: Terry, Pat and I went to Gioia this morning. We revisited two families we know there, talked to the women and played with the chil-dren and babies. We returned to camp about 9:30 with an American, who spent the night with us. (PM's visit this morning. There was talk of (1) Furlough, (2) Where we are to be used, (3) Rehabilitation.)

4 Sunday: To Gioia this afternoon for a few hours. Revisited the home of an Italian woman and chatted with her, her relations and a friend, and played with two babies there. After tea, I did some training, along with the guard, for camp duties tomorrow.

5 Monday: Reveille from today on—at 5.15! With other members of the Guard Camp, I got myself a rifle, etc., to be ready for the ceremonial pa-rade. After the inspection by the Depot Officer, we marched to the Guard Mount behind the Pipe Band. The changing of the Guard went off fairly well considering we are Artillery. I made two small mistakes. The Colonel inspected us at 0930. "Quite Good" was his comment. During the day and night, I played cards. There was a bad motor accident outside the camp in the early evening—four Italians being killed. (Parcels, 3 and 4 from M., and airgraphs, May 16)

6 Tuesday: D-DAY. I arose early, about 5:45. Just before the Guard change, one of the boys told us that the invasion of Europe had begun! This is the supreme event we and all the people at home—people every-where—have been longing for during the last two or three years. And now its has started, Pat and I went to Gioia del Colle later in the morning.

Another chap on the truck was an English seaman from Taranto who told us that he had been detained and questioned by the S.I.B. (*Special Investigation Branch.*) The reason for this was that Jerry has been dropping agents over that seaport of late, and the SIB, of course, are trying to locate them. From Gioia, we trudged for about four weary miles along the dusty Putignano road beneath a blazing sun. An Itie peasant picked us up in his cart. I spoke to the farmer, who told us he had never been to school. (He was only about 32 to 35 years old.). He told me he could not read and he could write only with difficulty. Such is not an uncommon thing in southern Italy. The peasants are shrewd in business in spite of this lack of education, but we were no sooner underway than one of our own trucks came along and we transferred ourselves to it.

In Putignano, the streets and shopfronts were gay with flags in honor of the liberation of Rome on Sunday. They did not seem to bestow any generosity on the representatives of the armies that had driven the Germans out! I don't know what the people of central and northern Italy are like, but I do know the southern Italian well. He is always pestering the soldiers for something—cigarettes, chocolate, matches, beef—in fact, almost anything. It goes without saying that we are forbidden to sell anything to the natives. These people have plenty of money, but they can't buy anything with it as there are no goods to be had. The vast majority of them live in filth and dress in rags.

In spite of this, and in the spirit of the celebration, we whiled away the day walking around the streets, having a few drinks, some eggs and vino, and a chat at a restaurant with an Italian who had lived in America for ten years. This man was interesting. He told us he did not like his fellow Italians as they were always trying to outdo one another! I heartily agreed with him! This man had lived in America for ten years and had only returned to Italy in 1920 at the request of his aging mother. He did not like Italy. The climate was beautiful, but the people were no good, they were always trying to cheat one another and that did not appeal to him. I need hardly say that his comments were very true. The shopkeepers and villagers are always out to fleece us. I heard an interesting comment on the radio last night that the Allies had been mobbed enthusiastically by the Romans today, then robbed enthusiastically tomorrow!

There was an unfortunate incident just before the Caves' Trip trucks left for the camp. One of our chaps—a little "merry"—was caught having "souvenired" an Italian flag from the facade of the Communal Theatre. The local constabulary and onlookers gathered around. The truck driver refused to leave until the flag was handed over. Eventually our friend was persuaded to hand back what most of us considered a worthless souvenir. At camp tonight, the Second Front was on almost everyone's list—following the BBC bulletin, Churchill's statements, and the King's speech. The day of reckoning has come for Germany for Dunkirk, etc.

Letter No. 37: Tuesday, June 6th, 1944

My sweetest beloved little girl,

....no matter what name you and I finally decide on, we'll both be equally satisfied with it.....

Your ever loving and devoted Alex—For Judy and the new baby—Roger?

Alex

DIARY ENTRY

7 Wednesday: To Taranto after lunch with Terry. We spent the day in perusing books in bookshops. Quiet and most enjoyable. (Airgraph from Mother.)

8 Thursday: Today I was placed in charge of the Caves trip. By way of a change, we went through Gioia to Putignano, and then on to Conversano. It was my first visit. We climbed the tower of the Norman-Swabian castle, which is mostly inhabited with twenty to thirty families living there. The panorama from the tower was a fine one. To the east, lies the blue Adriatic, while to the north, west and south, lie the rolling lands of Apulia. From the castle, we went to the old cathedral where Mass was being celebrated in honor of the Feast of Corpus Christi. The Gothic doorway with its two flanking icons was very good. However, I was not greatly impressed with the interior. A brief glance inside the beautiful little church of S. Cosmo, with its fine paintings and chapels, followed. We watched the colorful procession from the church. From what I saw of the people of the village, I could not help but conclude that they were of a better type than those of most other small town and villages I have visited. They were neatly clad and washed. It was a refreshing sight. We soon set off for the Grotto at Putignano, where we lunched, and then went to the village for the afternoon. With three other chaps, I passed the time at the home of an Italian family. A thoroughly enjoyable day.

9 Friday: To Bari, with Pat and Dudley, for the day. In the morning, we passed an interesting hour in the boat harbor where the fish market was in full swing. Here we saw Italians selling sea eggs, squid and fish and making a tremendous din while doing so. Some of the buyers sat at tables under umbrellas and demolished the sea eggs. They washed them down with a red wine known as the 'purple death' to we Kiwis. We went

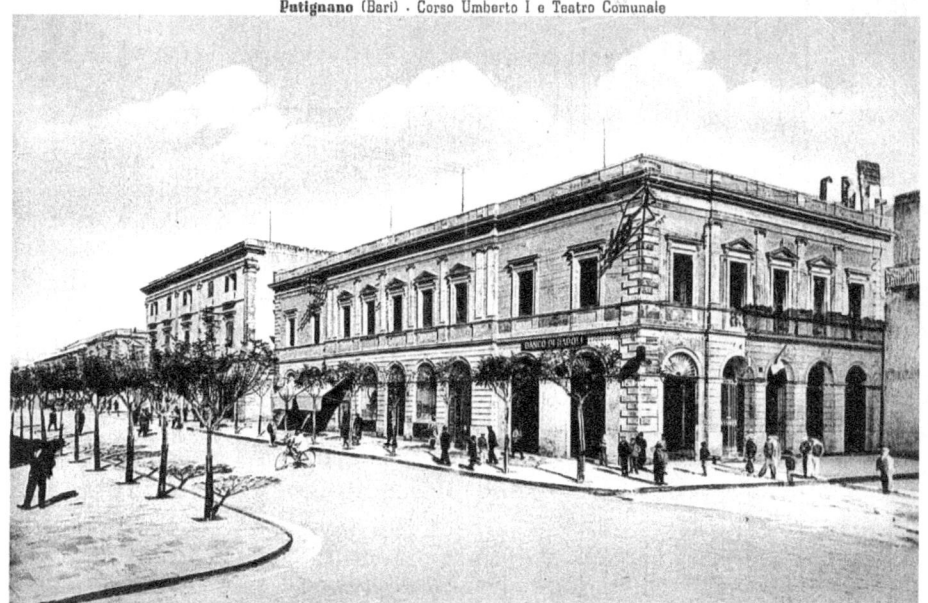

Putignano (Bari) · Corso Umberto I e Teatro Comunale

to old Bari, through its narrow, cobbled streets where we chatted with the inhabitants. A woman told us that a kilo of bread cost 90 lire on the black market. We spent the afternoon and early evening in modern Bari.

10 Saturday: Colonel's parade this morning. Afterwards, Alex Dudley and I went to Massafra. We passed the time in a wine shop with two Polish soldiers. One of the soldiers and I kept the conversation going by talking in Italian. They had no English, and we had no Polish. The Massafra villagers were, we found, sly and shrewd. They did not appeal to us.

11 Sunday: To Holy Communion early this morning. How refreshing, inspiring and necessary is H.C. for one who believes! In the afternoon, I went to the beach in the Gulf of Taranto. The outing was marred by a little light rain. Spent the evening in camp after a short walk.

12 Monday: This afternoon, Alex Dudley and I set off for Castellaneta, some five or six miles away. We were picked up by a small truck about half way there. The village was very uninteresting and we were glad to get away again. To the pictures at night—a Wild West film. The commentary on a short about the return of men from Puglia was met with a very bad reception. (23/5, M. Airgraph)

Letter No. 39: Monday, June 12th, 1944
My sweetest beloved little girl,

It is five months since that memorable occasion at Lyttelton when I last saw my homeland. Each and everyone of us in this country realizes to the full what a wonderful fine place is our little New Zealand with its happiest of associations, with its kindred spirits, its cleanness and freshness. The more we think of our own land, the dearer it becomes. Thank goodness there is such an excellent airmail service. Nineteen days only to the addressee in Italy.

All life is wonderful, but it falls down in adults where there is a lack of adjustment. By this, I don't wish you to think I mean one should have the fatalistic philosophy of the Muslim, or the passive attitude of the Buddhist, but rather a sense of joy in living whether the road be easy or bad.

You might be surprised to learn that we know less of the war situation than you people in distant New Zealand. The majority of us never hear the radio news, and in many areas one only gets a weekly summary of the news (from the *NZ Times*). One thing I do miss very much is radio music. You know how keen I am on good music. It will be a great day when I can turn on the radio and listen to those beautiful masterpieces of Chopin, Bach, Liszt, Wagner, Elgar, etc. Music gives me a tremendous amount of pleasure. It fascinates me and always will. Then, there are books—the books I love so well. I read nothing now. I don't think I have read a book since I arrived in the Middle East. I study Italian almost daily, but that doesn't give me half the pleasure that a good book does. However, the practice I get at speaking Italian with the natives gives me a little mental stimulation.

The new member of the family will now be at home in Whareora Terrace—whether it be Roger, or Geraldine/Alison.

Alex

DIARY ENTRY

13 Tuesday: The Caves trip today. The Route: The Camp, Mottola, Noci, Alberobello, Fasano, Monopoli, Putignano—then home. Our first stop was at Alberobello—("Beautiful Tree") in English—a quaint little village of *trulli* houses (beehive-shaped) in the heart of *trulli* country. The roof is usually adorned with a stone design. When we arrived we found the village getting ready for the festival of San Antonio that day. The local band marched through the streets playing religious music. From Alberobello, we drove along a particularly winding and narrow road over the hills to the main coast highway towards Brindisi. San Fusano came into sight—away below us on the plain between the hills and the beautiful Adriatic. We didn't stop at Fasano. It is a fine little town, and looked very attractive with its tree-lined streets. Monopoli was reached at 11:30. There, we spent an hour. The town nestles on the coast, and it has a particularly

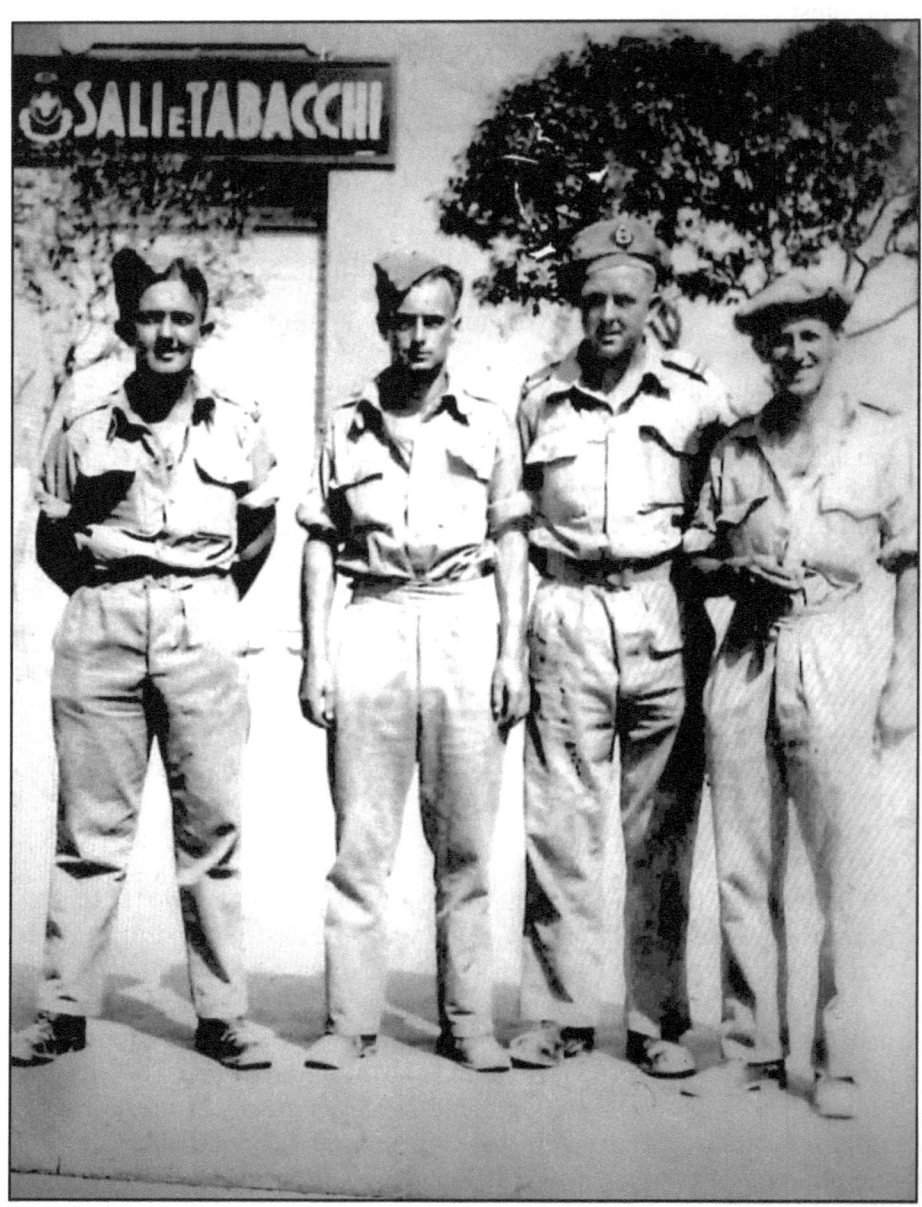

Alex Dudley, Pat Bowes, Terry Ellison, and Alex in Taranto, June, 1944

fine little harbor and a large piazza. An area we visited was occupied by the *Tedeschi* (*Germans* in Italian) not long ago. The Italian peasants told me a good deal about the German activities in the district. They said the Germans arrived at their one and two-storied farmhouses at midnight. The Italian occupants of the upstairs rooms were summarily ordered to the ground floor. The Germans did well for themselves at the expense of the local people. They fed off the countryside to no small degree.

Interestingly, this is how they made coffee. First, cow's milk, (not milk powder), then ten eggs, coffee, grain and marsala (a type of wine) were added to give flavor to the beverage. I should say that the brew would be excellent. Then they robbed the Italians of all their wine. One old woman took me to her storeroom. Here I saw a dozen huge wine casks and a similar number of huge glass bottles for wine. All were empty—the *Tedeschi*, so the old woman told me, had either drunk the lot, or taken what was left away.

We arrived at a farmhouse where they were making bread, and were given a goodly piece and found it very tasty. We were also given a little curd to eat with it.

Italy is a land of contrasts in weather. There are long periods of beautiful fine, sunny weather and when it rains the water usually comes down like a torrent almost all day for several days. The harvest is now under way. One sees the locals reaping the crops by hand. What tenacity and patience these people show in their labors. We left Monopoli and lunched at the Castellana Caves, then spent the rest of the afternoon in.

14 Wednesday: To Taranto this afternoon with Terry, Pat and Alex. We had a snapshot taken together in the Piazza Maria Immacolata. Visits to bookshops, and to the Royal Navy Petty Officers' Club filled in the day. There, we had two bottles of beer each! How welcome and refreshing after the awful Italian vino!

Moving North Again

15 Thursday June, 1944: Repacking once again. Convoy left at 12:30. At Bari, thirty of us to a (*train*) cattle truck with all our gear and rations. I, for one, slept little during the night.

16 Friday: Between 5 and 6 in the morning, we boiled the billy a few stations south of Caserta. Shunting operations caused a halt for a few hours. We reached Riardo (*south of Cassino*) about 11 a.m. A meal and a good wash. Then Pat, Dud and I went to the village. Joined at a wine shop by another Kiwi, we passed an interesting hour or two with an Italian, his family and his friends. After mess at night, we revisited the village for an hour or so.

17 Saturday: Packed again this morning, and then by truck to join the Div (*Division*). The chaps who had not seen anything of the Cassino area previously were most keen to get a sight of it. When the renowned Trocchio feature came into sight all eyes were alert. We gazed up at the ruined and desolate Castle Hill and the battered Monastery. Cassino itself was a scene of appalling devastation—shattered buildings, vast heaps of rubble, twisted girders. The town has been obliterated. Further north in the Liri Valley, with its holes and scarred trees and buildings, we gazed up to the monastery, which, on the northern side, is in surprisingly reasonable condition considering the bombardment. To the Division area at last. Back to the old gun and familiar faces again. In the evening, I met old many old friends. A full day. Thunder, lightning and heavy rain at night.

18 Sunday: There was heavy rain for most of the day. The bivvy is taking it well with the rain getting inside in a few places. Compulsory church parade for the Regiment this morning. First, there was a troop parade and inspection, then we marched along the sticky road to the Regimental Parade Ground. Padre Horwell was obliged to cut his address short because of a sudden downpour. Later, Jack and I attended a celebration of H.C., Presbyterian-style. I could not help but think how, in spite of the sincerity of the Padre, it lacked the beauty of the Church of England service. There was heavy rain nearly all day. I spent the time in my bivvy in writing and in reading a book by A. R. Burn on the modern Greeks, and rereading the sublime verses of Keats. What a genius he was! He will live forever in the realm of literature. During the day, we were regaled with music from the BBC, Berlin and other radio stations. It was mostly good stuff, thank goodness. A radio is a great boon here. It is good to have good books on hand, because it would be so easy to let one's intellectual self become stale.

19 Monday: The weather is still threatening, but there was no rain until the afternoon. Today, I am the NCO in charge of the Transport Check Post. A boring job, but at least I have plenty of time for reading and writing. A word or two about the countryside. The area here is thickly wooded with fine oaks and other trees. From our bivouac area, we gaze upon a countryside of gentle slopes and vales—richly green and undisturbed. The bivouacs of various units are dispersed among the trees over a wide area. What little I have seen of the Italians in this part of central Italy has caused me to conclude that they are a better type than their compatriots of the south. They look better, and I have been told they are much more friendly and hospitable. More anon on them. In the evening, with several other chaps, I passed an interesting few hours in the home of an Italian.

20 Tuesday: I finished my fatigue at 9 this morning. It is fine and sunny again. Our daily routine is roughly as follows: 0600, Reveille; 0630, Check Parade and Routine March; 0730, Breakfast; 0915 (circa), Parade and Inspection. Then after, maintenance and drill until midday. The afternoon is free. After mess at night, Jack and I visited a nearby farmhouse. We received a warm welcome from old white-haired lady (aged 75), her daughter, granddaughter and the father's five children. The womenfolk were busy baking bread when we arrived. It was done thus wise: the bread was placed in a stone oven, which was loaded by sticks and charcoal piled in the opening. It was an effective way of baking the tasty brown bread as we found out when the old lady gave us a goodly piece each; and a piece of curd as well. A little curd is alright. It is very filling. The old lady showed me her wine store. The large kegs and demijohns were all empty. The *Tedeschi* made sure of that. The daughter of the old

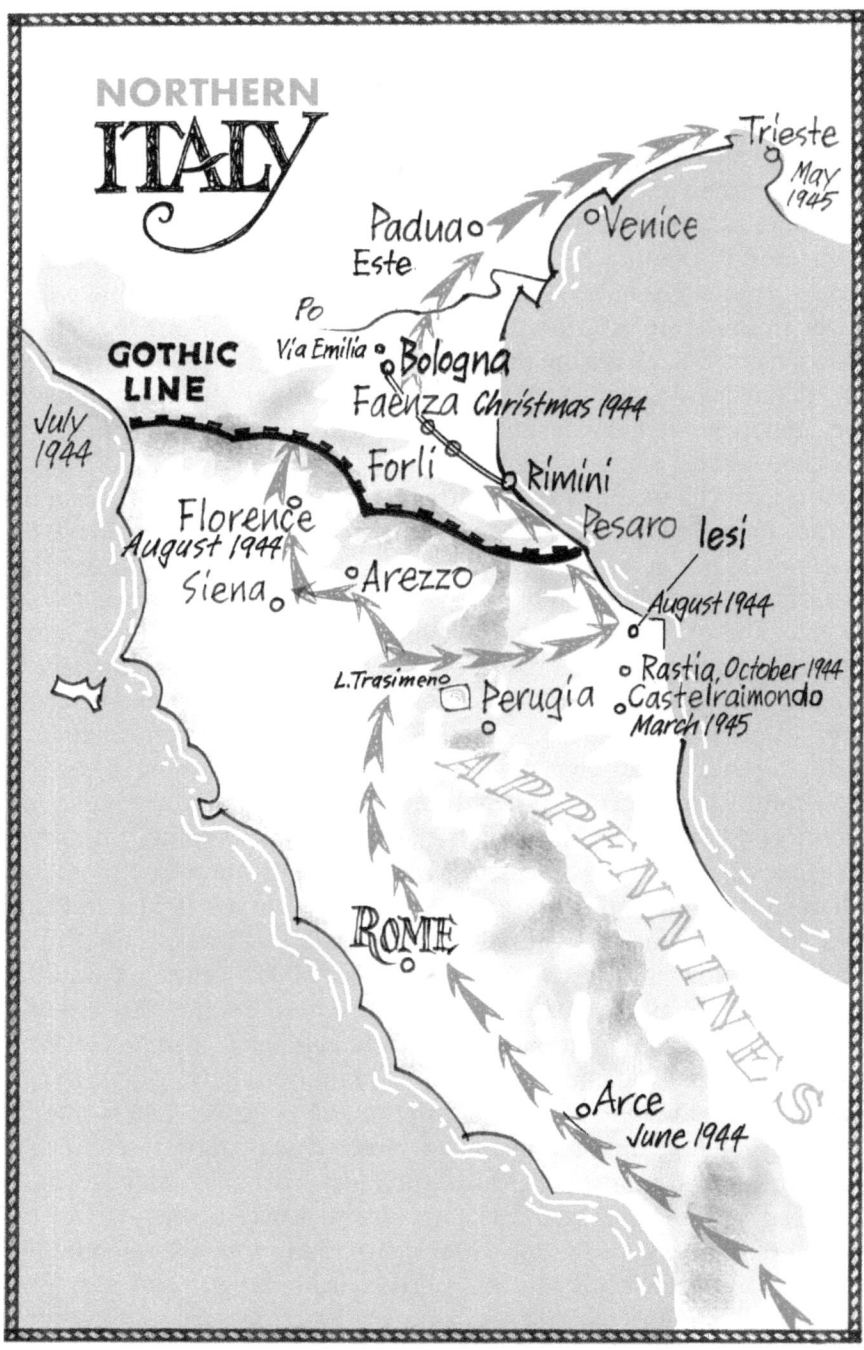

woman told me that her husband had been in America for thirty years, and had never returned to her.

21 Wednesday: We cleaned up our areas this morning in preparation for a visit by the G.O.C., but he did not turn up. I began a gun drill this morning. After lunch, Jack and I went to the hill village (*unnamed*). We found it to be a calamitous little place. At the former courthouse legal documents and books were piled deep on the floors. We got some stamps there. Deep in the pile, we found portraits of Il Duce. There was evidence of German occupation—letters, newspapers, illustrations from magazines, etc. At night to an ENSA show. The humor was most obscene. There was a remarkable woman contortionist, and a skillful piano accordion player. A battery party was in full swing when we returned. A night of much merriment.

22 Thursday: A morning of sore heads and bad stomachs. Attended a lecture on artillery concentrations. I spent an interesting half-hour watching ants at work. They were busy making a home. These busy little people came out of a hole with a piece of dirt or straw in their pincers. No sooner had they dropped it they were away for more. The head of the tribe—a big bull ant—showed fight when I put my finger near him. He didn't do any work himself, but left the house building to others. I learned something of gun laying late in the morning. In the afternoon, Jack and I and many others swam in the Liri River—a swift flowing river reminiscent of many New Zealand rivers. It was most enjoyable. At night, Jack and I went to see the Kiwi Concert Party. Theirs was a good performance. Later, we visited some chaps I knew in the Battalion. On the way home, we stopped to watch and listen to a concert by the M.D.S. Another very good show.

23 Friday: Lecture and practice in laying fire this morning. After Jack and I hitchhiked to Sora. The village of Fontana Liri was badly knocked about. It was thick with boobytraps, and one of the Division unfortunately lost his life there two days before. Jerry did indeed make a job of destroying the bridges on the Sora highway. Isola Liri appears to be a fine little place. Of course, the Liri River completes the beauty of this countryside of hills and beautiful poplars and other trees. Sora is an ancient village. Its most prominent features are the medieval castle perched on a rocky peak and a 14th century cathedral. We did not visit the former, but saw the latter. It is a fine church—beautiful Gothic arches and highly polished fine-grained marble. In the main piazza is the church of Santa Restituta, a modern version of the old cathedral. Here, as in most other

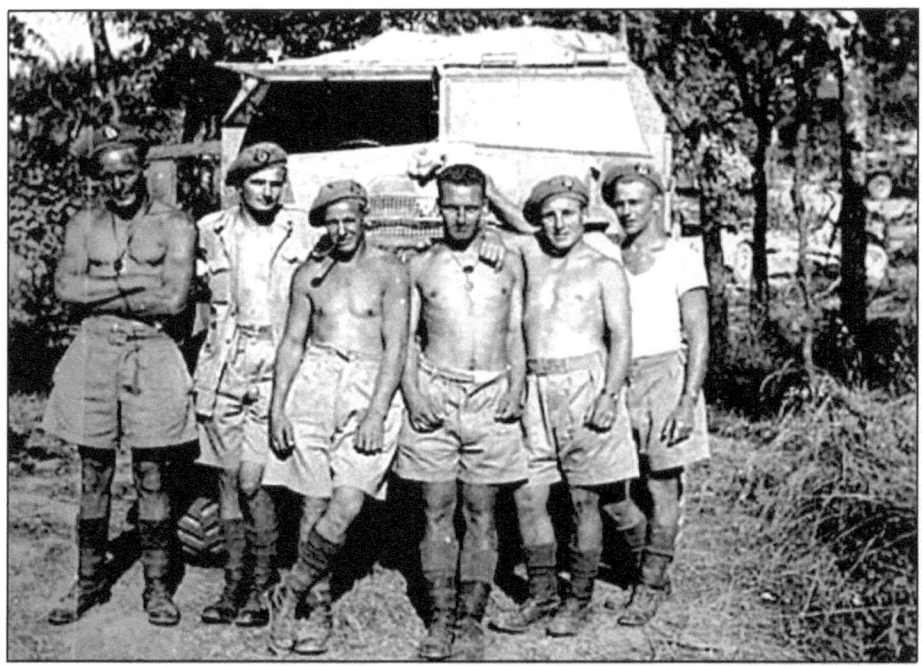

"The "sub." of which I was once a member (during the Cassino campaign.) From the left, Bill Harris, Stew Barber, Hugh Moorfort, Gil Patchett, Sonny Whitson and Stan Allot"—Alex Protheroe

places, the Germans robbed the townspeople of all their wine. We returned to camp in the late afternoon.

24 Saturday: A day of little activity. R.O.'s (*Regimental Officers?*) state that ex-officers are wanted for India. I must get details of this scheme. Several of us ex-officers discussed the proposal at the vino party of twenty-five in the evening.

25 Sunday: In the late morning, Jack and I went visiting. A thunderstorm occurred in the late afternoon, and I got very wet digging channels around the tent. I spent a good deal of the day studying Italian.

26 Monday: As usual, worked in the morning, swam in the Liri in the afternoon. Barry and I got details of the India scheme. It is hard to decide what to do for the best.

27 Tuesday: A hot sunny day. The usual morning routine was far from welcome because of the heat. A swim in the afternoon. In the evening, Jack and I discussed a variety of things, such as, religion and the church in the modern world, our University work, and our civil aspirations.

28 Wednesday: About half a dozen ex-officers of the Regiment, who have been recommissioned in the field, left for Advance Base this morning. I handed in my application for the British Army in India. Later, Jack and I attended the race meeting and vino party of forty-six. A well organized show. The party was the climax to the Regimental sports meeting held in the afternoon. I was NCO in charge of the prowler picquet at night.

29 Thursday: Very hot and sultry: the troop route this morning was turned into a bathing party. Swimming again this afternoon. To cinema this evening; a series of "shorts" shown. Quite enjoyable. (Letters 15, 16, 17, 18, 19 and 9 April, Mother. Airgraphs 1, 5, 9 June, M. 1 each M and M)

30 Friday: Regimental parade this morning. The C.O. Lt. Col. Stewart, DSO., gave a talk on the history of the Regiment, which I enjoyed thoroughly. The Regiment has undoubtedly done a very good job of work during the last four years. In the afternoon to Fontana Liri with Jack and Pat. We passed on interesting hour talking with some Italian women. Fontana is a pretty place: at least it would have been but for the ravages of war. We bought some plums and apricots just arrived from Naples at a cost of 35 lire a kilo. Visit to old women.

JULY, 1944

1 Saturday: A day of idleness so far as military training was concerned. This afternoon, Jack, Pat and I went to Isola Liri where we met a middle-aged woman, a school teacher, and her two intelligent, attractive daughters, one a school teacher like herself, aged 21, and the other, a secondary school girl, aged 12. The three of them spoke grammatical and pure Italian—a rare thing in these parts. They helped me a lot. It was refreshing for me to converse with intelligent people. I bought some more fruit—fine, juicy peaches at 30 lire a kilo and plums at 20. I then went on to Sora alone. I spent the evening in my tent.

Letter No.40: July 1st, 1944

To Judy, from her Daddy,

The Piggie-Wig and Doggie.

The other night, close by a house, played Piggie-Wig and Doggie. The Doggie jumped and barked with Glee. And Piggie snorted at the fun the two of them were having. But poor fat Piggie was tied to a cartwheel, big and heavy. And though he tried to get away the cartwheel was unyielding.

"If I could only break this rope," he thought as he was heaving.

Meanwhile our Doggie barked and jumped and wagged his tail with pleasure. He knew that Piggie could not move from cartwheel, big and heavy. The Doggie circled round and round intent on Piggie's curly tail, but Piggie said: "but you won't get it, my fine rogue. I'll teach you to be clever."

With one great bound through the spokes of the cart went Piggie in his hurry. Alas, for him, the rope was short and he got fed up with the sport. A contented smile came on his face when from the house emerged a friend to bring this comedy to an end.

Alex

DIARY ENTRY

2 Sunday: A trip to Lake Alban today. We arose early, and left the camp at 7 a.m. We followed the famous Highway 6 along which was evidence of the recent fighting—knocked out Tiger tanks, German trucks, guns, Teller mines, and other paraphernalia of war. Like main highways along which I have travelled, Highway 6 is excellent in spite of the frequent rough patches due to demolitions. Noble trees—poplars, oaks, planes and other varieties—flank the highway. Frosinone, the administrative centre of the province of that name, has been badly knocked about. Further on we drove through mutilated Ferentino and at the walled village of Valmontone. The road led to the foot of the mountain and the village of Artena. The grade from there to the top of the Alban Hills was steep. But what a view! To the west, lay the Anzio bridgehead area and the Pontine Marshes on the pretty plain beneath the Alban Hills. Lake Alban—or Il Lago di Albano—came into view soon after. Completely surrounded by hills, and bush clad on the southern side, this beautiful little lake looked enchanting with its deep blue water and unruffled surface. To the north, partly hidden by haze, lay the suburbs of the Eternal City. O, how I longed to be there, but that would be an impossible dream for that day. We stopped next to the walled summer palace of the Pope, walked to the bottom of the hill and the lake and took a swim. At the village on the outskirts overlooking the plain to the west and the lake are some fine villas of wealthy Romans. The entrance to the Papal Palace (*or the Castel Gandolfo*) is in a square in the village. We went to the Cardinals' Summer Palace, and was shown through the very extensive grounds—two kilometers by one and a half—by a servant. The lack of labor—there where were once twelve gardeners combined with the war have greatly affected the place, but we were still able to appreciate what a grand place it must have been. It is terraced, with beautiful avenues of trees, artistically planted shrubs, arched macrocarpa (*cypress,*) and other examples of the

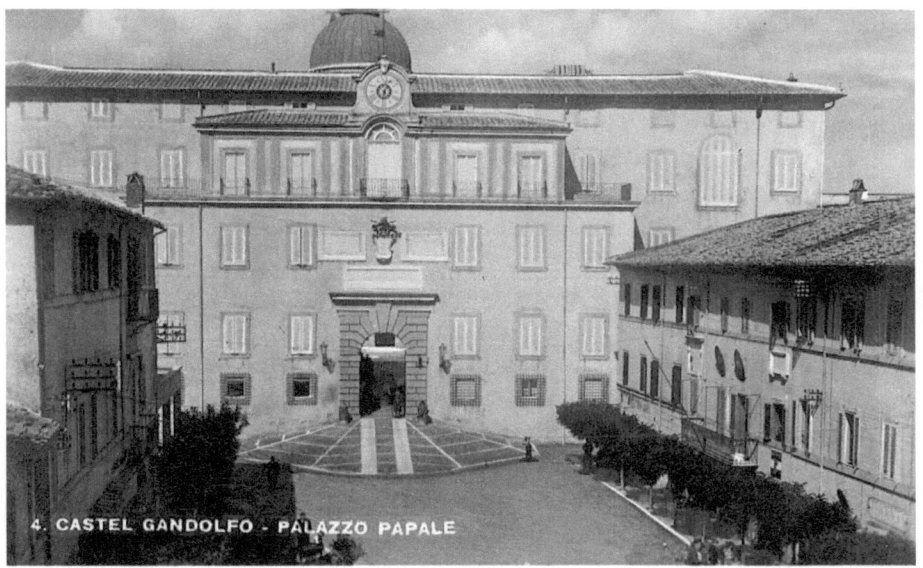

4. CASTEL GANDOLFO - PALAZZO PAPALE

gardener's art. In the grounds also are some Roman remains—a fine head of Constantine (*Emperor between 306-337 A.D.*) (from circa 700 A.D.), and a statute of Marcus Aurelius (*Emperor between 161 and 180 A.D.*) on a horse (circa 500 A.D.) Also, there are heads of Romans mounted on pedestals, columns, modern statues and an ancient Roman church built from brick with a circular roof. The floor of this ancient edifice was covered with piles of rubbish left by Italians who sheltered there during the recent bombing of the area. The walled grounds also contain a modern blue-tiled milking shed—now not used—and also a pigsty built on the same luxurious lines. It was a visit well worthwhile. Our homeward journey took us just over three hours.

3 Monday: Rifle shooting this morning at targets on the opposite bank of the Liri River. I was second. After lunch Stewart, Jack and I went to Isola del Liri. Here we passed the afternoon with an Italian chemist, (*pharmacist?*) his wife and two daughters. The school teacher daughter told me each village had its own dialect. She herself found it difficult to understand some of the remarks of her pupils. I greatly improved my Italian.

4 Tuesday: American Independence Day, and more important to me, the second anniversary of my little girl Judy: how I miss her and my beloved Margie! I pray the good God that our reunion—O, most happy of days—may be very close. With about a dozen other ex-officers, I was interviewed by the CRA, Brigadier Parkinson, this morning in regard to a commission to India. I have the conviction that I will be directed and safeguarded by the Almighty for His good purpose. In the afternoon, I revisited my Italian friends at Isola. There was a heavy rainstorm about 2:45 p.m. Here, I found Bianobe's fiancé at the house. He had brought his English grammars with him. His pronunciation was appalling, but I must not forget English is an extremely difficult language to pronounce correctly. Again, I improved my Italian. Later, I went to Sora where I bought a very good Italian dictionary dedicated to the ex-Il Duce for only ten shillings. At night, to the pictures with Stewart to see "George Washington Slept Here"—an amusing American comedy. (Letter 19 M. 2 Airgraphs Margie, letter Mona, Airgraph, Grace).

5 Wednesday: Although the weather was threatening in the early morning, it cleared and the day was hot and sunny. A Regimental sports meeting was held at the Isola stadium. Most enjoyable. Stew, Jack and I went to the town, and for the first time, saw the old town, which is on the lower ground below the pretty cascade on the Liri. Later Jack and I went to Arce to buy fruit—apricots and plums, and spent the evening in camp.

6 Thursday: Four years ago today my dearest Margie and I were united. Like thousands of other married men, I was separated from my beloved for a great part of that period. A swim this afternoon with Jack, then to the pictures at night.

7 Friday: Very hot again today. A swim in the morning and two in the afternoon with Jack. We did a little Italian. Both Jack and I expressed the view how much valuable time we were losing through our long army service. Both he and I want to get back as soon as possible to the life that is meant for us. To the pictures at night. We discussed the matter of going to India. It's a perplexing subject. I trust in the good guidance of God. (21 June, Margie.)

8 Saturday: Jack and I spent a pleasant afternoon at the river. At night, we went to the carnival of the 5th Regiment. We went off for a great walk and talk. The Army is no place for lovers of great contemplation and study. We both agreed that for people of our type—not understood by the average chap in the army—the R.N. (*Royal Navy*) would be a better place.

9 Sunday: To Holy Communion with Jack. Each time I attend a celebration I get new aspirations—of the great communion of Man with Christ, of God's love for us, and of the fact that each and every man can contribute something towards the establishment of the Kingdom. I spent the afternoon in studying Italian and in sleeping. Just before mess, a swim with Jack. At night, I began to translate Ovid's "Metamorphosis" from the Italian. Rain during the night.

10 Monday: Packing for the move. After lunch, Jack and I had a swim, and late in the afternoon we set off for Arpino, an ancient mountain town some eight miles from the camp. We arrived late. Arpino—or the main part of it—is built on the top of a steep hill. It has long been a popular residential area for professional people. Consequently, there are many fine villas there. In the piazza, there is a fine full-length Roman bronze of Gaius Marius, and above the pillars of a nearby building there are busts of Marius, Cicero and Agrippa. Just outside the piazza is an ancient stone fountain surrounded by the Roman eagle. Other sights of interest are an ancient Roman gateway, which we could not find, and a castle tower on the top of the hill. One thing that struck is particularly was the type of person we saw—nearly all neatly clad and intelligent looking. The lilac trees were in flower on the main street. I must find out what association that Marius, Cicero and Agrippa had with this interesting town.

11 Tuesday: Six months ago today my beloved Margie and Mother, my sister and the doctor, *(my father-in-law, the physicist, Dr. D. B. Macleod)* saw me off at Lyttelton. There was a great deal of activity this morning—dismantling tents and packing gear, burning rubbish and generally preparing for our departure. It is now opportune to sum up our stay here. Ever since our arrival, we have been invaded everyday by hosts of Italian peasants, old men and women down to tiny children, seeking food and anything which we were prepared to give them. The women about the place did our washing and ironing and they were more than amply repaid for their work. This camp of ours was so attractive to the peasants that they choose to walk here from Sora—some twelve miles away. All the units took the opportunity to engage an Italian boy or girl for various duties—washing dishes, and so on. These people were fed by us, and many of them slept here. They may never again be treated so well and so liberally. As each unit packed up, the area was flocked by Italians seeing what they can get or find. In our area, we were obliged to drive them away for fear of theft. It has been pleasant here—every afternoon and evening free. A film was screened in the Regiment area at night—Ginger Rogers in "Tom, Dick and Harry"—very stupid.

12 Wednesday: At one o'clock this morning, the convoy left on a long journey north. We travelled along Route 6 to the Eternal City. Thank goodness I awoke while we were passing through the outskirts of this great and ancient city. The light was steely. I was fascinated with what I saw. The broad highway was lined with fine trees, and on both sides of it was stately buildings, fine modern flats of six or seven stories, and wide footpaths. In driving through, we saw little of historical interest, except an arch in honor of Pope Pius VII, and what appeared to be a Roman viaduct. We went onto Route 3, and then the road began to climb. Rome glistened in the increasing light. Standing out above all else was the mighty dome of St. Peter's, and although the city began to disappear in the haze as we progressed, I could still see the great dome very faintly at 25 kms. I'm longing to visit the Eternal City. When we had travelled about eighty miles, about ten miles north of Rome, the three of us in the back were suddenly jolted back to wakefulness. It transpired that we had struck two trees, and thank goodness, they were uprooted instead of staying stable. The truck was somewhat damaged. I'm thankful to say that all we suffered were a few bruises. Our driver had dozed off, and then the accident happened. That hundred mile trip was very tiring. We halted for the day near the village of Civita Castellana, some thirty miles from Rome. In the afternoon, with some other chaps, I visited a nearby large shed. We found about forty Italians—men, women and children—living there. Each family had partitioned off "rooms" by stacking bales of straw one on top of another. On the side, there was the "living room," and on the other side the "family bedroom!" Apparently, most of them have lived there for the last ten months. They were obviously short of food. Their principal food is vegetables from the fields. And didn't they welcome some porridge they got from the cooks! A film was shown nearby in the evening—Noel Coward's "In Which We Serve," a fine film, ably presented on the work of the Royal Navy. The almost fanatical love that a sailor develops for his ship was a big part of the story. Back to the lines, a cup of coffee, and then the wait until starting time.

13 Thursday: At one in the morning, we started off again. We were all very tired. At 3:30, I relieved the driver, and drove up and down over the hills until 6:30. This was along Route 71, formerly a good road, but now badly worn. We passed through several villages, but none of these interested me until Barchi came into sight. This ancient little place has been erected on the almost razorback edge of a hill, and the centre there is a fine—probably medieval--church. Another thing that struck me was the relative sparseness of the villages in this region compared with the south, and the predominance of oaks. Other little places on the route whose names I can remember were Ficulle, Il Colle, and San Lorenzo, all of which are between twelve and fifteen hundred feet above sea level. We deviated from Route 71, and when we reached the layover area late in the morning all hands soon got to work to erect their tents. The 170-mile journey of the last two days has been most tiring. We camped for the day in the vineyard near the village of Panicale, just south of Lake Trasimeno.

Nearby, on a hill, stood the castle of the local count who, with the Church, owned most of the land in the area. Everyone spent the afternoon in having a much needed sleep. The evening was spent in repacking.

14 Friday: About midnight, we set out on the twenty-five mile journey to the area where we were going to establish our gun positions. Four of us travelled in the back of the 15-c.w.t., and it was not long before we were dozing or asleep. Suddenly, we were jolted back to wakefulness once again, with the truck lying on its side down a bank. Thank goodness nobody was hurt. The driver had apparently swung too much to the right when he was dazzled by the lights of a jeep. The two of us who were gunners were immediately whisked away to catch up to the guns. He and I rode on the top of the quad for the rest of the journey. The night was bitterly cold, and as lights had to be out, the convoy travelled slowly. We awoke just as we were entering the vineyard where the battery was to be established. To work immediately on the gun pit. The ground was frightfully hard and progress was slow. We didn't dig deep. Gun in, camouflage nets up, breakfast. Bivvy tents up, a wash and shave, and then to sleep. We are camped near the pretty little village of Castiglion Fiorentino, which I gather is almost deserted. The village's chief church has a very fine pointed tower. Nearby is a belfry whose sweet-sounding bells were rung at frequent intervals during the day. On the hillside to the north are several good villas and to the south stands what appears to be a fine castle with a high *torre,* or tower. At night we prepared ammunition for the barrage. (M June 25, Mona 22, H 24 , Mona 22)

15 Saturday July, 1944: Called at 12:30 this morning. We began our barrage at 1 o'clock, and each gun fired about a hundred and fifty rounds. The object was to dislodge Jerry from two hill points to the south of Arezzo. It was my first experience of a barrage. The noise was deafening, and the flashes blinding. The bombers went in before we fired. From the sound and the flashes, there appeared to be many regiments of artillery in the show. We finished at 2:30 a.m. A cup of tea, and then off to bed. Later, in the morning, we were told that the show was a success, the Germans having been pushed back towards Arezzo.

In the afternoon, Bill and I climbed the nearby steep hillside and spent an hour or two talking to an Italian peasant family in their ancient home. Above the fireplace was the date, 1764, and on a stone by the hearth, 1481! I was given the evening off, and went for a stroll. Surrounded by a high wall, and with a grove of fine cypresses on the inside about two hundred yards from our gun position is a monastery of the Capuchin Order. I spent a few hours having a few drinks and conversing with some Italians at a wine shop. I gathered that people here are unable to sleep because of the frequent heavy gunfire.

16 Sunday: A two-hour barrage was fired between 2 and 4 in the morning, but I slept through most of it. Apparently the attack twenty-four hours ago was only partially successful. Later, we were told that the attack had been a success, and our forward troops had lost contact with the enemy. We started to pack once again. I visited the farmhouse and bought some fruit. A woman there told me that the castle to the south was Montecchio. The ruined castle on the top of the range to the east was Montanino. I climbed up to the town. Castiglion Fiorentino—or "Castle of Florence"—is a most interesting place. The Municipal Square contains an arcade with fine columns and circular arches. On the wall are the armorial bearings of the families that governed the city from about 1200 to 1600, and in the streets I saw several houses where above the doorways were coats of arms. An Italian medical student who spoke English took me to the very old church of St. Francis. The Church itself was closed, but I was able to admire the enclosed courtyard with its fine colors and arches, murals and many tablets commemorating the lives of members for the Florentine nobility and other people. The medical student told me that Montecchio had been the home of an English soldier-of-fortune (or *condottiere, Ed.*) of the famous White Company. Unfortunately, I had to get back to the gun. After lunch, Bill and I revisited the house on the hill. The daughters were averse to being photographed until they had dressed in the Sunday best. We returned to the gun position to find that the gun and limber were ready for the road, but there was to be no move that night. After mess, we took a stroll to buy some vino. We got some two-liter bottles from a house which had been occupied by Jerry. It was a mess. To bed at a reasonable hour.

17 Monday: No barrage was necessary this morning as Jerry is well out of the range from here, some three thousand yards behind Arezzo. The C.O. spoke to the Regiment this morning. He reviewed the war situation. At the end, he mentioned that all 4th R. men in the Regiment would be going home on furlough. Naturally there was great jubilation by those concerned. With Gil and Stew, I revisited the village. We were lucky to find the Church of St. Francis of Assisi open. It has been restored. The interior is not impressive. In the courtyard, I ascertained that the murals—dating from 1546—depicted various features of the saint's life. Another mural in a room next to the church was done in 1300. We searched the large building that was once the Fascist HQ for souvenirs. Fascist literature, portraits, banners, were scattered everywhere. In one room was a magnificent glass chandelier somewhat damaged. In the afternoon, Gil, Bill and I revisited our friends on the hill. After mess, Stew and I went for a stroll along a dusty road. There was much celebration in honor of the 4th boys who were going home. (Airgraph June 28 from M).

18 Tuesday: In the late afternoon, with several other chaps, I was interviewed by Col. Walt Thornton, and two other Colonels, for transfer to the British Army in India. When I heard that some of the chaps had been asked if they would be prepared to remain in India for three to five years, I hastily told the officers, when my turn came, that I begged to withdraw. They were quite agreeable. A great walk with Stewart at night.

Letter No. 41: Tuesday, July 18th, 1944

My sweetest beloved little girl,

The rain is pouring down upon my tent. Just outside the entrance the BBC is broadcasting a glorious composition of Bizet. Most appropriate for a few minutes before a special item of news concerning France was announced.

How I love beautiful music. It eats right into me, hypnotizes and fascinates me. Regretfully, I find few chaps who can sit down and listen to a program of classical, or light classical music. Perhaps this is typical of the times. The boys want swing—a light, racy program. To them, swing is a tonic as classical is to me. I know I belong to a world of books and music. Some might call that world an unreal world, but I maintain that through books and music one is able to think and understand deeply. The man of a quiet and contemplative mind may not talk the same language as those not so inclined, but his study of the outpourings of the great imbues him —or should imbue him—with the qualities of tolerance and well being to his fellows. He suffers not the same loneliness as others, (the majority of men) who in their solitude know not the friendship of good books and music, but who are lost if they are not in the herd. So far I have only found four men with that intellectual make up which appeals to me so much.

The trouble with the Army is that one is likely to slip in the cultural sphere. There is ever present the thought that one might be required for duty at any time. Therefore one is inclined to say to oneself: it is a waste of time to sit down to study as I might have to dash away at any moment.

Alex

19 Wednesday: Jack and I had a discussion on Christianity this afternoon with Padre Button. I thoroughly enjoyed it, and what he had to say will be a directive to me. Our discussion led me to the belief of the vital role the Church could play if it took part in politics. With the teachings of

Christ as its platform, it should sweep to victory, and ultimately create a social and economic order which was basically Christian. Heavy rain fell. (Letter 20, 14 May from M, and 21 May).

20 Thursday: A day of almost complete idleness, except that in the late afternoon we were warned for a move. I began reading Archbishop William Temple's, "Christianity and Social Order."

21 Friday: Up about 6, beds rolled, breakfast, then we were ready to leave. However, nothing was doing in the morning. Stew and I went on a search for eggs, and after much hard work, we got a total of ten. We left at 3 p.m. The highway led to Arezzo, but we turned off onto the Siena Road. I could see Arezzo nestling among its trees a mile ahead before we turned to the left. The country leading to Siena was more open than the land we passed further back. There were many stacks of sheaves on the open, rolling countryside. The only place of interest we passed on the way was the hill village of Monte San Savino. As luck would have it, we bypassed Siena by a mile, instead we followed a steep mountainous route to our bivouac area, which we reached at 9 p.m. Siena could be seen away to the south as we climbed. I hope I will have the opportunity to visit the centre of the Renaissance art and culture. (Parcels, 3, and chocolate from Mother).

22 Saturday: We did not move early as expected. I was told that I was to be O.C., Rome party. We left at 11 o'clock and drove over the Chianti Hills to Siena. This ancient city has been a walled town, and are there still gates into the original part of the City. We drove through along the narrow, cobbled streets, past fine old buildings and onto the piazza, where stood a majestic pile which I took to be the University. After Siena was a good deal of rolling wheat country. Then we climbed a road through much barren land to Radicofani, where the truck broke down. The ancient castle town could be seen for miles as the peak on which it stands is a considerable one. On and on, we went along Route 2. The land got better, and there were olives instead of oaks, which are so plentiful in the north. We skirted beautiful Lake Bolsena, and at Sutri deviated to Route 3. Civita Castellana was crowded with people out for a gossip and a stroll when we went through. One of the chaps told me that Lucrezia Borgia had some connection with the castle in the town. We reached the rest camp at 9:30.

ROME, JULY 1944

23 Sunday July, 1944: Off to Rome at 6:45. Breakfast at the New Zealand Forces Club in the centrally-located Albergo Quirinale. Although all the fine furnishings, etc. have been removed, one can see that it was a first-class hotel in its day. With breakfast over, we were put in the charge of an English-speaking Italian for a tour of the sights. The Pantheon was first. It is a circular-shaped building with an opening in the roof, which was once the hot bathroom of the Imperial Bath. Our guide told us it was the temple of all the gods, but is now a church. A service was being held when we arrived.

Then to St. Peter's. No wonder this great pile is considered the best church in the world. I won't try to describe it. It beggars a just description. The superb art, the beauty—these are on every hand. You will get some impression from the booklets and postcards I will send home. In the centre is an obelisk brought from Egypt. Inside the scale is tremendous, and there is much movement in the architectural detail, sculpture and the painting. What one takes for paintings are, in fact, mosaics, the pieces being so skillfully cut and fitted that the eye is deceived. The original paintings of which the mosaics are copies are in the Vatican itself. The dome is one of the most famous in the world and was designed by Michelangelo, the font and most of the interior was designed by Maderno (1556-1629), and the curved colonnades in the square by Bernini (1598-1680). Being Sunday, the famous Sistine Chapel and Vatican Museums were closed to sightseers. Most disappointing. Up numerous staircases on which were stationed Swiss Guards to the Audience Room to see the Pope. Servicemen of all nations present. I could not help but note the precautions taken to guard the Pope's person. Armed Swiss stationed all over the place, and an excellent telephone system linking them. A period of expectancy. At 12:15 p.m., the Pope (*Pius XII*) was borne in on a chair, and he gave his blessing as he was carried to the dais. He spoke in English and French, but I could not catch his words because of the poor speaker system. A frail little man dressed in white, he blessed the throng and then chatted to officer representatives of the Allied armies gathered-ered around the dais. Back to the club for a meal. The afternoon visit was to the most famous part of all—the Roman Forum and the Coliseum. I won't describe these places. Excellent descriptions and illustrations are to be found in many books. A little persuasion on the part of some of us resulted in the guide taking us to the Protestant Cemetery to see the graves of Keats and Shelly. For many a day I had a longing to see Keats' grave. On the wall nearby is a plaque of the poet. Keats's tombstone does not bear his name but is inscribed with words that this is the At grave of a young English poet. His lifelong friend Joseph Severn lies next to him. "Shelly bequeathed his heart to Rome, his body to England." "Nothing of him that doth fade/But doth suffer a sea change/Into something rich and strange" are the words on the tombstone. His friend, Edward Trelawney, is buried next to him.

We concluded our trip to a hill from which we could see the City. Later some of us visited the Church of Santa Maria Maggiore where there are some superb mosaics on incidents from the Old Testament and the life of our Lord. There were other things here too and I must get more information on them from books. The Church itself is a very fine one. We then departed to a hill from the top of which we obtained an excellent view of the Eternal City.

Mussolini's sports stadium was our next halting place. Around the oval are statues of athletes symbolizing all types of sports. It is a very fine place and it is obvious Il Duce put much work into it. To the Club, a meal and then away. A hurried visit, no doubt, but still sufficient to give me the correct background when I reread the story of the Eternal City.

24 Monday: We began the long homeward journey just before 7 a.m. We followed Route 3. A road of beautiful views—hills, trees, valleys, rivers, mountains. Through Narni, badly battered Treni, and then the long drive to Perugia—built on the top slopes of a hill. Some fine homes and civic buildings on the outskirts. Then onto the Arezzo road; along the top end

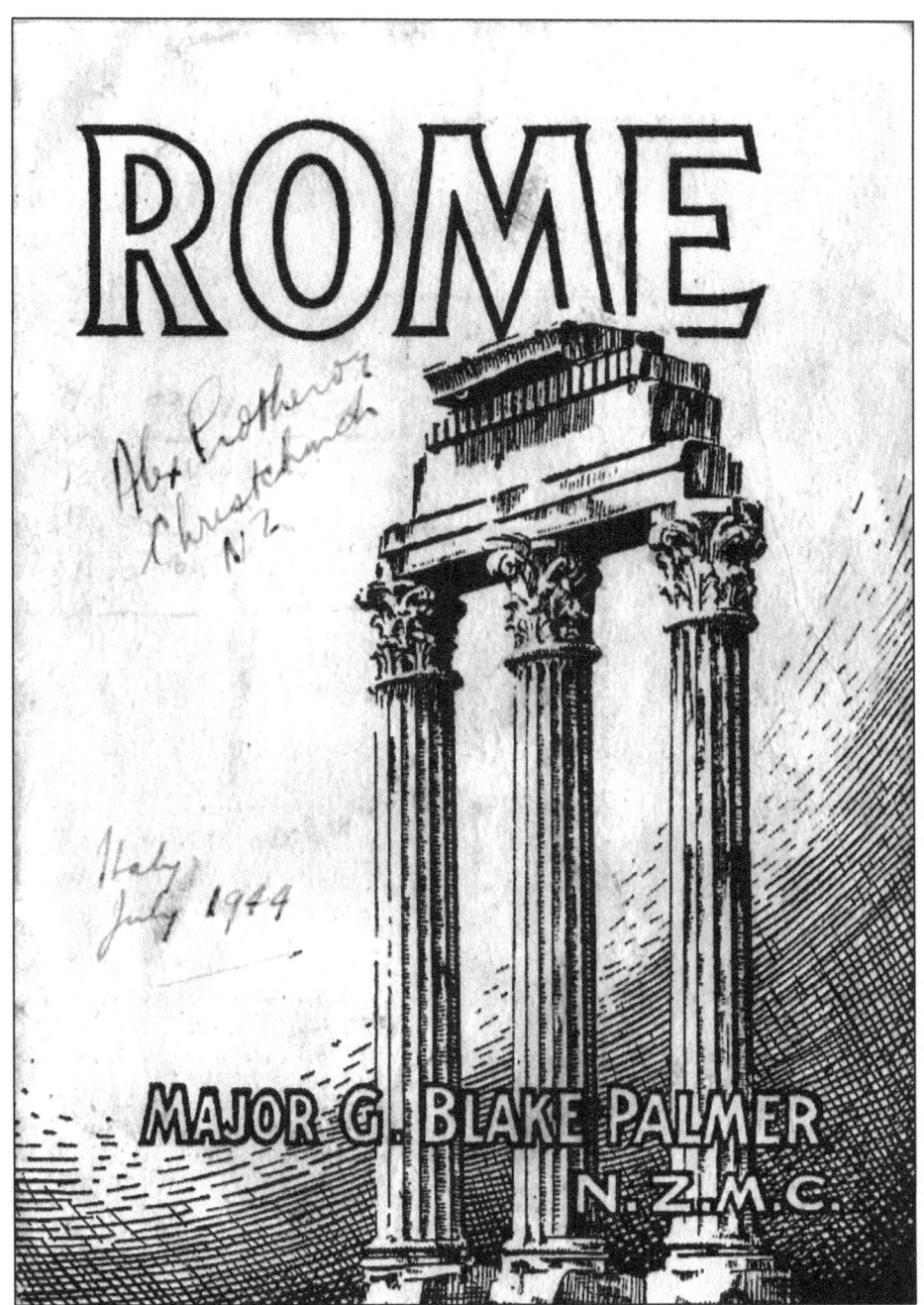

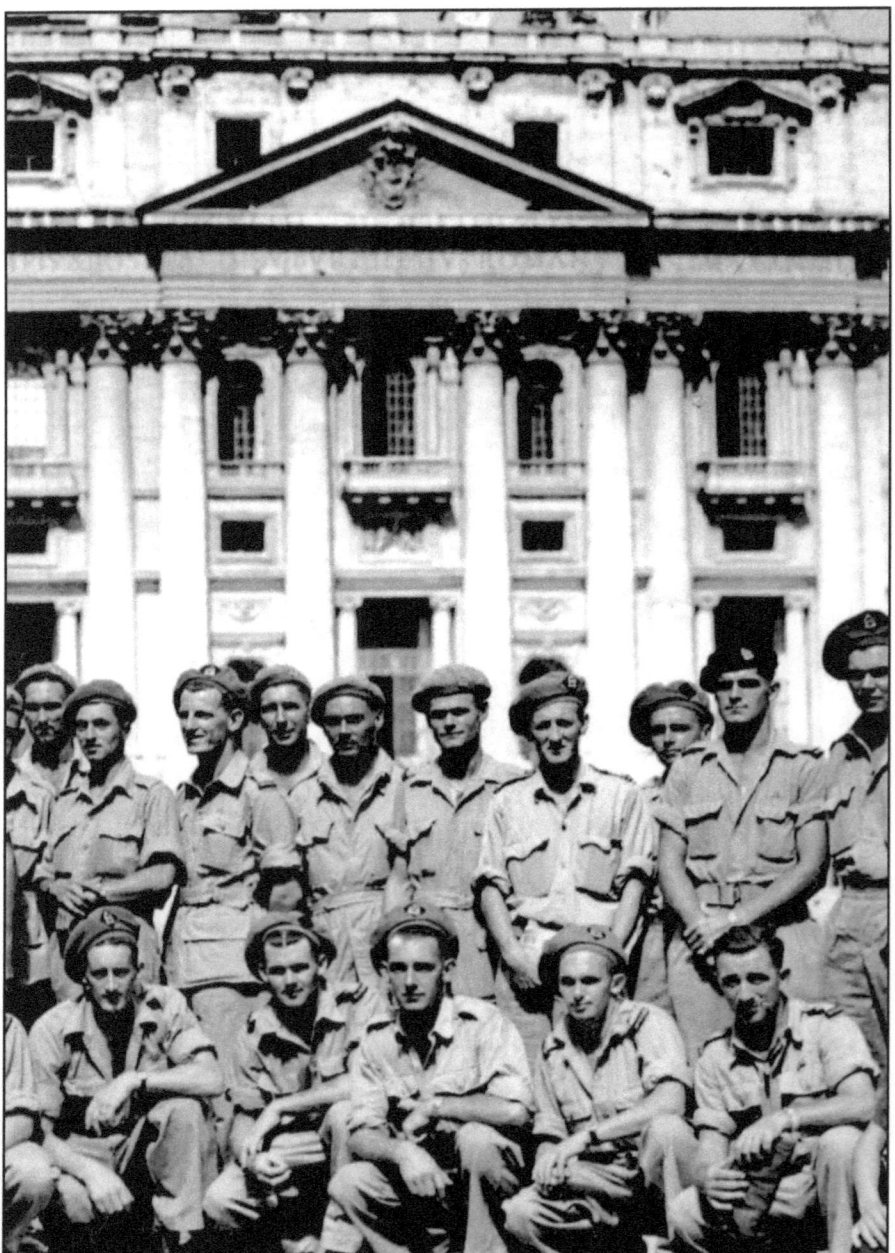

At the Vatican, July1944. Alex is in the top row, fourth from the right

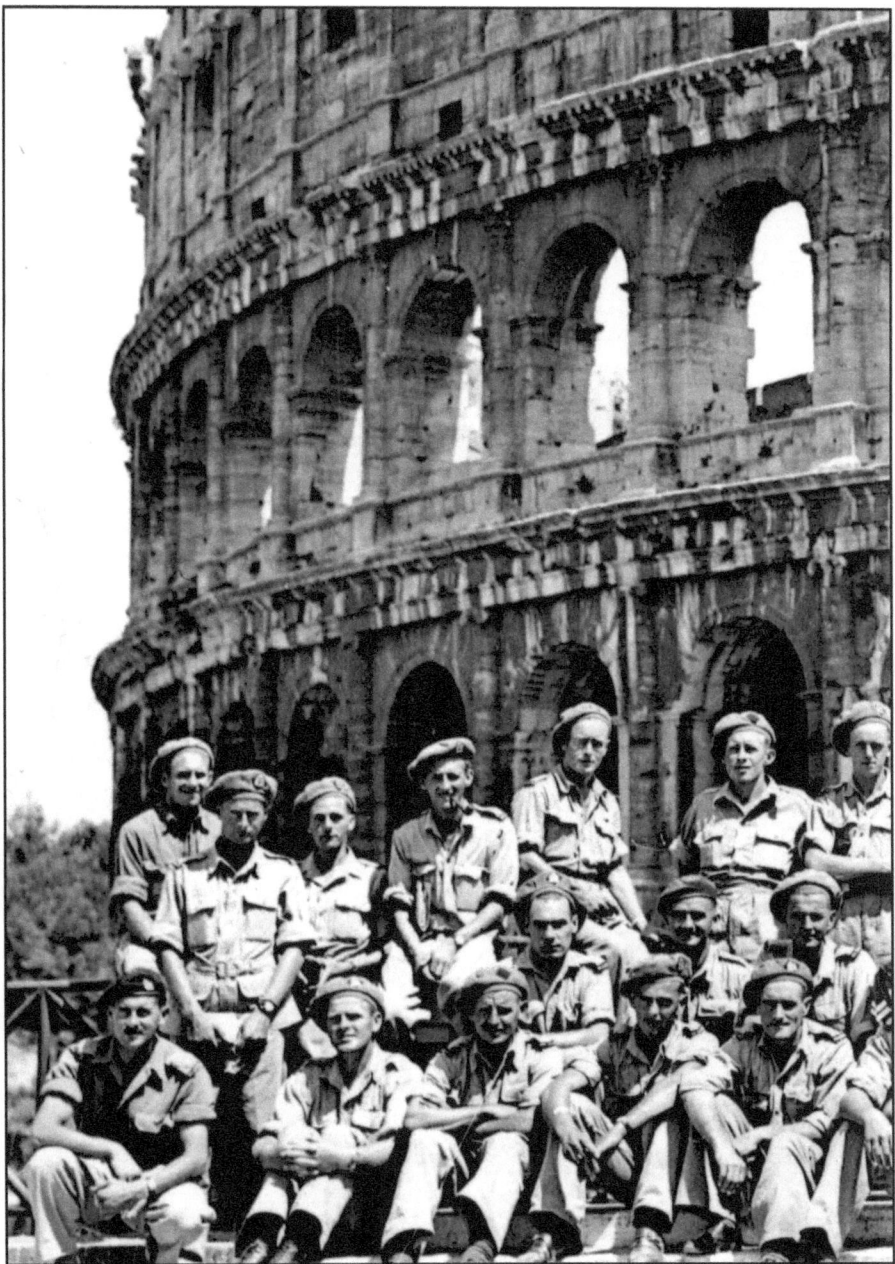

The Coliseum, Rome, July, 1944. Alex is on the top row with his trademark pipe, fourth from left

of beautiful Lake Trasimeno, with its three or four little wooded islets. Near Arezzo, we took the road through Monte San Servino to Siena. Then up into the barren tops of the Chianti Hills to catch up with the Division. The truck broke down; much rushing about, but eventually we reached 'B' Echelon about 8:15.

Back to the Line

25 Tuesday, July 1944: Spent the morning at 'B' Echelon, and returned in the afternoon to the guns just north of Tavarnelle, some fourteen miles down Route 2 from Florence. We did some firing, but not a great lot. The countryside in this area is rolling and grows grapes, wheat, fruit and maize.

26 Wednesday: Fired a few rounds in the morning. This is a rather pleasant spot, but rather hot. There was some heavy anti-tank and mortar fire in the FDLs (*forward defended localities*) over the hill in the early morning. A busy afternoon and evening. About 140 rounds fired in the afternoon in support of a dive-bombing attack by the RAF.

27 Thursday: Reveille at 4.30 after a night of little sleep. Gear packed once again. Pulled out at the 7.30 a.m., and set off to next position about four miles further north. To work on the gun pit immediately. When we had ours about three quarters finished we were told to stop, as we would be shifting! Cleaned up the pit, gun in. Jerry heavily shelled road above us. Fired about 40 to 50 rounds during the afternoon and moved again about 5:30. Back through Tavarnelle and then up Highway 2 to position in vineyard on flat south of San Casciano. No gun pit, thank goodness. Began shooting again about 10 p.m. in support of attack by (*an unnamed*) Battalion. Short of ammo, searching in the dark and so on.

28 Friday: Fired until about 3:30 this morning when night shooting by us terminated. Jerry was very active with his mortars on the FDLs after our tasks. The show resumed about 8 a.m., and was carried on all day and throughout the night. Near our position is the River Pesa with its fine little pools for swimming. (4 from M from 5 July), (Cable about 5 a.m.).

29 Saturday: Still the show goes on. Firing, firing, firing. Sorties, harassing fire, almost everything. This afternoon I was transferred to the Command Post. I know I'm going to like it. Jerry is very strong above San Casciano—plenty of guns, many mortars, and well dug in. Apparently not much can be done until the South Africans move up on the right and strengthen the line. (Airgraph 7 July M, 6 July Mona, Parcel 7, Margie)

30 Sunday: I'm being kept busy with ammunition for the almost continuous firing. We fired a barrage and other tasks at night to support the attack of the 5th and 6th Brigades. Went to a church service on the bank of the Pesa in the evening.

31 Monday: Another day of shooting—Early in the evening No. 1 gun had a premature. Tike McCaul and Jackie Mortimer being injured. The night, for once, was relatively quiet for us.

AUGUST, 1944

1 Tuesday: Although we were due for a move nearer Florence, we did quite a lot of firing during the morning and afternoon. Jerry lobbed three or four shells into our valley. We moved in the early evening along Highway 2 through thickly wooded gentle hill country to a depression near Cigliano. I had a hectic time with the ammo. Jerry did a good deal of mortaring and shelling in front of us. The troop's three active guns fired a barrage of about 120 rounds each. I slept very well in my slit trench being very tired.

2 Wednesday: Another busy day of firing. Jerry did much shelling himself of positions to our right and left. About 6:30, we fired 16 rounds of blue smoke for the fighter-bombers which came over and dropped their eggs. At 10:30 at night we fired a barrage in support of the 21st Battalion. One hundred and forty-five rounds in all, and two tasks completed the job.

3 Thursday: Learned this morning that the 21st had been successful. Another busy day of firing, with harassing tasks against Jerry transport predominating. The ammo situation began to look bad and I had to dash around transferring from one gun to another. RHQ had ordered that no further ammo was to be delivered. About 11:30, the embargo was lifted and we got more than 600 rounds. But little of it was used, Jerry being mostly out of range. (July 12 M, July 8 Mona, July 13 Margie)

4 Friday: Our 'recce' party left at 9 a.m., so we started to prepare for the move. We left about 4 p.m. The winding road led us through some thickly wooded hill country. There was much evidence of warfare—badly battered houses, shell holes, burnt out tanks (including two Tiger tanks destroyed by us), and Italians trudging back to their houses in the area. We received warm welcome from the people of the little village of La Gora, who lined the roadway and waved, smiled and shouted as we drove in. We pulled into a fruit orchard in torrential rain, and all got frightfully wet. Some from the troop spent the night sleeping in the basement of a large stone home of a Marquis, who we were told was in Florence. Of course, we were not in the bedrooms. Quite a number of us slept next to huge vats in the wine store. Very comfortable too. The Germans only left this area last night. There was some heavy shelling by Jerry on both sides of us during the night. We did a little harassing fire.

5 Saturday: The weather cleared this morning. We did some firing up to about 3 p.m., but not a great deal. The Canadians were taking over from us here. It is only two miles direct to Florence from here and we are very disappointed that we have to leave when we are so close to the city of Dante, Boccaccio, and others. We left about 4 p.m. and retraced our steps. We took the road through La Romola—very badly battered, and pulled into a vineyard in the Cerbara area. The Canadian convoys were on the road when we left La Gora. I had my second egg for five months at night when we had a supper of eggs, tomatoes, fried bread and bacon.

6 Sunday: A fine, hot sunny morning. With others I attended a church service held by the Padre in the riverbed. The padre stressed the need of the spiritual in our lives to make them complete. Threatening weather in the afternoon compelled us to erect our bivouac. Very necessary too as there was a very heavy storm. We will be moving tomorrow to take over from the 8th Indians, south of the Arno and to the left of Florence.

7 Monday: Our brief period of rest was all too brief. The weather cleared this morning. We left at 5:30 for our new position, and we in the non-gun vehicles arrived at the village of La Luna—some four thousand yards south of the Arno—about an hour later. The troop's gun positions were nearby in a depression, but it was necessary for vehicles to follow a circuitous route to reach them, traveling both in daylight and under observation from Jerry's excellent OPs (*Observation Posts*) on the hill on the other side of the river. We established ourselves in a house on top of the hill occupied by an Italian *contadino* (*farmer*) family. We took over from a Tommy troop belonging to the 8th Indian Division. The house was of three stories—built of brick and stone like most Italian houses. Although

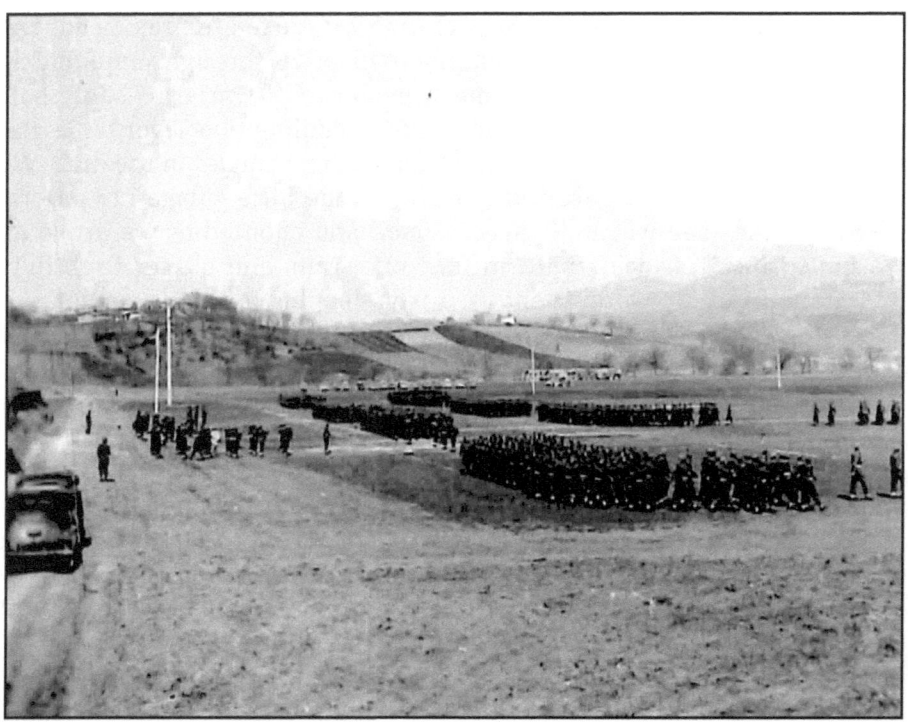

Parade, possibly in Arce.

the family showed no outward hostility to us, I feel they resented our intrusion into their house. We established the CP (*Command Post*) on the first floor, and our sleeping quarters on the second. The guns arrived about 9 p.m., and the gun crews worked all night digging pits.

8 Tuesday: Up fairly early to find the battery cookhouse about three quarters of a mile away in the village. Far too far. In the clear air and bright sunshine today, we appreciated just what excellent observation Jerry had on us, and throughout the afternoon we learned to respect it. He fired numerous rounds in the area—some very close to the house— and shelled and mortared houses and roads nearby. This is a so-called quiet position, but it is the worst we've been in for some considerable time. He has the area taped. Things are aggravated by traffic throwing up a lot of dust on the roads. This mortar fire on two sides of our house was heavy. We decided to evacuate the first and second floors, and moved onto the ground floor in the afternoon. Harassing counter battery and counter-mortar fire were the order of the day for us, but owing to the ammo expenditure being limited we did not fire many rounds at one time. With us in the house, (besides the Italian family, who dislike the *Tedeschi* even more than we do), are fowl, and rabbits, plus myriads of mosquitos. (Airgraphs July 17 and 19 from M.)

(The letter I just received, in my little girl's own hand, was written at St. George's Hospital, Christchurch. Roger was born at 9.20 on July 18, and weighed 7 lb. 14 oz. Both very well. What great and good news!)

9 Wednesday: Quieter today, thank goodness. About 12.30, Jerry lobbed two shells very close to our house, and we thought our washing, which was lying on the grass just behind where one shell landed, had had it. Inspection when things quietened down showed it to be alright. Jerry also did the road below and the village very effectively too. The dust made by the speedy traffic let him know that the road is a good target. Two and a half tons of ammo were brought in. Each gun is to be built up to five hundred rounds so something must be coming off. In bed by 11 p.m. (Letters 22, 23 24, M; June 6 and 13, Mona).

10 Thursday: The "Boche" was not so active today. He did some shelling of the roads well away from us, and lobbed a few near the house I visited in the late afternoon. Early this morning, I went to the BC (*Battalion Command?*) at Regimental Headquarters—a fine villa with a fountain, coat of arms, "show" shrubs, trees and ornaments—to see the Colonel. The bombshell from him: I was to be reverted to guns "in accordance with the regulations." I know—or at least feel—that things will turn out alright.

Letter No. 48: Thursday, August 10th, 1944
My sweetest beloved little girl,

You must of all been thrilled with the news of the (*D-Day*) invasion. It had been something we have all been waiting for a very long time.

Apparently Barbara has not forgotten Keith. (*Dr. K. Macleod, brother-in law*) I have not seen her fiancé for some time...

I am sure no one will settle down in civilian life more readily and happily than me. There's no honor and glory in this present life of mine.

Alex

DIARY ENTRY
11 Friday: Jerry resumed his shelling of this locality about 1:30, and two or three landed unpleasantly close. Jerry put down a murderous mortar stonk on the house on the ridge beyond ours. We did a little hostile battery shooting.

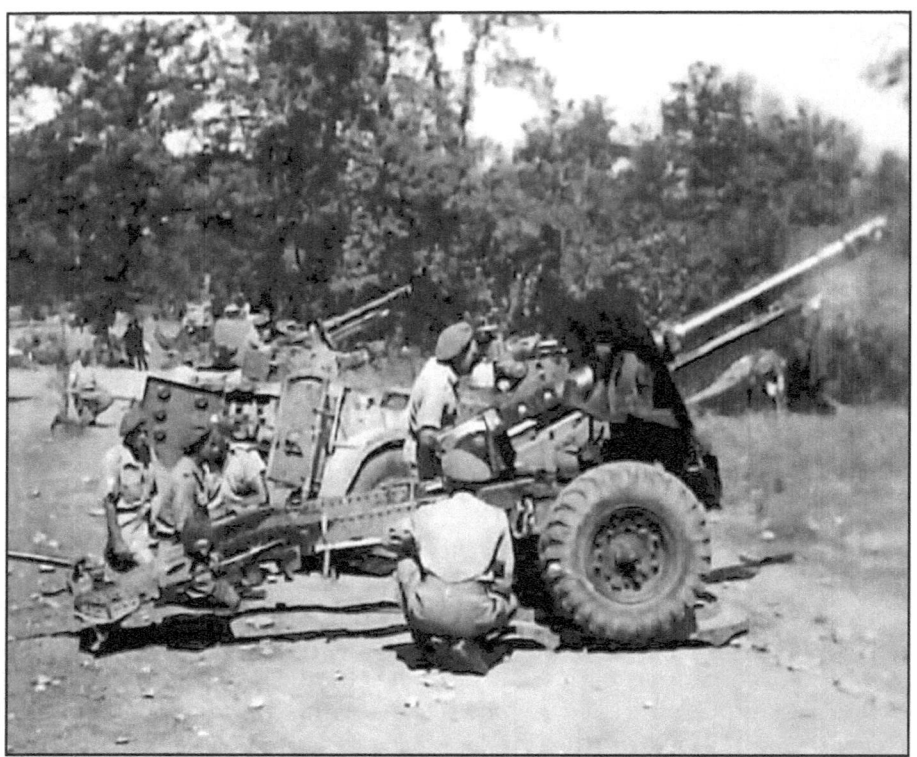

Artillery in training, near Arce

12 Saturday: Up at 3 a.m. for harassing fire—only sixty rounds in all. We had just finished some troop target firing about 12:30 p.m. when Jerry lobbed three shells next to No.3 where Don McGregor and Bill Hitchon were preparing lunch. They were killed instantly. Jerry was vicious in his shelling of the area—plastering houses and the road. We replied with many hostile battery tasks. Those of us who could get away paid a final tribute to Don and Bill. The night was fairly quiet, but we could hear the mortars exploding in the infantry positions a few thousand yards ahead of us.

13 Sunday: I spent a fairly busy day on the phones because of the harassing fire conducted by our O.P. (*Observation Post*). At night, I came down to 'B' Echelon for a two-day rest.

14 Monday: I didn't get up until about 9 a.m. I awoke about 1 in the morning, because of the heavy shelling within a mile or two of us. The R.S.M. (*Regimental Sergeant Major*) told me that the guns would be coming out of action tonight. With Jack, I paid a visit to the village of Ginestra, a most uninteresting and dirty little place. I went into the FSS (*Field Security Section*) office where I found Barnard Wilson, a Varsity contemporary and he and I had a great chat. He told me the FSS had to run the village, because the AMG (*Allied Military Government*) were not there. After lunch, Jack and I visited the house of an Italian, where Jack played the classics on the piano. I couldn't help but think of the happy days at home. On the wall was a coat of arms under which were words to the effect that the family's ancestor had come from Spain in 1517, and had changed his name to Pandolfi. We later had a swim. About 8:30 at night we set off for La Luna.

George S. stopped outside a building which, on closer inspection, turned out to be the local police station. Its rooms were crowded and outside were Italian policemen and "patriots" armed with rifles. The Fascist prisoners did not seem to resent their compulsory confinement. No doubt they would at least be certain of a meal. The drive to La Luna was uneventful although it was still daylight and Jerry could see us from Monte Albano. With the gear onboard, we wasted no time in getting away. The Italian family pressed us hard to take a farewell drink, but we could not wait. I learned that the heavy shelling in the morning was C-Battery(?) work by the Germans on our position and the positions of the other two Batteries of the Regiment. In one building, he hit a dump of chargers and caused a fire. In our area, the shells fell to the right of the house near the AA—but no-one there was injured. An AP (*Armor Piercing round?*) fell very close to the house. The battery pulled into 'B' Echelon for the night. In the afternoon, truckloads of U.S. infantry went up to take over from our troops.

15 Tuesday: Up at 4 a.m., a cup of tea and then away in the dark heading south. As light came and the sun rose we were able to appreciate the beauties of the wooded hillsides of the Chianti. We passed through several villages, including San Pancrazio, mentioned by Boccaccio in the "Decameron," and Castellina in Chianti to our bivouac area just south of Castellina, where we settled down among the rocks and the oaks. We are fairly high up here.

Due south (eleven miles by road) can be seen the towers of ancient Siena. As luck would have it, there was a truck going to Siena in the afternoon. Naturally, I jumped at the chance to go. I resolved to see as much as possible of this famous city of medieval art. Siena, which I had passed through previously, is a city of about forty-seven thousand inhabitants. It has narrow, twisting, flagged streets flanked by four to five story buildings. I won't describe what I saw. This has been done most ably in several books I bought. First to the superb black-and-white marbled Cathedral to see its world famous art treasures—its pulpit, inlaid stone floors, library of blazing colored frescoes, statues and figures. Then to the Public Palace (*"Palazzo Pubblico"*) to see frescoes by Sodoma, Lorenzetti, Vanni de Bardolo, di Pietro, and choir stalls by di Niccolo in the Duomo; then to the churches of San Martino and Serri di Maria, and the Loggia of the Merchants. In the Saracini Palace, I was shown oils by Sodoma, and others no less famous. The music room, the musical instrument room (with a viola by Stradivarius), chandeliers, exquisite floor paintings resembling mosaics, and a host of other treasures were also shown to me by a butler. Finally, to the Museum of the Duomo from which most of the treasures had been moved to safety. Home about 8 p.m. (22 July M. No. 28, 20 and 21 July M and M).

16 Wednesday: To Siena again this morning—officially on business. Again to the Cathedral. After lunch, with others to a private home to purchase wine. There was a pleasant few hours with the *signore* who spoke good English. The wine was my downfall unfortunately. I was very ill and learned a lesson. Today was the anniversary of *Il Palio*, (*the famous horse race around the Campo*, Ed) but no pageant was held.

17 Thursday: A day in camp. In the evening, Jack, Dud and I walked to a nearby house to get our washing done. Then we went on to the little, dirty war-torn village of (*unnamed,*) where we spent an hour or so conversing with the natives.

18 Friday: Heavy rain this morning compelled us to cover up our gear under a canopy, which leaked like a sieve. Jack and I went off to Siena in the afternoon, purchased an excellent guide book by Lucy Olcott, and "allowed" her to take us around. Before we bought the book, we went to the famous church of San Domenico where a friar conducted us and an English soldier around. Of this visit, and other visits, more anon. We revisited the farmhouse in the evening. I got confused over the words *"pane"* (*bread*) and *"panni"* (*clothes*) but when I had comprehended the latter word, all was sweet. Then farmer's wife told me of the German's activities, and how they had taken away all—or most of—their clothes. To bed about 10:30.

19 Saturday: Soon after lunch, Jack and I set off for Siena, and continued our tour of its art centers—San Bernadino, San Stefano, Fontebranda, Oratorio delle Contrada, Confraternita di Santa Caterina, Oratorio del SS Crocifisso, Porta Romana, Santa Maria degli Angeli, San Raimondo, Porta Pispini, San Spirito, San Giorgio, Loggia del Papa, Sant'Andrea, and others. In the Campo, we saw a display of the costumes and banners carried by the representatives of the seventeen wards at the Palio, which I gathered, had not been held for four years. The Siennese, I noticed, were well dressed when taking their evening stroll. We got back after dark.

20 Sunday: Compulsory church parade this morning. I remained for H.C., and afterwards had a chat with the padre. I did not go to Siena today.

21 Monday: Early this afternoon to Siena, with C. Shoemark and Jack. We contented ourselves with one visit only—to the Public Palace. We thoroughly inspected all the object of art detailed by Lucy Olcott in her excellent "Guide to Siena." One needs to visit a place of art more than once to get to know its works. Later, Jack and I visited the Museum of the Cathedral. Most of the famous works have been moved to a safe place in the country, and rightly so. A few remain. In addition, there are some Roman sculptures—some of which are well preserved, and others not so.

22 Tuesday: This morning about 9:30 half of us set off for the beach resort of Follonica for a rest. The country en route was mixed—large areas of oak in some places, and nearer the coast, some grain-growing land. But it was almost invariably hilly. We found Follonica considerably damaged by warfare in some quarters. Some miles off the coast lies the mountain island of Elba. I only wish I could visit it. In the afternoon most of us had a bathe. The water was deliciously warm; and most of us admitted that we had never found the sea so warm in New Zealand. Bathing finished, we took a stroll to the town. Follonica is once again getting into its stride. After mess again to the *paese* (*town*). George, Gordon Rogers, and I were invited by an ex-naval officer into his house for a drink. Luckily, for the other two, the officer could speak English (with an American accent). We passed a pleasant few hours with the officer, his wife and elder child (about eight) and his wife's sister. I was told by the *signora*, who has a baby, two months old, that it is difficult—in fact, impossible—to get the correct foods for children. The little son, she said, had spent some time on their farm, and there he had picked up many dialectical expressions and words, such as "*Male*,"and "*cattivo*." (*bad,* and *evil.*) I learned much of the people of Italy from this family.

23 Wednesday: Cork is grown in this vicinity for the heels of *scarpe* (*shoes*), and this morning we saw a woman sticking layers of cork together, then pressing them, and putting them in the sun to dry. In the afternoon, we bathed as usual. Really delightful. We revisited our Italian friend in the evening. The outing proved most enjoyable. I learned of the *mezzadria (sharecropper)* system of agriculture, whereby the *contadini* (*farmers*) worked the land for the *padrone*, receiving half the yield, and how it had started in Tuscany before spreading north and south. However, the ex-naval officer did not think *mezzadria* operated in Fascist Italia. For refreshment, we had dried cherries, and then cherries that had been soaked in a solution of sugar and water. They were tasty. We talked of the war and other topics. To bed about 11.30 p.m.

24 Thursday: Up at 6 a.m., breakfast, then away from this fine holiday resort. We arrived back at base to find everyone lined up on the roadside awaiting Churchill. A siren on an advance car heralded his approach. With Churchill in an open car was the G.O.C. Freyberg. Churchill, dressed in a brown "duck" suit, topee and sunglasses, leant over the windscreen and alternately waved his hat and gave the 'V" sign to the cheering troops. The Maori Battalion made the best job of the cheering. He returned the way he came, this time seated. At night, Jack and I went for a walk to the house of the local *padrone*, and there talked with some of his tenants.

25 Friday: The Battalion Commander spoke to us this morning of the present military situation in Italy, and outlined the arrangements for our move to the Adriatic. In the late afternoon, I had a swim, then visited an Italian here at night. (No. 24 M. June 26).

26 Saturday: We packed during the afternoon, and set out about 9 p.m on our long journey. In the early stages, on either side of the road, were views of hills and valleys with their olives, hornbeam, and oaks, as well as farmhouses, and villagers in groups chattering in the fading light.

27 Sunday: Even in the black, the villagers were still sitting or standing chatting outside their homes. We branched off at Siena, then took the road leading to Castel del Lago on Lake Trasimeno. We crossed the top of the lake before passing through Spello and arrived at our halting place—just outside Foligno—after daybreak. A sleep. In the afternoon, Jim Covice and I went to Foligno—a fair-sized town badly damaged by aerial bombardment last January. We visited the ruined Church of San Feliciano—in a frightful condition—and chatted with a female custodian and her family. She had lost four or five daughters in the bombing. One of the surviving daughters was a mute who attended a special school. We saw examples of her embroidery learnt at the school, which were very good. After mess at night, Jim and I climbed and climbed a twisting cobbled street to the village of Trevi. There were no signs of past warfare there. We chatted with the villagers, and reached camp on foot at about 11.30 p.m.

28 Monday: We started again about midnight on our way to the Adriatic area. I slept most of the way on a journey of about ninety miles. The nearest point of importance to our new camp is Iesi, or Jesi, a town of about forty-two thousand persons. I walked to the nearby hamlet of Santa Maria di Monsano in the early afternoon. There I was surprised to find a stone statue of Dante ("Onorare Altissima Poeta,") (*"Honor the Ultimate Poet"*) next to the church. A jeep took me to Iesi, of which the greater part is walled. With two other chaps, we visited the home of an architect and his two sisters where we were passed a most interesting few hours in conversation. From them, I learned the name of a tree which has puzzled me for long—the *"gelso,"* or in the dialect, the *"moro"*—namely, the mulberry tree. The silkworm cocoons appear for about forty days (in May), and the foliage is also used for cattle feed during the winter. I must get more details about this interesting tree. The landscape is less hilly around here from where we were, in fact, the areas of flat around us appear to be quite extensive. There are the usual olives, poplars, and vineyards, as well as maize. To bed early.

29 Tuesday: After lunch, I hitchhiked to the *podere* (*farm*) of the Marasca family, some three miles on the other side of Iesi where the parents, their two daughters and I sat on chairs under the trees and chatted. For refreshment, we had red wine and large fresh peaches. Some of the children of the *contadini* on the farm sat nearby and looked in wonder at the foreign soldier. I learned that the children of the *contadini* receive three years of compulsory schooling while those of the *operai* (*workers*) five. I also learned more about the system of *mezzadria*, and something about the construction of houses—the use of brick, lime and paint, and the placement of wooden ceiling beams. I returned to camp about 8 p.m.

30 Wednesday: Moving again. We packed up in the morning and were moving off after 1 p.m. The journey was very dusty for most of the way. We passed through many villages, but the only names I remember are San Giorgio di Pesaro, Piagge, (both war scarred,) and M. Maggiore. We reached the main highway at Fossonbrone, and very soon after got into very bad traffic jam. We pulled into a field for half an hour or so, then moved again along through narrow, exceptionally dusty roads experiencing many halts in packed conditions to the halting area. Eventually, we got ourselves a meal that the cooks turned on after 9 p.m., then went to bed. (Airgraph August 10, Margie and Mother).

31 Thursday: On the road once again. We set off about 3 p.m., got onto Highway 3 and pulled in at a halting place next to an exceptionally dusty road and in a very dusty paddock. Jerry departed from here last Saturday. There is a collection of houses next to us—no vines—no eggs because the fowls are *ammaliato* (*bewitched*)! With the other chaps, I walked to the village at night. Its name is Montemontanaro, and is a very lonely place on the brow of a small hill. The area was shelled by German 170 mm and 210 mm Howitzers last night, and the people are much afraid. An example of this was a line of women kneeling outside their *case* (*houses*) praying to the V. M. (*Virgin Mary*) for protection.

SEPTEMBER, 1944

1 Friday: The Battalion Commander spoke to us about the present situation at the front. He said the Gothic Line had been breached in several places. Our job was uncertain. We had first been attached to the Canadian Division, then to the (*unnamed*) Division. Now we might have to wait until the rest of the Division comes up. In the afternoon, John Sellar and I visited the parish priest, his three sisters and their niece. They were liberal with the wine. We talked with them for about two hours. Next to the church was the temporary residence of some nuns of the Benedictine Order. What I noticed particularly was the way the memory of their departed was cherished. The walls were lined with photos of the deceased, each photo containing the name and dates of birth and death of the person concerned. Later, we went on to the village and talked with a number of *contadini,* and a girl studying for the teaching profession. She told us of the cruelties practiced by the Germans—the stealing of cattle, goods and chattels from the *contadini,* and other crimes. After mess I returned to the village and chatted in the rapidly fading light with the peasants. The village was very poor in appearance—the people too.

2 Saturday: We moved again this morning after 9 a.m. The road was very dusty and the countryside grew hillier with fewer trees than many other places we have passed through. We crossed the river Apsa (?), a tributary of the Foglia, and put guns in positions on the side of a deep valley near the hamlet of Il Gagli (?). The hill to the north in front of us was very high. Digging of pits was cancelled. I (*Intelligence*) reports received during the day revealed that the Gothic Line had been well and truly breached. We did not fire. A point of interest: we saw peasants plucking coarse weed-like plants for boiling and eating. The taller ones—the fibers of which are gathered with the stalk—are dried, soaked in water, and finally woven into a coarse fabric for clothing: nightgowns and nuns' clothing, and sometimes pants. We have heard the Allies in France are only fourteen miles from Germany!

3 Sunday: After 8 this morning, we pulled out and returned to the vineyard near the badly damaged village of Saltara to which I walked in the afternoon. At night there was a compulsory church parade on the account of the national day of prayer on the fifth anniversary of beginning of the war. (*September 3, 1939*). I remained for Holy Communion. The Colonel spoke to us after the service and told us what our future activities were to be. (M 14, M and M16, Parcel 9 from Margie.)

4 Monday: This morning parties from the regiment went to Fano, some twelve miles away, to bathe in the Adriatic. The road en route (Highway 3) showed much evidence of war—potholes, smashed and demolished houses. When we reached Fano, we headed along the coast highway to a beach about two miles south of the town. It was shingle, and today the surf was strong. George, Gordon and I went back into the town. With the exception of Allied soldiers and officers and a few persons who have returned to their houses, the place was deserted. Looting had been rife there—shops broken open, all that was worth taking removed. The locks were shot out to enable an inspection of the interiors. The same applied to the houses, offices, and flats we inspected. Home about 5 p.m. At night, Sam and I visited a nearby *casa* of a *contadino*.

5 Tuesday: Spent the morning writing letters. After lunch, Jack and I visited several *case*. In one place, the *contadino* had a spare spring mattress in his bedroom covered with silkworm cocoons. We chatted with another household, including some refugees from Fano. There we drank new wine which was "*poco buono*" ("*quite good*".) Everyone, except the children, had a job—men ploughing, women washing and ironing, mending *scarpe* and so on. At night, I revisited the *casa* above the camp. When the household went upstairs to the only remaining room—the others being wrecked by shells—the adults downstairs sat down by a kerosene light to remove the corn from the cob. They were very dexterous at it.

6 Wednesday: Up at 5 a.m., and on the road at 6 to the Division concentration area some twelve miles away on a rise overlooking the Adriatic located a mile away to the east. We have been forbidden to fraternize with the natives! What utter nonsense! What of the wine, the eggs, and our washing! Our course, as usual, we are far from a village. San Costanzo is three miles from here. The countryside to the west is more open with large fields set aside for cereal crops. The farmers are now busy "de-cobbing" the corn for winter feed for their animals. (Airgraph, Aug 11, Margie).

7 Thursday: There was a light rain in the early hours, but it cleared away for a time. I went for a stroll to the farm of a *contadino* in the evening. Surprising as it may seem, there was a good radio (not working now) in the house. The family was of the better *contadino* type. The daughter, aged about twenty-two, is keen to follow her uncle and go to

Canada after the war. She appears to be keen and intelligent, and it is a pity that she has had so little education.

8 Friday: Mud and slush everywhere after frequent and heavy showers of rain. This afternoon and morning, I walked with Norman to San Costanzo. We spent some hours with a woman shopkeeper and her family, and had potatoes cooked in oil for lunch. Afterwards to the temporary home of a *padrone*. (His house is in Fano.) The household consisted of a father, mother, and two daughters. The daughter with a broken ankle was with her fiancé (a student of English.) The other daughter (with two children) was from Bucharest. A most entertaining afternoon was spent sipping delicious Romano cognac. I carried on a lively conversation with the daughter from Bucharest, and the younger daughter and her fiancé, while Norm spoke in English with the father who had once been in the coal business at Newcastle-on-Tyne. We got to the bottom of *mezzadria* system (at least from the *padrone's* point of view). The Bucharesti girl was vivacious and charming—such a contrast from the *contadini* women we see in our travels. On the way home, we obtained some eggs and had four each for "lunch-dinner." (Aug 22 and 28 from Margie).

9 Saturday: This morning Norm and I went to the seaside town of Senigallia, twelve kilometers to the south. The war has knocked the stuffing out of it. Business has not regained its feet. Outside the old town stand numerous fine villas, many of which are badly knocked about. Senigallia is far from an impressive place now. (Cable, Sept. 4, Margie).

Letter No. 67: Saturday, September 9th, 1944

My sweetest beloved little girl,

Your air letters arrived, only eleven days from New Zealand to an isolated spot in Italy! What an excellent service. Whatever name you chose, Paul or Roger, will suit me also.

I'm so glad to hear that your Dad has had good news from England about his paper. The Faraday Society is no mean body. I only hope his paper goes to the Royal Society and that they consider it along with his past achievements worthy of his receiving a Fellowship.

(*On the subject of awards,*) the OBE (*Order of the British Empire*) is awarded generally for good administrative work. The DSO (*Distinguished Service Order*) goes to an officer who gives outstanding service in the field, or whose men bring him the honor and glory. I certainly don't intend to work all out to get to the rank of Bombardier. Others can have those ranks, if they so desire. Certainly not me!

Alex

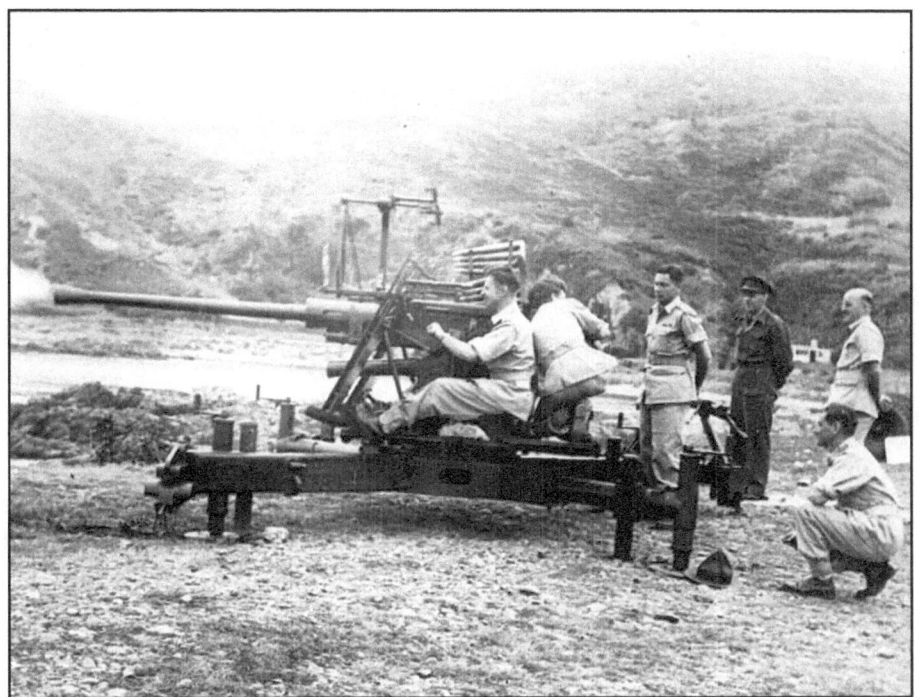

Bofors firing

DIARY ENTRY

10 Sunday: Compulsory church parade this morning! We packed in the afternoon, and after an early mess, set off for our concentration area about 5 p.m. Along Route 16 through Fano and Pesaro (with its sycamore-lined highways) to fields just east of Gabicce. On the top of the hill next to us is a rather fine castle with a castellated tower. We dug "slit-ties" because the Luftwaffe has the bad habit of bombing the back areas at night.

11 Monday: I was awakened about midnight by the bombing and the AAs. The hundreds of Bofors rounds—red and glowing—looked like a fireworks display. Jerry bombed again about 3 a.m. We packed for the move, and left about 3:30 p.m. The battery was established on a flat among the vines. We are a few miles west of Misano in the Villa Vittoria. A busy afternoon and evening of digging in; there was a bit of firing throughout the night, but none from our battery.

12-Tuesday: It turned out fine and sunny. Gun pits and bivvies were completed. We started the fireworks at 6 p.m. and carried on throughout the night in support of an attack by the British and Canadians. The RAF was also very active. The troop fired in all about eight hundred rounds.

13 Wednesday: Bright and sunny. The mediums (*bombers*) were again very active. They made a tremendous noise. Jerry dropped two large calibre shells into our gun area during the night. Thought to be a (*German*) 9.2 (*inch howitzer*). He dropped others in the D troop area and behind us.

14 Thursday: Today we fired 450 in support of another phase of the attack by the Canadians. The RAF bombers and fighters were very active over Jerry's position. A quiet night, thank goodness.

15 Friday: Rain seemed possible this morning. The C.P. (*Command Post*) packed up to move. The signal to ceasefire at 2015 was given at 2013, and at 2015 came the peremptory order: "Fire orders—ten rounds!" When the orders came through, the guns started quickly. Then: "Move 1000," then: "Stop!" It was an awful mess up. However, we got away about 9 p.m. We passed along Highway 16 through the seaside villages of Abissinia and Riccione—both utterly deserted—to our new position near Riccione. Digging gun pits and slit trenches again was hard. We all worked well into the early hours to complete them.

16 Saturday: The situation changed a lot during the day in our favor: advances were being made against stiff resistance. Jerry put down very heavy fire in the Coriano area to our left. After mess—about 6 p.m.—he shelled our area. Gordon Rogers was wounded and Don McKenan slightly wounded.

17 Sunday: A message came through at around 10:30 that Jerry was heavily counterattacking the Greeks—(*from the Greek 3rd Mountain Brigade)*—at the southern end of the airfield. We had to post anti-tank sentries and have our small arms ready! Up to 3 p.m. today the troop had fired eight hundred rounds in the previous twenty-four hours.

18 Monday: The big show started about 5 this morning. About five hundred dive-bombers were on the job, and to 3 p.m. our troop had fired twenty-three hundred rounds. Jerry's morale must be exceptionally high to stand up to such a hell as this we are launching. He is holding on like grim death to the airfield four thousand yards ahead of us. No wonder he fights so well; his corps commander has told him that upon the zeal of the German soldier rests the fate of the Army Group in Italy and the whole of the southern front. The show restarted with a vengeance about 10 tonight.

19 Tuesday: Another exceptionally busy day. To 3 o'clock, we fired twenty-five hundred rounds in twenty-four hours. About mess time, a RAF S/Cdr. and an American Captain visited the gun site. They told us that in the big show yesterday only eleven planes had been lost in two thousand sorties. A thousand tons of bombs were dropped on Rimini. I was on duty as the Telephone Operator overnight.

20 Wednesday: We prepared to move about 9 p.m. As was to be expected, the guns got "Take Post," but no firing was done. Rain fell heavily. The guns left at 10.15 p.m. I remained with the BSM (*Battalion Sergeant Major*) at the CP (*Command Post*) to await the return of the ammo trucks with the balance of the ammo. It rained, and rained, and rained. (Airgraph Aug. 30, Sept. 4, Margie, Sept 1 Mona).

21 Thursday: The ammo trucks got back about 6 a.m. They took seven hours to go seven miles. Mud, slush, narrow and jammed roads. To 'B' Echelon for breakfast, then to the guns about midday. The destruction to be seen on the way was appalling—trees stripped of their leaves, shell holes everywhere. About thirty knocked-out or broken-up tanks, dead cattle in the paddocks, shattered buildings, and so on. It rained again, and the area was like a mud pie. Thank goodness there were plenty of good, deep Jerry dugouts. Jerry must have moved out in a hurry. Besides domestic gear, he left a good deal of gun ammo on the position. When the Canadians left the dugouts, we moved in. The San Fortunato feature is about two thousand yards ahead of us. A good night's sleep in the former German Command Post. (A/L Sept. 3 M and letter from Mona).

22 Friday: The weather cleared and there was bright sunshine this morning. We did some firing—three hundred rounds (range 7400 yards) —then prepared to move after the recce parties went out. We left in the mid-afternoon through the Rimini suburb of San Andrea to a position to the west of that place. I was kept busy with ammo. The bridgehead here is narrow; Jerry is only fifteen hundred yards to the left. We started firing about 11 p.m.—a program of 900 rounds. Jerry was very active with his artillery in the locality.

23 Saturday: The troop began banging away with bursts of twenty this afternoon. We had packed to move, but did not do so. A good night in bed, although the gun teams did a little shooting during the night. Jerry was also very active.

24 Sunday: This morning I went on the Battalion recce to a position near San Giovanno di Bagno, north of Viserba, some four to five miles north of Rimini. On the way up, we saw South African engineers beginning to make a bridge to replace the one blown by Jerry. The site selected for the guns was only one thousand yards from the FDLs (*Forward Defended Localities,*) and from a little rise I could see the *Nebelwerfers* and shells landing on our FDLs. The *Nebelwerfer* has a most unholy sound. On the way home, we stopped to inspect a German defensive position. It was a concreted-in Tiger—a wonderful a job of work. The river had been two thirds bridged when we reached it! We are to move early tomorrow. At night, I was on duty in the CP (*Command Post*) during the barrage for the 6th Infantry Battalion attack. Jerry started two fires farther back when he hit ammo dumps. He was again very active at night particularly with his 170 mm Howitzers.

25 Monday: On the phone during the small hours and early morning. We moved at midday to a new position. The usual digging in and preparing for action. It rained fairly heavily for a time. The troop did a little firing.

26 Tuesday: A bright sunny morning after the rain. Our aircraft dropped news bulletins and leaflets on Jerry with the question: "The Allies are in Germany. Why do you stay in Italy?" Some drifted down to us. A fairly quiet night broken only by the firing of the mediums and Jerry's 170s.

27 Wednesday: We moved at midday up the coast road to the somewhat battered village of Bellaria—"fine air"—on the coast. Apart from a few Italian police, partisans and a few other persons, the place was empty so far as the local inhabitants were concerned. The guns went into a paddock in front of the road, and the GPO (*Gun Position Officer*) selected a two-story house of blue-pointed stone for the Command Post. Firing began about 3 p.m. We all selected a *casa* for our sleeping quarters, except the gunners in artillery. A little firing was done during the night—but five rounds were fired on 2800 yards, "Charge 1!"

28 Thursday: George S. and I weren't called at 4:40 this morning for picquet duty around the guns because there were only scant elements of two of our Battalions between us and Jerry who, incidentally, left this village on Monday night. Instead, we prowled the area armed with Tommy guns for about an hour. The rain came down in torrents during the day and at night. Number 4 gun pit was flooded with water up to the layer's seat and had to be removed, and No. 3 was pretty bad too. We were called in early evening to lump "smoke" to No. 1 and No. 2 guns that were firing in support of the infantry. What foul weather! Thank goodness we have houses for the night.

29 Friday: There was no rain during the day, but the weather remained threatening. Throughout the day refugees from the FDLs two miles to the north arrived at the village to take refuge in many of the deserted houses here. A really tragic sight. "*Che è la guerra!*" (roughly, "*That's war!*") On duty at night, but little doing before midnight.

30 Saturday: From midnight to 2 a.m., I was awake for the harassing fire by our guns. The weather was beautifully fine today. We did not do a great deal of shooting. Jerry a/c (*air cover?*) was over us about 8 p.m. AA very, very lively. Jerry was active with a 170 (*mm Howitzer*) about a quarter of a mile away in the late afternoon. There were casualties when he hit a truck.

OCTOBER, 1944

1 Sunday: Little of interest to record today. George and I were on picquet for about an hour in the early evening. Two Greeks (*from the Greek 3rd Mountain Brigade)* were shot by the 5th Cols (*5th Columnists*) in the area last night!

2 Monday: Jerry kept us awake early this morning with persistent shelling in the vicinity of the village. One shell went through the roof of a house near Battalion HQ. It was fairly quiet during the day, but Jerry was active again at night.

3 Tuesday: The same old tune early this morning. Jerry persisted in his shelling of Route 16 and other areas all day and all night. A large dud shook the house to its foundations.

4 Wednesday: A beautiful morning reminiscent of spring weather at home. On duty all day as an Assistant (*to the GPO, Gun Position Officer*). In the late afternoon and early evening, we did a fair amount of CB (*Counter Battery?*) work. There was also about five hundred rounds of harassing fire at night. Jerry was quieter, thank goodness.

5 Thursday: Bad weather again and a little rain. CB work this morning and afternoon and again at night, when I was on duty. (Margie Sept. 14)

Letter No. 50: Thursday, October 5th, 1944

My sweetest beloved little girl,

I had a letter yesterday saying at last he (*brother-in law, Dr. Keith Macleod*) had arrived in Italy. He has asked repeatedly to tell you more about myself.

About two months ago, one of the officers asked me how I would like going off the guns and into the Command Post, i.e. be a part of the troop which works out all the corrections for firing, controls the shooting, and does administrative work. I jumped at the offer because it meant that I would have the opportunity to learn something of the mathematical side of gunnery. At first, I did little in the 'ACKing' line, but was kept busy with the ammunition. Only when the Sergeant-Major resumed control of the latter I was able to get down to the 'ACK' work, and I must say that I greatly enjoy it. It would have been better if I had learned the work at a course rather than in the field. The very frequent, almost deafening, noise caused by gunfire and the shelling doesn't make learning of fairly complicated work easy.

We are housed in a '*casa*' with breakfast and dinner coming from the Battery cookhouse.

I have done quite a lot of reading lately—one excellent book, "The Case of Sergeant Grischa," by Arnold Zweig. The Continental novelists paint a more realistic portrait of mortal man than the average, or even most of the best English novelists. He makes his characters very real individuals and does not hide their human weaknesses. He is able to transport his reader to the scene of his tale. The book was all-absorbing. Even though one's enjoyment in reading such work is great, how much more so it would be if one could read them in German and Russian, and thus get a "little more" from what is lost in translation.

What a proud Daddy I would be if our little girl could recite a few of Keats's, (*Edward*) Lear's, or Wordsworth's lines to me when I stepped inside the door. We must ensure she is well versed in our great heritage of literature.

Alex

DIARY ENTRY

6 Friday: We fired a DF (*Defensive Fire task*) at about four thousand odd yards at 5 this morning. I had the rest of the day off. George and I walked along the beach to the river, and then home. We couldn't help noticing Jerry's strong dugouts, wire, dragon's teeth, etc., on the beach.

7 Saturday: On duty all day and all night with H/F and H/Bs (*Hostile Batteries?*). Not a great number of rounds fired, but they were spread out right throughout the day.

8 Sunday: More rain, but only light, in the morning; heavier in the afternoon. A fairly quiet day. Some shooting at night. I visited the local school mistress (We are living in her house.) at the place where she is now living with about twenty other refugees. It was an interesting visit: a little talk on language, Bellini, etc. Bellaria is so-called because its keeps down the mosquito populations (that are so prevalent in other parts of Emilio-Romagna). (Sept 9 Mother, September 14 Margie)

9 Monday: Rain in the early morning gave place to bright sunshine. Like a bolt out of the blue came the message that we were to be prepared to move by 6 p.m. However, we had bad weather again, and we did not shift.

10 Tuesday: Away on the road about 8 a.m. It began to rain after a while. We passed trucks bogged down in the ditches near San Vito, and watched others go in. The rain came down heavily. It was grim—wet through, mud everywhere. It was hard to get the guns into position. The former lightly covered green paddock was cut to ribbons by the quads. Then we got to our slitties. We found it easier to throw the mud out, or bag it by hand rather than use a shovel. About 18 inches deep was the safety limit—there was water below that depth—then sandbags and the tents. Straw on the bottom, empty sandbags on top, and then finally our bedrolls. To bed at 7.30 p.m. The towers of the village of Santarcangelo are a mile or two away to the south and the three-towered peak of San Marino lies in a line behind it. We are more or less in a diamond—San Mauro (northwest), Savignano sul Rubicone (west), and Santarcangelo (south) being the other points.

11 Wednesday: Jerry woke some of us this morning with his shelling. The sun replaced the rain. How grand! We did some harassing fire during the night. Jerry was very active with Nebelwerfers and some guns, but not in our area. Two Jerrys buried. (20 and 25 Sept, Margie)

12 Thursday: Again fine and sunny. Recce parties went out this morning to recce our new position. Just why a new position, I don't know, because Jerry is not more than seven thousand yards from here. They returned later to tell us that there was a veritable hail of metal—Nebels and mortars—in the FDLs about fifteen hundred yards ahead. We did not move, and had to dig the dirt out of our slitties again for the night.

13 Friday: We moved around 7 a.m. up through battered San Mauro and across the Fiumicino, which I gather Mussolini claimed was the historical Rubicon, but which is in fact the Uso further south. The banks were about fifteen feet high and the actual stream was about six to eight yards wide. We took up positions near Gatteo, and began firing in coordination with the OP (*Observation Post*) after lunch. Fighter-bombers were very active nearby in the late afternoon. I spent the night at 'B' Echelon, where I had a good sleep.

14 Saturday: We got a fright about 3 o'clock this afternoon. There was the telltale noise of the Nebelwerfer, and then everyone dashed for cover. Shells went over the top of the house and one landed near the forward gun making a mess of some of the chaps' clothing. He put down some shells at the same time. A little later Battalion HQ was hit by a single shell. A very unpleasant period. Our guns supported a move forward in the San Angelo area at night.

15 Sunday: To Holy Communion at 7 a.m. at RHQ just outside San Mauro. On duty for the rest of the day and overnight. Harassing fire, and H/B, neutralization and H/M (*hostile mortar*) tasks. Our Battalions are advancing. In evening, there was a vino party in honor of J.B., who is going to a job in Florence.

16 Monday: A good day. In the afternoon, walked to Gatteo, which was full of New Zealand Armed and Infantry personnel. Gatteo is battered—very battered—principally by shellfire. Saw Coy Moore. The Battalion is coming in from the line. Played bridge all night.

Letter No. 77

40455 Gnr. A.G. Protheroe
26 Battery
4 (NZ) Field Regiment
2 NZEF   MEF
Monday, 16th October, 1944

My sweetest beloved little girl,

I'm hopeful of receiving a letter from you this afternoon, and so I won't complete this until the mail arrives. As a matter of fact, the mail has not been so good of late, but let's hope there'll be a big surface mail-in soon to compensate for the comparative shortage. As I have already answered your last two air letter cards, there's nothing I can answer. However, here are one or two items which will be of interest.

The ex-officers, who left us about three months ago for the R.A. (*Royal Artillery*) OCTU, have now finished their course. All but two (one of them was Charlie Williams) passed, and they have been recommissioned. Charlie Williams returned here a few days ago, and he, like the rest of us who weren't lucky enough to go to the course, has been demoted to gunner. I must say quite candidly, dearest, that I had pangs of jealousy for awhile. I think it most unfair that all of the ex's did not have the same chance, i.e., to be recommissioned, even though some of us were unfortunately away when the Colonel had his interviews. I am no mathematical genius, but I can hold my own with fifty out of the hundred in maths and some of the chaps who have got their star back did not do as well as I did at the RAF course at Tauranga. Now these chaps—most of them single—are receiving sixteen shillings and sixpence a day; I am getting only seven and six. I don't often refer to this subject, dearest, but I feel as if I must vent my spleen a little here. Of the five of us that joined the Regiment on the hills at Cassino, only Wally Tyrrell has now been recommissioned. Charlie Williams had his chance, and Barry Diamond, John Rogers and I have had none as yet. John Rogers is no longer connected with the guns: he is now a gunner helping with the ammo, while Barry has been away sick for more than month. I have told you that for a month or two I have had training as a Gun Position Officer's Assistant, and it is rumored that I have been recommended for a course in that work. Naturally, I am keen to learn more of the work. (I can do a good deal now, thanks to the good instructions I have been receiving under ideal conditions), but the maximum rank for a GPOA is Bombardier. I have no desire to hold NCO's stripes, and I certainly have no intention of seeking them. All I want—and I consider it only fair—is to have the same opportunity as Charlie Williams, Wally Tyrrell, etc. to get my commission back. If I failed on such a course, well, that would be my own fault, wouldn't it? The chap who was GPOA here for many a long day (a 5th Reinforcement, like me) left yesterday to take up a job at the New Zealand Club at Florence. He thoroughly deserved it, didn't he? Now, another Aucklander has come to take his place. I believe I told you that the Colonel assured me, when he demoted me, that my chances of being recommissioned were in no way jeopardized. I trust that is the case. I have, however, heard a rumor that that it is false. Don't ponder over the above unduly, dearest. If I don't have a chance of going to OCTU, then I'll have to grin and bear it, won't I?

Incidentally, I am making good progress with my series of short stories. I have finished two and have started a third. It—the last mentioned—is about a wealthy man—a landowner or *padrone*—I met sometime ago. He and his family and what they had to say make excellent material for a short story. I have a fourth story in mind, and I'll begin it when I am able to do so.

I have seen very little of Jack Mercer these days. He spends nearly all of his time at 'B' Echelon, where he is officially classified as a maintenance signalman. He has only been associated with the guns about three times in the last four months, and thus I rarely come across him.

I believe I told you that Bob Baker is back. He is the C.P.O (*Command Post Officer*) i.e. the person responsible for the direction of the guns in action.

I wonder to which unit Keith will be posted? Won't it be grand when he and I can get together and have a good chat.

I am afraid there is little news, beloved. All I can tell you had already appeared in the newspapers.
Later:

No mail, sweetheart. Most disappointing.

I have harangued about myself too much in this letter. Now for more important persons. How are you, beloved, our little girl, Judy and the wee boy? I'm most keen to get your cable giving me the final decision in regard to our little boy's name. Roger or Paul. He will be three-months old in two days! I have sent Judy another special airgraph, and I'm sure you'll all laugh at my attempt to draw the "Wee Bubby Buzzer." I trust your mother and dad are in good health. I suppose your Dad will be starting tennis again soon? I well remember stacking the fire ready for the after-tennis bath. May God Bless the three of you so very much, beloved, and reunite us in His good time, which I trust will be very soon.

> Your ever loving and devoted,
> Kisses for Judy and the baby,
> Alex

DIARY ENTRY

17 Tuesday: We moved from our position near Gatteo this morning, passing through Gatteo itself, and through Gambettola—also badly knocked about—to our position just outside the town. The Command Post was established in a really filthy *casa*—No. 26—which had once been used by a German battery. The old woman who inhabited the place was like a bulldog—no threats or shouts would drive her away. (She was not actually inhabiting the place, but come to pick up this and that), and so one of the chaps finally shouted out "Where is the *pistola*?" She then beat a hasty retreat. (September 28 M and Mrs N, and 25 M and 1 Mother).

18 Wednesday: With George and Lloyd to Gambettola this afternoon. Full of Division troops. Badly knocked about, but many Italians still in residence. Barrage at night in support of attack by Division troops.

19 Thursday: Warned for move. Recce parties out, but Jerry still active at no great distance from the new area selected. We did not move. Jerry did some shelling away behind us.

20 Friday: Moved this morning to a new position about 5 miles away at Gattolino in the *campagna*. For the first time for about a month, we were able to get the Ities to do our washing. Beside the family in the *casa*, there are refugees who are relatives and friends. Part of 24 Battalion is also quartered here, an A/T (*Anti-Tank*) Unit. The infantry have been telling us about our shots on the barrages. Our tanks are going ahead very well today. Did not do much firing overnight.

21 Saturday: Fire orders—as were to be expected—just before we moved about 8:30. We took up positions just outside the village of San Giorgio di Cesena and had to dig slitties in the mud. A program was fired during the night in support of the Canadians, and a platoon of our own Battalion was counterattacked by about a hundred paratroopers.

22 Sunday: At 2:30 a.m., I awoke suddenly to find the side of my slittie had collapsed on top of me. Sandbags were on my chest and feet and a pile of mud on top. It was quiet during the day. The Division is to be reorganized—the Armed Regiment and the Divisional Cavalry are to become infantry as is the Motorized Battalion. The A/T (*anti tank?*) Unit is to be organized into three battalions; the Regiment is to be disbanded and its members are to become artillery reinforcements, and an ATD (*Anti-Tank Division?*) is to be established in Italy. The (*unnamed*) Regiments are to go home soon. The infantry have been relieved by the (*unnamed*) Division, but we do not know yet when we are to be relieved. George and I saw the infantry coming out when we visited the village in the afternoon. I was on duty at night. Jerry was very active with HF. (3 Surface letters, from Margie, snaps of children, and one from Mother and Mona.)

23 Monday: Cold and miserable. Jerry did a lot of harassing in the morning. Light barrage for attack across the river overnight. Visited house full of refugees in afternoon and evening.

24 Tuesday: Attack was successful. Canadians are finally established across the river. The ammo was picked up in the afternoon and we went out of action at 5 p.m. Visited Itie refugees for a chat and vino at night.

Regrouping in Le Marche

25 Wednesday, October, 1944: We packed up in the morning, had poultry for lunch, and left at 2:30 on our long journey for the Fabriano area (*in Le Marche*) near Iesi. A circuitous route through Gatteo, etc. took us to a road junction on Highway 16—some ten miles south of Cesenatico. Knocked out Tigers and Shermans were prominent on the road. The journey was long and tiring. We ran into rain, and got tangled up with a tank transporter convoy going north. We reached Iesi in a torrent, wet and with nothing to eat, about 10 p.m. Some quads and trucks were lost. Slept in the back of the truck, and a good sleep too!

26 Thursday: Left Iesi about 9 a.m. Rain off and on. Through the limestone, steep hills towards Fabriano. Chains on at one village. Finally to the hamlet of Rastia, deep in the hills. Everyone ensconced in a *casa*, thank goodness. Nice and quiet here but very, very isolated. Sat and chatted around the hearth at night.

27 Friday: A day indoors. The family here consists of a woman and a girl of fifteen, her brother, a repatriated POW from England, and her niece. Her husband is a policeman in Iesi. At night, we sat around the fire, reading and talking. The former POW did not like England because it rains too much there. More of the family anon.

28 Saturday: Again wet and miserable. A talk by the T.C. (*Tank Commander*?) in the afternoon. The subject: the upshot of him conferring with the C.O. in the morning. Most interesting and amusing. We learned we are to

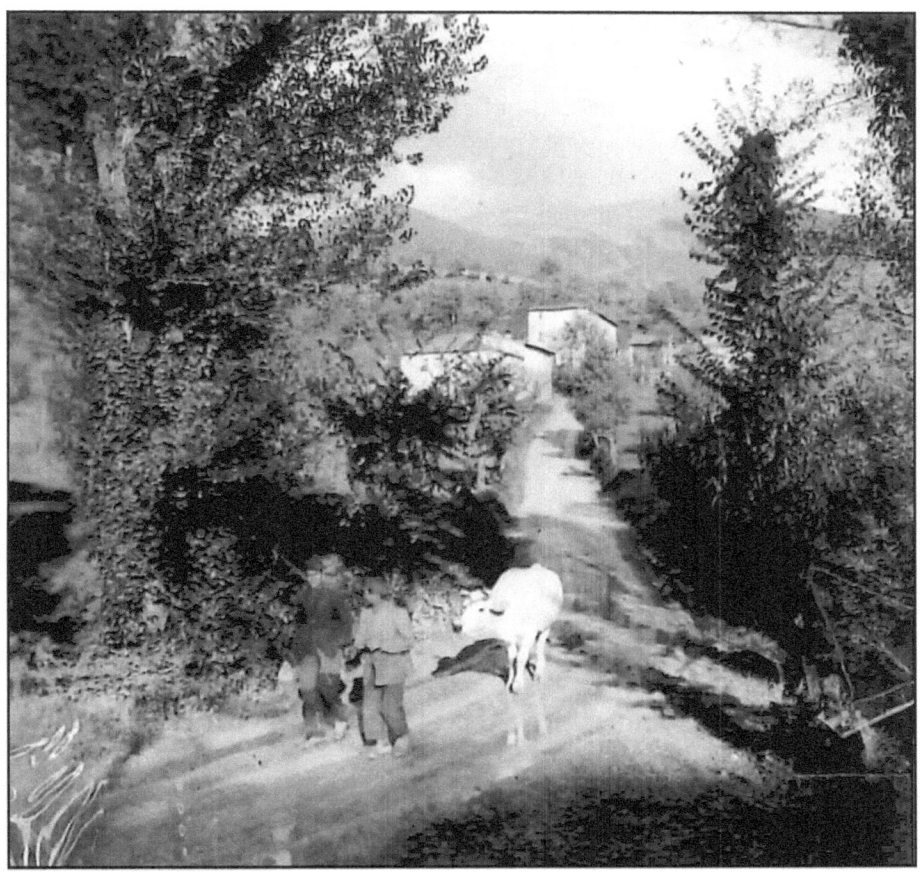

Rastia, near Fabriano, Le Marche

be here for about a month, during which time the Division is to be reorganized. Parades begin on Monday. Also in store: maintenance of equipment, rank marches, sport (?), gun drills (?). No drinking during daylight(?) Compulsory showers in a *casa* (?), no thieving (?), numerous guards, no selling of goods and clothing, foot inspections (?), no rape (?), no stealing of transport, or rifles indoors, or buying of plonk. A night around the fire in the *casa* with the family. Chat and "plonk." About 11 p.m., an officer and another came here. The officer became involved in a violent argument with one of the gunners, which nearly ended in blows. To make matters worse, someone went upstairs to the Ities living quarters. Things became very tense when the Itie upstairs came down with a loaded pistol in his pocket!

29 Sunday: How bitter is the weather! All "a stew" today over the fray last night. A report was demanded by the C.O. and the "Itie" from upstairs was interviewed. A curfew is in effect on this house at 9 p.m.—the door is to be locked. The Itie was relieved of his pistol. To Holy Communion in the kitchen of a farmhouse in the morning. One of the Ities stood by the door and watched the service. He was not at all embarrassed. Showers— most welcome—at the outskirts of Matelica (six kilometers away) in the afternoon.

30 Monday: Rastia is an isolated little hamlet of about two hundred souls at the head of the valley in an oak and poplar-dotted mountain area. One reaches it by a side road running off the Maletica road. The *contadini* here live very simply. The little settlement must be isolated from the rest of the area when the snow comes in December. The Francini seem to live on spaghetti, yet they all seem healthy.

31 Tuesday. The TC (*Tank Commander*) saw me this morning, and asked if I would like him to recommend me for a commission in a supporting service (some type of specialized work). I expressed my appreciation of his action and naturally agreed with his suggestion. This afternoon to Maletica with two other chaps from the troop where I saw two films and drank a couple of bottles of *creme de menthe* ("*crema alla menta*" in Italian). A little merry, but not inebriated.

NOVEMBER, 1944

1 Wednesday: A fine early winter day. A quiet day writing letters.

2 Thursday: To Matelica this afternoon. Since I and the other chap with me had already seen the movie, we spent the best part of the afternoon in the back of a wine store having a chat with a *contadino* proprietor. We missed the truck and were obliged to buy some bread (only ten lire for a kilogram loaf) from an Italian bakery. We went back to the cinema at night and sat it out.

3 Friday: This morning a lecture by Lt. Moffatt on c/b work. Informative and good. Rain intermittent during the day. One of the blackest nights I have ever seen.

4 Saturday: A fine sunny day—the best we've had for some time. Tonight to Fabriano—a biggish town with some large buildings—to the Canadian concert party and later to the cinema. A bitterly cold journey home in the 3-tonner. I finished, "In the Village, Italy."

5 Sunday: Very cold early this morning, but fine and sunny later. Went for walk in hills this afternoon with Jack. This region—I ascertained it is the Macerata province—is very mountainous.

6 Monday: Training for Regimental Guard this morning and later writing in the afternoon.

7 Tuesday: Regimental Guard this morning. Only fair. The usual two hours on, and four off for the following twenty-four hours. (Air. L. from M., Oct. 18).

8 Wednesday: Through the flutter over the Colonel's inspection, the Battalion forgot our breakfast. When he finally came, the Colonel asked if we had plenty of *vino*. Three good jobs advertised in Gazette this morning. NZPRO., A., NZPRS and M.P.C. Also Editor, NZ Times, and reporters. In a quandary because of previous recommendation, but I know things will turn out alright.

9 Thursday: With M., I went on a vegetable buying expedition today. First, to Fabriano, where we inquired about *legumi (peas and beans)*, and *verdure (vegetables)*. We were told to go over the hills to the market garden area. An interesting day was spent in haggling over prices. Briefly, costs were as follows: Cauliflower, 10 lire a kilo; onions (very scarce) 18 lire; cabbage, 10 lire; and potatoes, 16. The Italians have literally thousands of lire, but there is nothing to buy with them. Tonight to the home of my friends, who confirmed my opinion on the financial condition of their countrymen. (letter, Keith)

10 Friday: A day in the house and a vino party at night. Enough said. Our first fall of snow early this morning. Very cold.

Letter No. 84: Friday, November 10, 1944

My Sweetest Beloved Little Girl,

Keith and I met yesterday. He looks very well. He is still in the 5th Field, but still expects to be posted to a Battalion Unit soon.

I went away yesterday morning with an officer on a buying commission for the Battery. The area where we are at present is not rich in vegetables, and thus we had to go further afield than we expected. I acted as interpreter. We called here and there to acquire potatoes, onions, cabbage, cauliflower, celery, and anything else we could get in quantities sufficient to feed a large number of hungry mouths. I thoroughly enjoyed the day. I have been commissioned for a number of other translating jobs on behalf of the Battery. I thoroughly enjoy doing them. Of course, I get stuck at times.

As you know, I haven't had any good fortune as far as positions are concerned so far.

Snow has come at last. Very pretty, but very unwelcome. I doubt very much that it will disappear. We will probably have snow on the ground

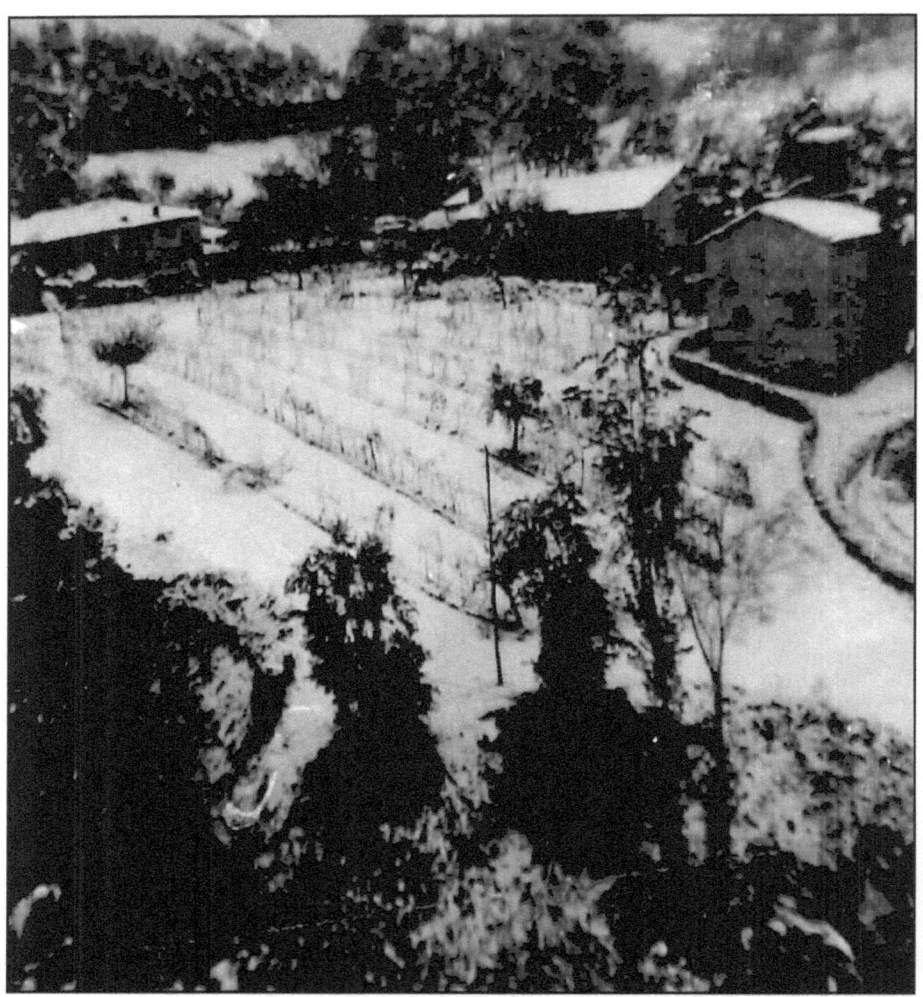

Snowy landscape in the hills, possibly near Rastia

for several months ahead. The Italians have just finished the sowing of grain before the winter. Surprisingly, they seem to feel the cold as much, if not more, than we do.

Alex

DIARY ENTRY

11 Saturday: No more snow, thank goodness. Papers in from New Zealand. Spent afternoon and evening answering letters from sixteen of Mina's pupils.

12 Sunday: Cold and rather dull this morning. An ultimatum issued by (*the mistress of the casa*) Ginevra, this morning—we can have two rooms only: either a bedroom and the storeroom, or a bedroom and the kitchen. I think Ginevra objects to two of the boys sleeping in the kitchen not getting up when she and her family come storming down about five in the morning! We intend to ignore her protests as we will be leaving again for the front in a few days. A lot of parties in the various *case* tonight, it being the birthday anniversary of one of the officers.

13 Monday: Cold early, but fine and sunny. On cookhouse and fatigue duties this morning and late this afternoon. Party at night with Hugh and others.

14 Tuesday: Decision is to be made at 5 p.m. by G.O.C whether or not we will move tomorrow. This afternoon to Iesi to buy cauliflowers for the Tank Battalion. Went into to town after ordering veggies. Quite candidly, the women in Iesi I saw walking in the piazza and main street were the best looking and best dressed I have seen in Italy! It was very dark when we arrived back at camp.

15 Wednesday: Cold and miserable, with some rain. No move today, thank goodness. An interpreting job this afternoon over a broken cart. I'll need to watch the Itie, who is causing all the fuss. This evening a conversation with Maria. Later, she sang some beautiful songs in French. Then later still, to a drinking party given by the D Troop drivers in honor of some of the local Ities. I left early. (Air Letters, Oct 26 and 29 M)

16 Thursday: The day was spent mainly in packing up for the move back to the line tomorrow morning. I was told by the GPO (*Gun Position Officer*) in the afternoon that I was to remain behind as I would be required for an interview at the Division HQ on Saturday morning. I took my gear down to Piane in the evening, but went back to Rastia to have a few farewell drinks with the Ities.

17 Friday: By 11 a.m., all the vehicles had left and were on the road. We spent several hours hanging about for a truck to take us to Matelica. Our party comprised footballers, boxers, and four ex-officers going to Division for the L of C (*Lines of Communication*) interview. Eventually, we left and passed through Matelica on to Esanatoglia, a quaint village wedged in a narrow valley, and then went up the hill to the former Division Artillery HQ that was a Benedictine Seminary for priests. Erected about twenty-five years ago, it is a huge place of three-stories built around a central courtyard. The view to be obtained from it of the surrounding hills and valleys is really magnificent. Spent the evening playing bridge.

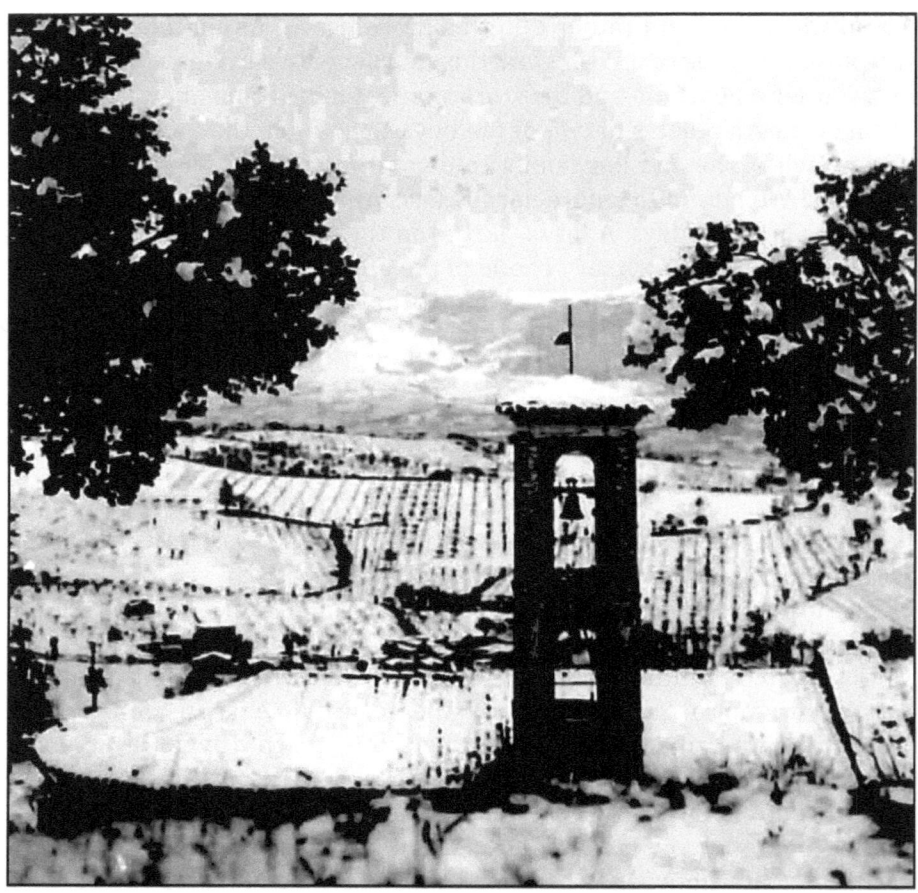

Early winter snow, Le Marche

18 Saturday: About thirty of us ex-officers were interviewed this morning by the Col. L W T, (G), a Lt-Col. and a Major, who after asking us our age and marital condition, got us to tell our own stories. They gave us no information about the jobs, but I presumed they were P.D. (*Professional Development?*), and L of C offers at camps, etc. I gathered that most of the chaps before the board were married men with families. No decision was given as to whether we were successful or not. I pray to God that, for the sake of my dear Margie and our little children, I shall be successful—the extra money will help so very much.

Later to the art exhibition of works of chaps in the Div. Excellent painting, recalling to mind many scenes familiar in various actions. Then back to the Seminary with Laurie L., and onto the village in the afternoon where we chatted with old associates in the Army back home. Early in the evening, the Archbishop of Ancona and Macerata, accompanied by the *capo* of the Seminary and other priests arrived to check the inventory taken when the Div. Artillery took over. I acted as interpreter between the Archbishop and the only officer in the building. It was agreed that the *capo* should come tomorrow morning and go around the building with me. Before departing the Archbishop presented two bottles of good vino to the soldiers present.

Moving Back to the Line

19 Sunday, November, 1944: We left Esanatoglia after 10 this morning with a returning Rome leave party on our journey back to its unit. Morning tea-lunch at the YMCA Iesi, then along Highway 16 to Rimini and up the road to the Regimental HQ 'B' Echelon, just short of Forli. Hugh Weir and I spent the evening with H.D. talking to an Itie family in a *casa* on the position.

20 Monday: Early this morning Jerry lobbed over a good number of heavies, but none was close to us. Left about 7 a.m. for our own 'B' Echelon, and after breakfast passed through Forli, a large manufacturing town not badly battered, across the river to the gun position a mile or so out of the town. There is a large *casa* for two of the gun crews and the Command Post. We fired a few smokes and H.E *(high explosive?)* this afternoon.

Letter No. 86: Monday, November 20, 1944

My Sweetest Beloved Little Girl,

I didn't get another opportunity to see Keith. Let's hope I run across him again.

Just what is our wee boy's name, PAUL or Roger....? Please let me know definitely whether you have registered him as Alexander Paul, or Roger Broughton.

Judy must have caught the New Zealand 'Trade Union' bug to remark,"That's enough for today!" when she was helping you in the garden.

A few weeks ago, I received a letter from my young cousin, Bill, who has arrived in Italy after a considerable period in Sicily. Regarding my short stories, I have not been able to get on with them during the last month or so because there are too many interruptions. I pray there will be good news, which with the extra pay, will enable us to send our wee girl to kindergarten next year.

This afternoon, I posted home some more snaps of Cassino and some of the sports meeting and celebrations we had at Arce some months ago. I received three volumes of short stories from Basil (*brother-in law and husband to Hilary*), and the '*Listener,*' (*the magazine of the New Zealand Broadcasting Service*) containing the photos of himself at the listening watch, and the article on the reception of the news of the invasion. I will be very pleased to hear that Basil has at last got a job where there is a prospect of advancement and opportunity for his talents.

I can hardly believe it is twelve months since I was in Burnham (*Military Camp*). So far my luck in regard to status and advancement has been far from favorable, but I feel that everything will turn out all right shortly.

Alex

DIARY ENTRY

21 Tuesday: About 2 a.m. this morning, three of the guns fired about forty rounds each in support of an attack by units of the British 46th Division to which we are attached. The attack across the river was by no means as successful as was hoped. The fighter-bombers and mediums were very active during the day. Chatted to Italians at night. We are now on a "silent role."

22 Wednesday: Cold early, but later beautifully fine and sunny. About 2:15, I was a witness to the tragic sight of one of our bombers being shot down in flames. There was a good deal of argument about whether any of the crew got away. We fired a few H/Mortar (*heavy mortar*) tasks before midnight. Jerry bombers were over Forli about 5 p.m. A/A very active.

23 Thursday: I was on duty in the Command Post overnight. A few H/Mortar tasks during the early hours, and about 7 a.m. a smoke program to cover the bridging of the river. Further smoke later in the morning. In the afternoon, I went to Forli, a big town with some modern buildings. The town is almost entirely occupied by troops. I inspected a refugee shelter—no light, very little air, pitiful human beings. Forli is very proud of its famous citizens as there are tablets on the walls of the houses in which they are born, lived, died, etc.

24 Friday: Fire and sunny morning. The (*British*) 2 and 5 Hampshires, the Bedford/Hertfordshires and the 2 Kings are going well towards Faenza. We received their "sitreps" (*situation reports*) stating that there is little or no enemy contact.

25 Saturday: This afternoon Mark and I went with the recce party to our new position. We went up Highway 9 for about 9 kilometers, and a position was "reccied" just off the road. The country was very flat and open. Many of the trees in the fields en route had been felled by Jerry obviously to give him better vision. Two chaps from HQ, plus Mark and I remained to secure accommodation in the houses for BHQ and the Troop respectively. Our *casa* was the crossing keeper's home. If I recall correctly all his family were there—the crossing keeper himself, his wife and four daughters and four sons. At the time, there was eight all told in the premises, plus three refugees. What a charming family: they were honestly pleased to see us as Jerry left here (Faenza Corleto) on Thursday evening. In the evening, we sat around the fire, and the mother got me to sing "Tipperary." She recalled the English soldiers singing it during the last war. The children slept in the *rifugio* (*refuge*) across the road with twenty other Italians. Jerry shelled Highway 9 and Forli and about a mile to the east of us during the afternoon and evening.

26 Sunday: I asked Justina (sixteen years old), whom I called "little woman" to do my washing, but she didn't want to do it on the Sabbath. However, when I told her that we might possibly leave, she did the washing. I mustn't forget to be thankful for the hot water that was brought into our room, and the little boy cleaning our boots. The digging parties came up and got on with the gun barricades: one couldn't call them pits because it was impracticable to dig pits. However, we got a shock when the family, all highly excited, rushed in to tell us that the major had ordered them away to Forli. It was hard, but I'm afraid very necessary. They hurried about and the girls put on skirt after skirt, chemise after chemise, and jersey after jersey, their best shoes, grabbed a few rings and rations and then we took them to Forli in a 3-tonner. Permission was given for three men to remain behind at the two *case* to watch the cattle, etc. Throughout the day until after dark, the rest of the Division—tanks, infantry, etc.—went up the road. There was a tremendous amount of congestion. We got a real fright in the early afternoon. Six Thunderbolts (as we found out later) peeled off behind us and we didn't know which way to run. Two of them dropped their eggs about seven hundred yards ahead of us on the railway line, and the other four not much further forward. Bad briefing—as Jerry was about four kilos away at least. At night, some of the boys raided a turkey and duck pen, and we also had a cognac and vino party.

27 Monday: The guns came up about 8 a.m., and in the rain and foot-deep mud the quads sweated and the gunners bled to get them into position. Then the question arose of accommodation—only a four-roomed house for the whole troop. The GPO decided that four on each gun, the officers, a TSM (*Troop Sergeant Major*), signalers, one ac. driver and a tiffy (*gun repairman*) should remain. It was impossible to sleep outside in the "bivvies." Those of us who did not stay at the guns, returned to our old position and had to search for accommodation again. However, I persuaded Tonina, who had moved back to her room upstairs, to evacuate it and thus six of us got a good dry spot for the night.

28 Tuesday: I learned from the cooks that the guns did not fire overnight. To the dentist in the morning, and letter writing in the afternoon. At 5:15 p.m., when I was preparing a fire to roast a turkey and the majority of the chaps were lined up in the mess queue, two Jerry planes swooped over and dropped bombs near the vital bridge on Highway 9 at Forli. There was a hail of AA fire. The Jerry plane I saw hedgehopped to avoid the AA. I don't know if they did any damage. We had turkey and plonk about 5 p.m. It was only when we were cutting it up that we realized I had forgotten to remove the gullet when I cleaned it.

29 Wednesday: This afternoon Jack and I went to Forli. We heard in the morning that Jerry had slightly damaged one of the two Bailey bridges with a bomb the night before, but there was no sign of damage when we saw the bridge. We made a point of inspecting the Rocca of Caterina Sforza (*Rocca di Ravaldino*)—an ancient sturdy pile of brick. A good deal of the moat still surrounds the castle. For many months, the ancient fortress has been used as a refugee centre and the Italians were well set up as far as beds accommodation were concerned. The spiral staircases, the narrow passages and the great rooms showed the medieval architecture of the building. We talked with some of the refugees and they could not believe that it was possible for private soldiers to go to Varsity. All men who had gone to the University in Italy were officers, they said. The barrage for the 10th Indian attack began at night.

30 Thursday: A cold, miserable day. I woke about 5 a.m. with the beginning of our and Jerry's shelling. Our troop fired in support of the 10th Indian Division at Faenza Corletto early in the morning. This evening to a concert given by Tommy talent at Forli. A first class show! No wonder, with so many professionals from London on the program.

DECEMBER, 1944

1 Friday: Back to the troop this afternoon. We did some harassing fire during the evening. One could hardly realize that the roads could become such mud pies.

2 Saturday: Early this morning we shot counter-mortar and harassing tasks. Quiet during the day. After dark, Jerry was over, probably with the object of his bombing being the vital bridges again. The AA presented a glowing spectacle.

3 Sunday: About 9 a.m. this morning two Jerry Focke-Wulf 190s flew over us from the direction of Forli at no great height. The AA did not realize what they were until too late, and could only give them the hurry up. We also fired about this time, a hundred propaganda shells with safe conduct leaflets enclosed. To the new 'B' Echelon, east of Forli, after mess at night. I managed to get a fairly decent room for Fs (*Files*) 1 and 2 from an Italian family.

4 Monday: A morning around the house. After lunch to the showers at Forli. I walked home. In the country, I visited another Italian family, and after I had done some 'singing' myself, one of the girls sang some delightful Italian love songs and excerpts from opera for us. Most enjoyable. As it was fine all day, our bombers and fighter-bombers were on the job until dark giving Jerry the works. Chaps down from the guns say bridgeheads were put across the river. Jerry lobbed over a few 170 mms last night, but none was very close, thank goodness, as those badly damaged and cracked houses of ours might have collapsed about our heads.

5 Tuesday: Dull, misty and miserable with rain. However, the weather improved in the late morning. Back to the guns again. Ravenna has fallen after stout work by Canadian and United Kingdom troops. Very little firing has been done here during the last two days.

6 Wednesday: Another miserable misty day. We plowed about in the mud in the afternoon lumping ammo. No firing by us at night. A heavy barrage to our left front indicated an attack there. There was heavy rain in the early evening. Jerry was also active with heavy concentrations in the vicinity of Route 9 and elsewhere. We received part of a big shipment of mail. I spent the day reading "The 1890s," by Holbrook Jackson, a book full of information on the art of the 1890s, and of criticism and analysis on the works of Wilde, Beardsley, Davidson, Beerbohm, Shaw, etc. Fascinating! I also read J.D. (*John Donne?*). Also, J. D. Beresford's remarkable story, "The Hampdenshire Wonder," took all my attention. (Chocolate from Mona, 12 and 13 from M. and another)

7 Thursday: Again cold and miserable. In the evening, I visited the Italian family next door with other chaps, and again Bianca sang for us. About 10:30, there was an AA barrage over Forli. Probably a German plane on the prowl.

8 Friday: To Forli this afternoon with J.R. All shops, or most of them, closed because of a *festa*. Jerry was very active further north tonight with shelling.

9 Saturday: To Forli this morning for a shower. A bright sunny day for a change. Back to the guns in the afternoon. Other chaps told us they had only fired a few rounds in the last forty-eight hours. One round of GF (*gunfire?*) early in the evening. Jerry was active during the night with harassing fire.

10 Sunday: A beautifully fine and sunny morning. Each gun fired twenty rounds of harassing fire between 5:30 and 7:30 at night.

11 Monday: Dull but fine. A big day for the bombers and fighter-bombers. The mediums went through a terrific barrage of flak to do their job. One of the bombers must have been hit as four of the five crew bailed out behind our lines, the pilot kept his ship going. We all hoped he would get home alright. Also, heard that a Spitfire was shot down. Jerry bombed Forli last night, and one chap told us that fifty chaps were dug out of the ruins of one building. In the afternoon, I went to 'B' Echelon at Casina on Route 9. Spent the evening drinking vermouth and chatting with an Italian family.

12 Tuesday: Jerry woke me about 6 a.m. with his continued shelling of the locality. A day around 'B' Echelon.

13 Wednesday: A squadron of tanks went up this morning. The weather today was entirely suited for air activity. I did some swot in Italian this morning, a little in the afternoon. Sat in front of the fire at night.

14 Thursday: Cold and dull, but fine. Back to the guns this afternoon. The "show," as we shall call it, is part of the Battle of Faenza, which started at 11 at night.

15 Friday: Each gun had a program of about 400 rounds, F1 did not complete it because of a jammed cartridge. But we gunners didn't mind. I couldn't help but think of the hell those Germans and Italians around Faenza must be suffering from the thousands of rounds fired at them. We performed DFs (*Defensive Fire*) and other tasks more or less continuously throughout the day; us gunners firing on despite a lack of sleep. The day was fine and bright and the fighter-bombers were fairly active.

16 Saturday: Up at 6 this morning. Unlike when we put the guns in, we had little trouble in getting them out. Up Highway 9 we went for a short distance, and then along the recently-constructed Lamone Road, one built of bricks, etc. on top of the mud, to our position at Faenza Errano on the bank of the steep-sided, deep-flowing Lamone. We had a halt of an hour or two on the way as we waited for a convoy of wounded to go out. The Maoris are also in the farmhouse where we are quartered. Fired a little AP (*armor piercing?*), but not the two hundred round barrage as was expected.

17 Sunday: A little harassing fire in the early morning. Spent the day in building a barricade in front of the gun. I couldn't help but notice on the way up yesterday the complete absence of burnt out or other Jerry vehicles. An engineer showed us a Jerry propaganda pamphlet addressed to us saying we were "the boys who are put in when things get grim." There is a girl of nineteen in this house who studied English for three years in Faenza. She speaks it quite well, but does not understand fairly fast speech. This afternoon the Maoris prepared a pig for the boys in the line. They got the hair off by first washing the pig with hot water, and then pouring petrol over the pig, and setting the petrol alight. Very effective. The BBC announced that Faenza had fallen to us. We only fired about four tasks tonight.

18 Monday: A cold and miserable day with a little rain. Harassing fire at night.

19 Tuesday: Up till 3:30 this morning on harassing fire. Spent the day in preparing ammo for the barrage which started at 9 p.m. The Maori boys were on the job with us—loading and ramming and enjoying themselves thoroughly.

20 Wednesday: We finished the barrage after 2 a.m.—a total of about 440 rounds. No DFs from Jerry, thank goodness. All very tired. To "A" Echelon in the late morning, and to bed very early in the evening.

21 Thursday: This afternoon I hitchhiked towards Faenza to the family that had left the house next door. They were pleased to see me. In the evening, Jack and I ran back another family from the house to their own home—about four kilometers from "A" Echelon. "Their" house—there are other relations there as well—is a great big one with a huge room below ground where all the Italians are living now for safety. It was dark when we went down below, and I was taken aback for a moment when I was confronted by some plaster casts of friars. I returned to 'A' Echelon where I conversed with a girl from the University of Bologna who spoke quite good English. She has been studying chemistry there for five years. Back to the guns as the Maoris have gone back to Forli for Christmas.

22 Friday: L.L. came to see me this morning. He told me of the fortunes of the boys interviewed with us who have gone back to Egypt with their commissions. The three of us from 4 Fd (*4th Field Regiment*) seem to have missed out. Another visit to the family near Faenza this afternoon.

23 Saturday: A day of preparing for the festa. Cookers (for ovens) constructed from charge cases provided the means to cook our pork. Then there was an issue of a patriotic parcel containing about sixty cigarettes, two sticks of chocolate, an orange, and three bottles of beer. The festa started after mess at night, (We did no firing, having been given the evening off.), then carried on until such time as the fellows had had enough and went to bed. Snow—a light fall—fell during the day. I went to Forli in the afternoon to take a middle-aged woman from here to hospital who has gone mental through the bombing. What Jack and I did notice was that the Italian man who accompanied her was more interested in kissing and embracing his friends at the hospital than worrying about the old woman who was left outside sitting on a stretcher in the cold. We came back to Faenza—one of the most scarred cities I have seen. Jerry must have defended the riverbank stubbornly as the whole bank is pitted with many German slitties. Faenza is really a frightful mess. The boys were generous to the Ities giving them beer, chocolate, etc.

24 Sunday: CHRISTMAS EVE. Up at 6:45 a.m. to fire a short barrage of about seventy rounds a gun for an attack. As soon as we had finished Jerry put down a lot of stuff on the FDLs (*forward defended localities*). It was a novelty for me to work the guns in the snow. Roast pork for lunch. A good night around the fire eating nuts, then to bed. Did not have to get up because there was no shooting.

25 Monday: CHRISTMAS DAY. Bitterly cold and miserable outside, but no more snow or rain. This morning I went to Church and Holy Communion conducted by the padre in a Nissen hut. We had Christmas dinner in the late afternoon—turkey, pork, vegetables, fruit salad, jelly, plum pudding and cakes. An excellent meal.

26 Tuesday: A fine sunny day, ideal for our a/c (*air cover,*) which hammered Jerry all day on the other side of the hill. We were called about 4:15 this morning for three rounds from each gun. I went into battered Faenza in the afternoon and got many postcards. Jerry, as usual, dropped eggs on Faenza just after dark tonight.

27 Wednesday: To Faenza this morning to see Keith with whom I spent most of the day. At night to an Italian family and refugees at "A" Echelon,

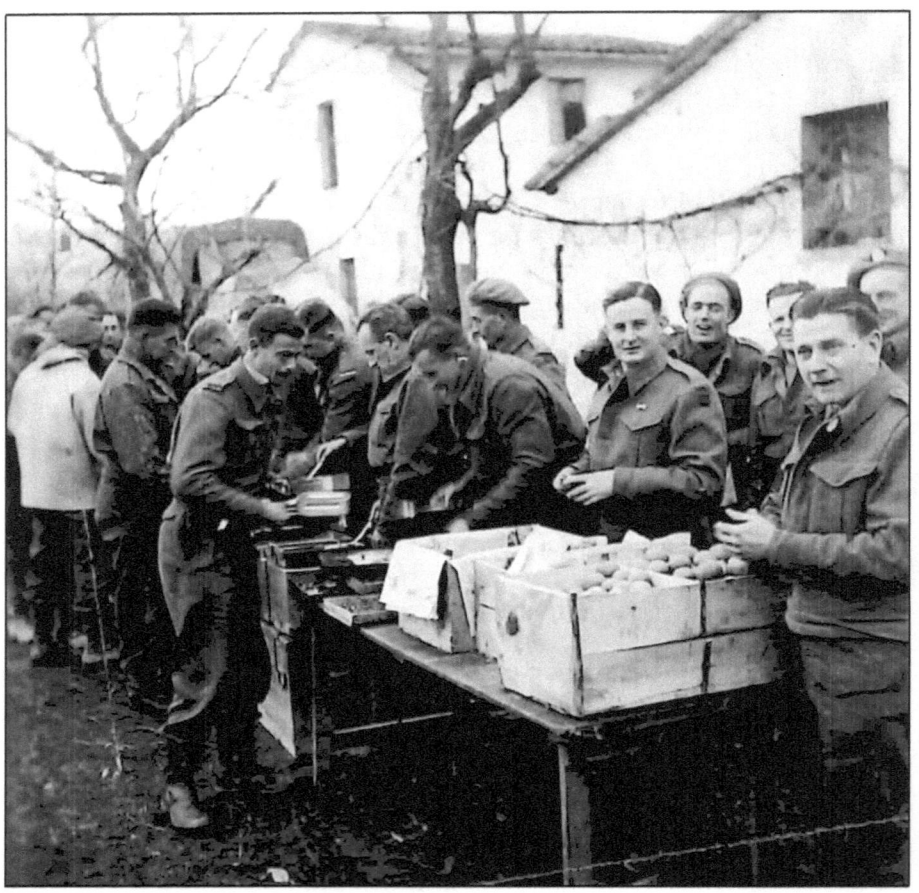

Christmas dinner, Faenza, 1944

where I spent an enjoyable evening. Jerry again over Faenza in the early evening.

28 Thursday: I heard today that one of Jerry's bombs uncovered a lot of interesting "material" in Faenza, which our chaps were not too slow in investigating. Visited Italian families in the afternoon and evening.

29 Friday: Today we fired twenty-four rounds for the operation. Later reports confirmed we had scored three direct hits on a house at the crossroads. The troop also did some harassing fire before midnight. A bitterly cold day. Snow likely.

30 Saturday: Some harassing fire between 4 and 7 a.m., and then, during the morning, when we started digging a gun pit—a proper one—snow began to fall. The digging kept us warm, thank goodness. The excuse is that it is thought Jerry might launch a counter-offensive here, and I wonder, seeing that we've had a very easy time lately? The snow ceased early in the afternoon when we completed our pits. Spent the evening chatting in the house. Two of ours were wounded by a mine this morning.

31 Sunday: NEW YEAR'S EVE. Jerry awoke several of us early this morning with 'vicious' and concentrated shelling and mortaring on one of the sectors. This morning, Pete and I dug slitties around the pit. A really beautiful spring-like day. As was expected, there was the usual conviviality at night when we saw the Old New Year out and the New Year in.

JANUARY, 1945

1 Monday: Many sore heads this morning. I went off to Faenza to wish Keith a Happy New Year, but he was out. Returned to camp in the mid-afternoon, and went to bed fairly early. The Ities of this locality at least did not celebrate the birth of the New Year because of the conditions. Recce party out this afternoon. We are to dig gun pits in a new area tomorrow.

2 Tuesday: After breakfast, we were away on two 3-tonners to the new position at Faenza San Silvestro, about one and a half miles north of the town and three thousand yards from the FDLs near the Senio river. Twenty-one Ities, including a Sicilian family, occupied a big damaged house next to the wine factory. It was my duty as interpreter to tell all but the Sicilians that they would have to go. Then a FSS (*Field Security Section*) chap came along and ordered all out. We started on the gun positions, and then came a message to stop as we would be going to another position! In front of the house was a huge cross above the grave of seven Germans killed there. Our dive bombers bombed and shelled Jerry vigorously and continuously while we were at the position.

3 Wednesday: We were told early this morning that we would be moving today. Guns out of action at 10 a.m., and away soon after. Through Faenza across the Lamone to Commenda, a tiny little farming settlement. Digging gun pits all day—ground sticky, but not unduly hard work. Jerry again opened up on the OP (*Observation Post*) with air cover observing over the bulge in the line on this side of the Senio. He fired about sixteen rounds at "Pippo," *(the euphemism Italian parents used to describe Allied bombers to their frightened children.)* There are several families of "*operai dei contadini*" here—these are people who are compelled to work for the peasants. Their's is an extremely hard existence. They have to buy everything—wine (5, 10 and 20 lire a liter) from the *contadino*. Jerry was very active with shelling during the night.

4 Thursday: A beautifully fine sunny day. Our fighter-bombers on the job early. Some work on the gun pit. Judy is two and a half today.

5 Friday: As tomorrow is Epiphany; the Italians began making preparations today. I watched women cleaning a fowl. They eat almost everything—comb, heart, liver, ova, kidneys. The only parts they throw away are the contents of the intestines, the eyes, the beak and the nails. One round from the guns tonight.

6 Saturday: EPIPHANY. A cold, miserable day. This afternoon I went to Forli to hear the Kiwi EP (*Entertainment Party*). Snow began to fall about 4 p.m., and by the time we got home the whole countryside was covered with a white mantle. A very quiet Epiphany for the Ities here. Most of them had a fowl and managed to get something for the children, but nothing like their prewar celebrations. Some O.S. (*offensive support*) by F1 this morning. (Letters M, B and K.F.)

7 Sunday: A frost during the night hardened the snow. A propaganda shell was fired. I spent the morning and early afternoon preparing for my trip (leave) to Florence. To 'B' Echelon at Faenza Corletto in the afternoon.

Florence

8 Monday January, 1945: After waiting around RHQ 'B' Echelon for some time, we eventually got on the road at 10:15. The mountain area was soon reached and chains were ordered. We climbed and climbed for some hours through country covered with deep snow. After the top of this section of the Apennines our vehicle struck another going the other way. The bumper was badly bent, and in efforts to straighten the bumper out we were turned to almost right angles on the road. There was a slight blizzard at the time. Eventually, we were righted and once over the highest point of the road, we made good progress. Although the journey over the mountains had been very long and most tiring, and most of us had headaches, I resolved I would not waste valuable time during my visit. The snow decreased as we neared Florence, and in the vicinity of the city itself there was none. We reached the Australian Club about 4:30 p.m.— booked in at 30 lire a day and prepared for dinner.

With dinner over (A good meal considering army rations only were used,) a chap and I went to the Apollo to see the Ballet. I was under the impression that there was to be a performance of one of the classic ballets, but this proved to be wrong. The ballet I saw was composed of a series of ballets written around modern and semi-modern music, including Strauss, Gershwin, and Dvořák. They were well executed. An American girl announcer explained to the audience that all the ballet dancers were well known to the lovers of the ballet in America. Also she and another woman played on the piano several classical numbers. The whole performance proved to be most enjoyable. It was novel to say the least.

Strict blackout in the streets.

9 Tuesday: A really beautiful day befitting this lovely city. Cold and fresh in the morning with a thickish haze. I began my tour early. The atmosphere was heaving with moisture. I bought a guide book, poor and inadequate, and then walked in the direction of the Duomo, St Mary of the Flowers. On turning the bend in the road I saw the most majestic pile rising before me. What better atmosphere could one hope for when approaching the majestic building. The great dome and sides rose out of the haze as I drew near. Then, when the structure was clear with the sun shining on it my first thought was 'how wonderful and glorious is the work of man for the adulation of God!' We went inside. There is a vast octagonal space below Brunelleschi's cupola, which was painted with great frescoes by Vasari and other artists about 350 years ago. It baffles description—so magnificent it is with all its exquisite art—its facade, sculpture, bas reliefs, frescoes, and mosaics. Much has been removed from the interior to a safe place, and rightly so.

I climbed the spiral staircase to the interior of the dome. Those who have been there consider it an achievement to have climbed so high and to have scrawled their initials on the frescoed cupola. Once outside, I had to pluck up a good deal of courage to lean over the stone rail and gaze down on the tiny human figures way below. As I descended, I was amazed that men could lay on their backs suspended from above to paint the frescoes of the 'Last Judgement,' which took nine years to complete.

Once down, I saw the marble chair with a very fine series of bas reliefs by Bandinelli and Bandini in the centre of the octagon. The bronze doors that opened onto the Old Sacristy by the great master, Donatello, were not to be seen, however, although once inside I did see Donatello's beautiful marble "wash basins" (*lavabo*) and Luca della Robbia's "Angels bearing Wreaths," which more than justified my visit to the Sacristy. In the nearby chapel is the Ghiberti masterpiece, the sarcophagus of St Zenobius of Florence. Another place of great artistic value is the New Sacristy, where I saw the following art treasures: the "Angel's Head" by the sculptor Mino da Fiesole, inlaid cabinets in walnut, and boys carved in wood by Donatello, plus the lavabo by Buggiano. On a wall in the left nave is a panel by Domenico di Michelino in honor of Dante. For 394 years, this was the only Florentine monument in honor of the poet. The exterior of the Cathedral is also adorned with a host of monuments. The Baptistery outside is now but a shell of its peacetime self. There is almost nothing to be seen, either inside, or out. The three famous bronze portals, including Ghiberti's famous doors, are not there. I did see the font in marble executed by Pisan artists in 1370—the grand font is carved from a single slab of marble.

I contented myself with a glance at Giotto's famous tower, which is separate from the Cathedral. The steeple is familiarly known as "Giotto's Campanile" because that great artist initiated its construction. Undoubtedly, this is considered a jewel in worldly architecture. Unfortunately, the bas reliefs were bricked up. After lunch, I walked to the Piazza della Signoria, the most important in Florence, not only because of its monuments, but because of its historical associations. By far the most dominating—the most striking of the Piazza's arts is the famous Old Palace (*Palazzo Vecchio*)—a perfect parallelogram with square-shaped battlements and surrounded by a really elegant tower built five and a half centuries ago. An English captain, (Much traveled, he told me!) said, "This is the most famous building in the world!" Almost in front of the Palazzo, on the pavement is a bronze dais recording that here in 1498, Savonarola, the belligerent Dominican Friar and his two companions, were first hanged and then burnt. To the right of the Savonarola plaque is the entrance to the Loggia, unhappily for the art lover, now without its famous statues.

The first courtyard of the palace itself contains a famous work, a fountain consisting of a porphyry bowl finely sculptured by Battista del Tadda, but now, (at least during the war,) is without the delightful bronze cupid, which can be seen on the postcards. A great staircase leads to the Sala dei Cinquecento (Room of the 500). This huge room is 170 feet long and 95 feet wide. On its walls are frescoes of battle scenes by Vasari. Although this great chamber gave me pleasure, other rooms in the palace pleased me more.

I have purposely mentioned many famous works I have seen so that you too, if you have illustrated volumes, will be able to get some idea of the great engagement which was mine when I saw these works. The various rooms—those from the great Cinquecento room down to the very smallest—are most rich in their treasures of the Renaissance. I can't detail what I saw because so many pages would be necessary.

Then to Santa Croce, the burial place of many of the famous (Michelangelo, Machiavelli, etc.), but I realized that the day was too short for me to see the church at all adequately. After a stroll in the pitch black streets and on the Santa Trinita Ponte to see the Arno, I returned to the hotel. A day well worthwhile.

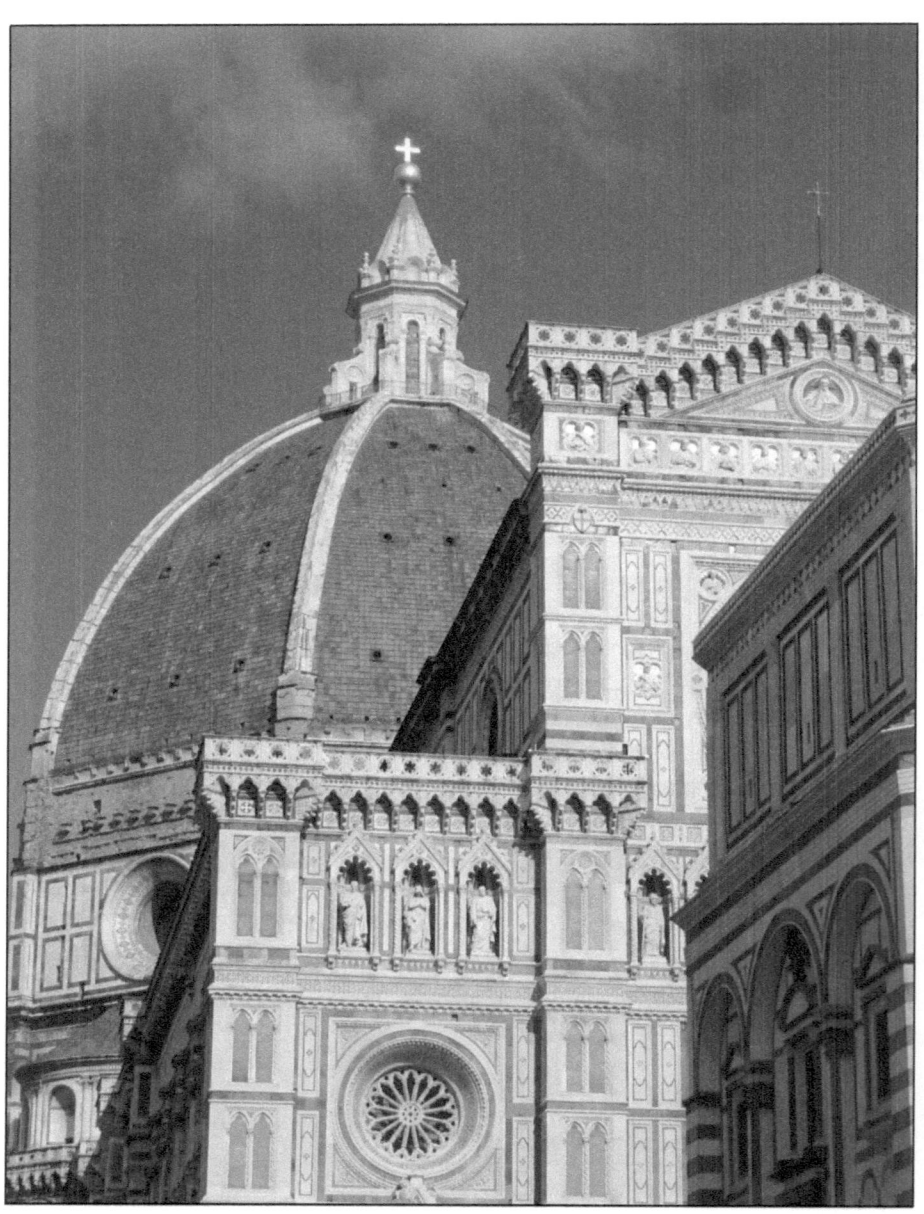

Santa Maria del Fiore, Florence

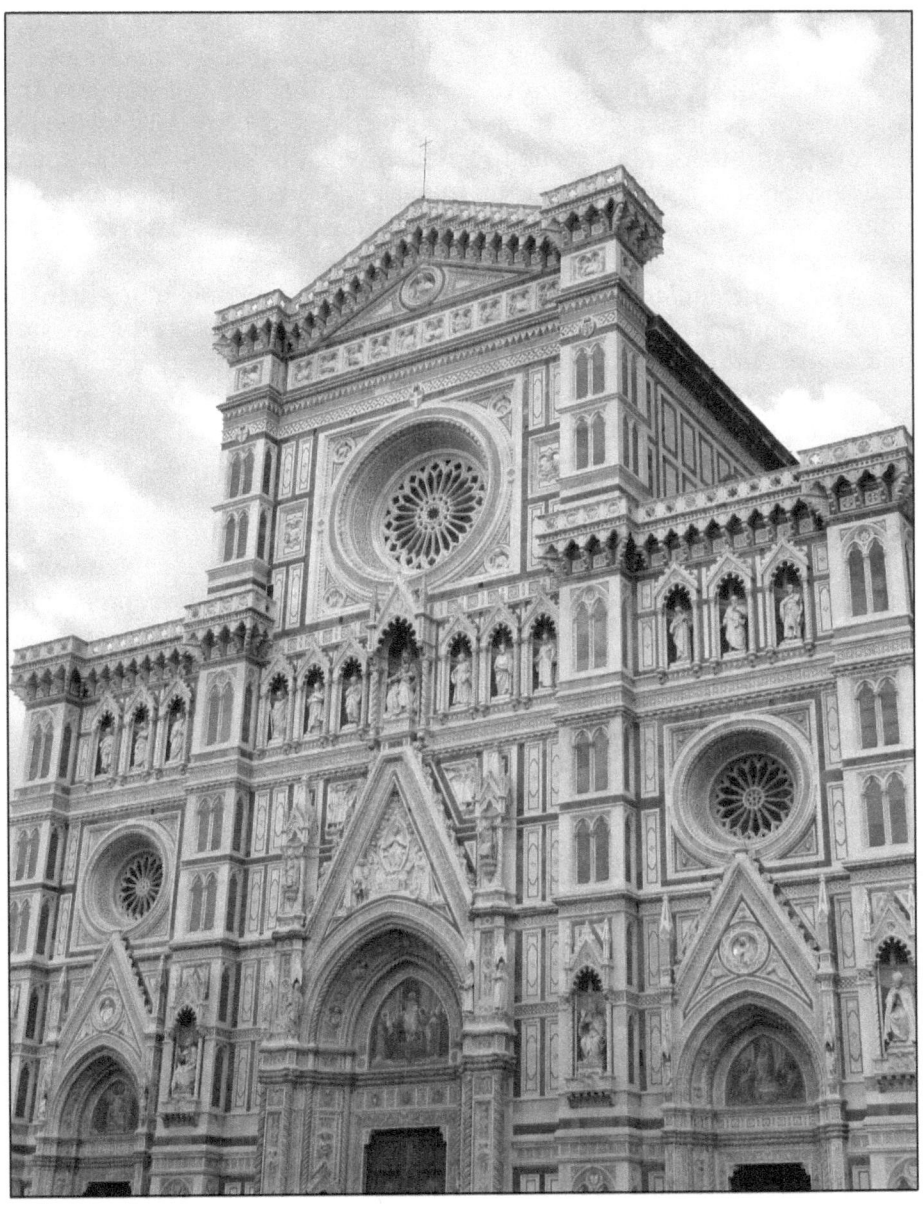

10 Wednesday: Another fine but bitterly cold day. I continued my tour. I walked to the Church of Santa Croce from Palazzo Vecchio. I stood for a time in the Piazza. While I was doing this a man approached me and asked me if I would like him to guide me around the Church. Instead, I approached a Franciscan monk escorting some other soldiers and requested that I would like him to conduct me through the building the following day, but he agreed to me doing it then and there. He started his discourse in English, but turned to Italian when he knew I could speak and understand it. What a contrast from the ignorant man I had foolishly enlisted as a guide yesterday and soon dropped when I discovered his ignorance of art.

As the burial place of so many distinguished men, it is more than an ordinary church. I saw the tombs of Michelangelo, Machiavelli, Rossini, and the monument in honor of Dante. John Ruskin, in his delightful and enthusiastic way, talks about these monuments and the Church generally. Apart from the frescoes, the outstanding works of art in the Church which have been covered or hidden include the delightful bas relief, 'Madonna del Latte,' that masterpiece of ornamental sculpture. The pulpit is by Maiano. The frescoes by Taddeo, Gaddi and Giotto were magnificent. Many years ago some of these lovely works were covered with whitewash during the restoration of the Church and they remained hidden for many years. In this Church, one sees ruined masterpieces destroyed deliberately so that mediocre oils could be used as altarpieces in their stead. In the Sacristy, I inspected the really fine ancient cabinetry of inlaid wood and the large illuminated scrolls contained in them.

Before lunch to the Santa Trinita church—beautiful—but so much has been removed from it. My visit to Santa Trinita was very brief. It was very ancient and dark inside, so much so that it was impossible for me to study the architecture and art. Then later I crossed the Arno to the Palazzo Pitti, a superb, regal dwelling. Firstly, I made for the Boboli Gardens, next to Pitti Palace. The construction of the garden began in 1550. I did not see a great deal of the garden. After I had rid myself of the keeper who showed me the garden, (I gave him a packet of cigarettes), I was escorted through the palace by a custodian. The Palace itself is a truly magnificent and regal building. Although the palace only contained about five hundred works before the war, they were almost all masterpieces, with works by Titian and Rembrandt, Van Dyke, Raphael, and Rubens, Perugino, Velasquez, and many others. The Gallery remained private for almost two centuries. The ceiling decorations of the large first floor rooms must be seen for one to appreciate their beauties. These fine rooms are dedicated to Saturn ("Earnestness",) Jupiter ("Majesty",) Apollo ("Splendor",) Mars ("Energy",) and to Venus ("Sweetness"). As I expected, all the masterpieces had been removed. The plaques at the base of the empty frames told me that Van Dyke was meant to be here, etc. I passed through the other rooms quickly and was able to admire beautiful mosaic tables, porphyry, antique Chinese and Japanese vases. I must return when all the treasures are brought to light again.

The Church of Santo Spirito is beautiful. Built by Brunelleschi, it is one of the best creations of the Renaissance. Inside there are thirty-eight Corinthian columns, and thirty-eight chapels along the sides of the church. The high altar is in the centre of the transept under the cupola. Here is a grand display of rare marbles and valuable stones. In the Apse stands a wooden crucifix, a youthful work by Michelangelo, which he sculpted when he was hardly twenty. The vestibule was inspired by the Pantheon in Rome. A service was being held in the Sacristy. I descended into the Cloister, interested because of the frescoes and the numerous tablets of old Florentine families which were delightful with their old world air of quiet and calm.

Finally, to Santa Maria del Carmine, noteworthy for Chapel VII (The Brancacci) and the marvelous frescoes of Masolino, Masaccio and the great master, Filippino Lippi, which were bricked up behind a wall to protect the chapel. The Church of Santa Maria del Carmine has had a troubled history. Imagine my great happiness when I found that a small opening had been left in the brick wall. It was dark inside, but I struck many matches so that I could study the masterpieces on the walls. The frescoes are of capital importance in the history of Italian painting. I believe the works of Masaccio in this chapel constitute the sole remaining works of that great master. (*Alex is mistaken in this belief.* Ed.) I thought how real these persons were compared with the hundreds of others I had seen done by lesser artists, how grand, how magnificent was the color, how natural was the manner in which the incidents were depicted. Many of the people are portraits of contemporary artists. I also saw into the sacristy with its vivid frescoes relating to Saints Cecilia and Valerian. The frescoes are by an unknown artist. It was almost dark by the time I reached the hotel.

11 Thursday: Until lunchtime today, I thought today was Wednesday—more's the pity because that would have meant more time for me here. A full morning. Santa Maria Novella—very rich indeed in artistic treasure; San Lorenzo, where most unfortunately, I found the superb Cappella dei Principi Medici to be locked against all comers. Most disappointing, but

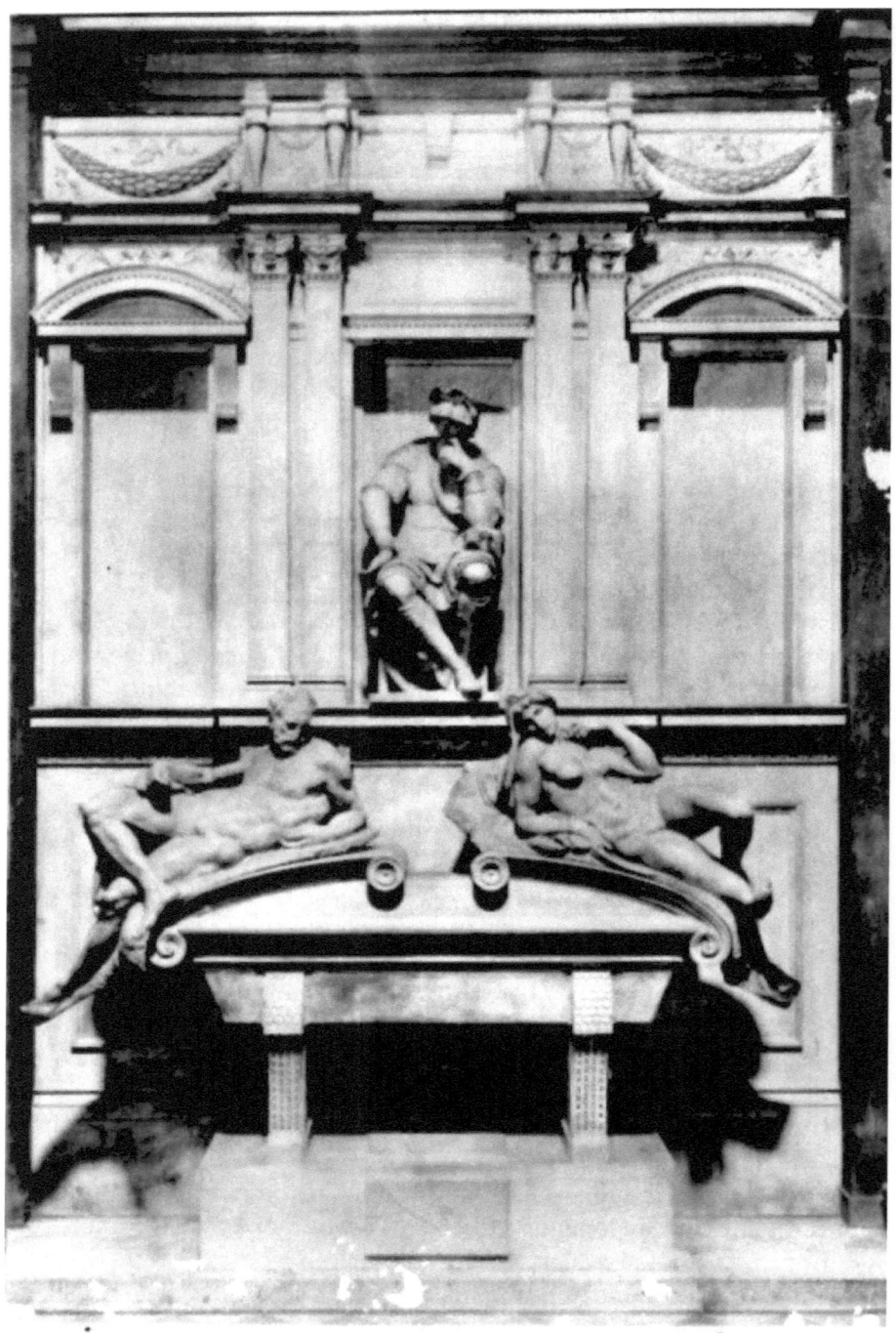

FIRENZE - Cappella Medicea - ' mento a Lorenzo de' Medici: Michelangiolo. 331

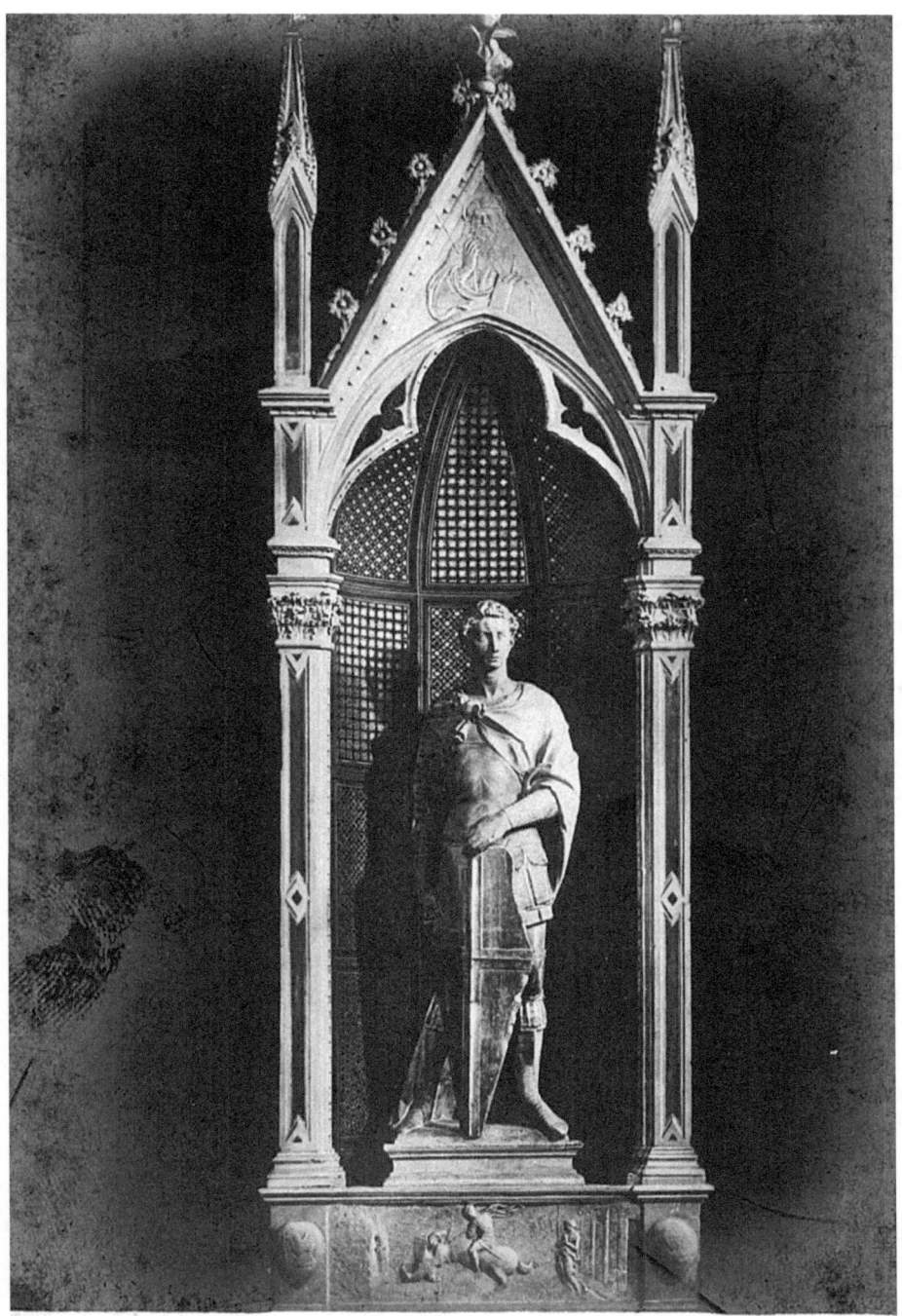

FIRENZE - R. Museo Nazionale - S. Giorgio (Donatello)

this has been my experience in many places. The best of the art has been taken away or bricked up. I continued to SS Annunziata, then to San Marco, which did not impress me much. Finally before lunch to the Medici-Riccardo Palace to the glorious chapel! Here also are the very rich reception rooms of the Riccardi, and the most beautiful *sala* of the Provincial Council, with its magnificent tapestries of the seventeenth *secolo*. After lunch, across the Ponte San Trinita, through the Porta Romana to visit meet a Belgium woman, her Italian friend and the latter's niece. A grand afternoon of it, if I may say so, with elevated conversation. "Questa e la mia vita; la via della vita il quale e data a me." (*"This is my life; the way of life which is given to me."*)

12 Friday: I continued my tour of art and other historical places today. As usual I started early. Since my guide book told me the Strozzi Palace was near the hotel, I went there first. Unfortunately, this palace is now without its treasure, just the same, there was much there to interest one —the architectural conception and execution among other things. It is still one of the most beautiful in Florence, which together with the Medici-Riccardo Palace and the Pitti Palace, are among the most notable monuments of the 15th century. You would need to see this place to get an appreciation of its grandeur, strength and solidity. As I climbed the tremendous staircase and walked through the huge reception rooms, I thought what immense riches Phillip Strozzi must have possessed to have built such a palace as this. Few of the tremendous pictures and sculptures where on display.

Unfortunately, other palaces in the vicinity, such as the Corsini Palace, were either out of bounds, or occupied by civilians, but my luck was good with my visit to the Church of Ognissanto. The Father Superior offered to show me around. He was a very wise man. He told me that the masterpieces of Ghirlandaio, Botticelli, Gaddi were covered. He led me out to the Refectory—really a museum—where I saw works by Vasari, Perugino, Agostino di Duccio, and others. The end wall was bricked up for the protection of Ghirlandaio's masterpiece "The Last Supper," which is reportedly the inspiration for Leonardo's painting of the same name in Santa Maria delle Grazie in Milan.

I then set off for Santa Maria Novella to see the Spanish Chapel and High Altar frescoes, and Santa Maria Maggiore before returning to the Loggia of the Uffizi, and the Uffizi Palace, which, before the war, was the most important collection of paintings in Italy and one of the richest in the whole world. In the niches of the columns near the Loggia are twenty-eight statues representing illustrious Tuscan personages. These statues are modern so far as art goes, only having been executed a hundred years ago. No wonder a guide conducting American soldiers led his party first to the statue of Amerigo Vespucci.

After lunch, I crossed the Arno and climbed to the top of the hill on which stands the famous church of San Miniato. It is a glorious little place with a most beautiful facade decorated in white black and green marble. Above the central window is a marvelous mosaic in Byzantine style (1297) representing Christ between the Virgin and St Miniato. The interior rafters of the roof are exposed and were decorated in colors six hundred years ago, which give the church an air of lightness and originality I have not seen elsewhere. Sadly, the famous chapel of the Crucifix was not to be seen: "Perche della Guerra!" (Because of the War!")

Finally there was the view from the Viale dei Colli. Florence looking entrancing....I am baffled for words.

It is twelve months today since I left home.

13 Saturday: I knew I could not leave Florence without seeing the Palace of Podesta, *(now the Bargello Museum)* one of the most notable monuments of the city. It is a fascinating old place, this home of Justice. I was conducted through the almost bare rooms, which formerly comprised the National Museum. What wonderful works the lover of art must have seen before the war! Here, in the courtyard, I saw many cases containing famous works of sculpture, etc. Also Dante's house, and other places. I did see a portrait of Dante in a fresco of Paradise attributed to Giotto. I spent the rest of the morning shopping.

14 Sunday: I went to the NZ Club this morning where I was greatly surprised to meet Keith, who was just on the point of setting out on guided tour. I arranged to see him after lunch. Meantime, I went for a long walk to the Protestant cemetery particularly to see the fine monument over the grave of Elizabeth Barrett Browning who, as you know, lived for several years in Florence.

In the afternoon, Keith and I drove out to ancient Fiesole from which a magnificent panorama of Florence—glorious Florence—in the valley of the Arno is seen. Unfortunately, Il Duomo was closed, but we saw something of the Roman and Etruscan excavations. It is interesting to note that the excavations here were undertaken by a Prussian Baron at the beginning of the last century. In the piazza, we stopped to have a glimpse of the ancient church of Santa Maria Primerana, (built before the 10th century but almost completely rebuilt in the 17th century.) The most fascinating part of our visit was the view which baffles a just description.

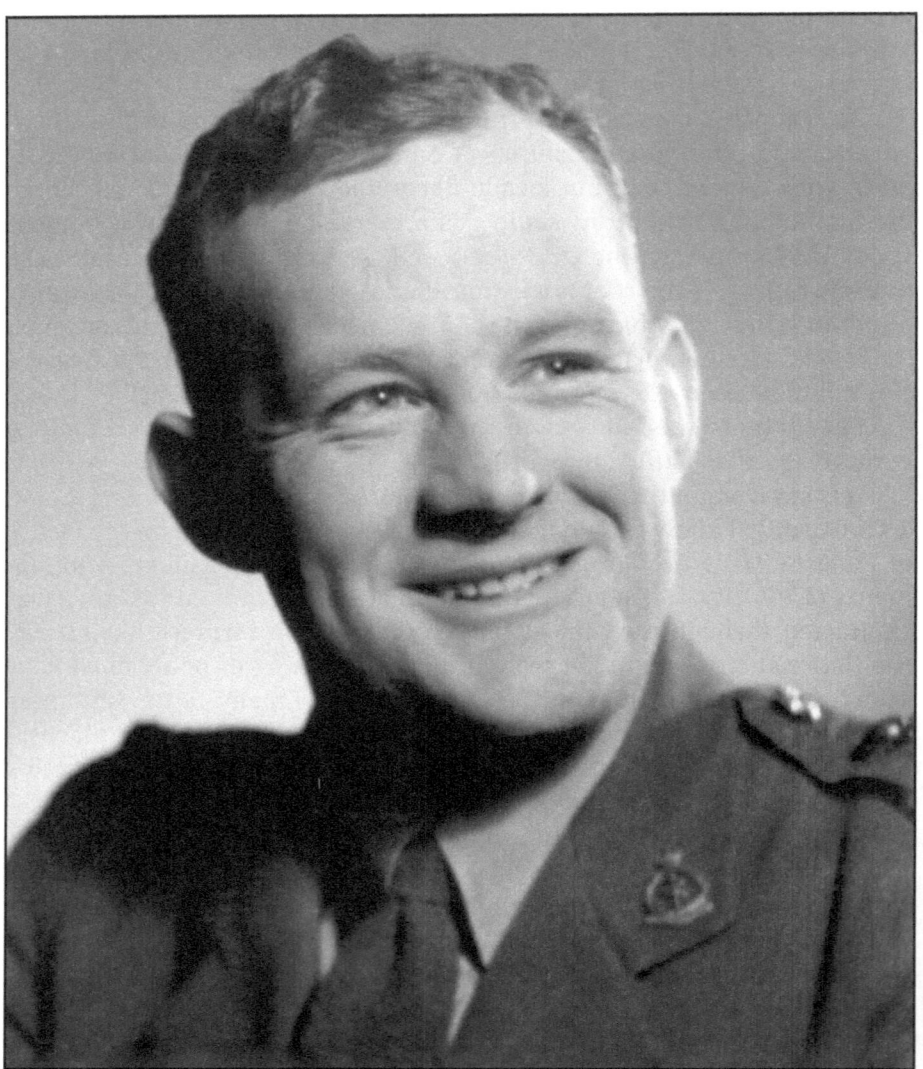

Dr. Keith Macleod, brother-in-law

But for the cold and limited time, we could have gazed about for hours drinking in the scenes, which were truly superb.

Then, we crossed back over the Arno to St. Miniato for another panorama in a second visit to that beautiful church. We delighted in the panorama after inspecting the Church. We returned to the city with the conviction that it would be well nigh impossible to find places which could offer more delightful and more fascinating panoramas for an afternoon's excursion. We must go to Florence together one day with Judy and Paul. I am sure the wonderful enjoyment that was mine will be yours also and that you will form as high an impression of noble Florence as I have done.

15 Monday: A really perfect morning. The reflection of the Ponte Vecchio on the Arno was something not to be forgotten. We were on the road by 9:15. It has been a really wonderful week—by the far the best I've spent since I left home. The mountains with their light blanket of snow were superb in the bright sunshine. We left the perfect weather behind but soon after we crossed the top struck bleak and cold weather from then on. Back to the guns by about 4:30 p.m. Hardly any shooting has been done of late.

To Faenza and Beyond

16 Tuesday January,1944: To RHQ this morning where I filled in a form applying for a job in the FSS (*Field Security Section.*) Did some rifle shooting with Len in a dugout this afternoon.

17 Wednesday: A fine day here. I spent the day writing letters. As usual, no shooting. This morning to Faenza to do some interpreting over a wine problem.

18 Thursday: Fine and sunny. On picquet at the window for the Huns early this morning. After lunch, I walked to Faenza. As I walked along the road, the sight of the white-coated town across the river was very fine. Not much has changed in Faenza since I was there some weeks ago. A night at "home," and to bed early.

19 Friday: Some rain late this morning. The guns left this afternoon for the alternative position to do some harassing fire. This morning to Regimental HQ to do some translating (over the taking of wood) for the Colonel and 2 I.C. (*Second-in-Charge.*) How I enjoy such work!

20 Saturday: A beautiful fine day following a cold night and frost. The sun is now beginning to make inroads into the frozen snow. Early this morning (or was it late last night), Jerry was very active with shelling and possibly bombing near Faenza. Our RAF active today.

21 Sunday. Another beautifully fine day following a severe frost. RAF active all day.

22 Monday: Packed this morning to move to the alternative gun position to relieve the other half of the crew. All quartered, thank goodness, in a large farmhouse. No firing during the night. Did maintenance in the afternoon. The boys have started skiing on the gentle slopes in this position.

23 Tuesday: Fine and sunny today. I spent the morning and afternoon "swotting" Italian. In the evening, from 6 p.m. to 4:30 a.m., I was on picquet watching for flares. (With air cover, Jerry was on the job last night and early this morning bombing Faenza. One of the chaps counted twelve bombs.) There was a good deal of activity while I was on picquet duty: Spandaus, our own M/Cs (*Machine Carbines*), flares, mortars and gunfire, (it being mostly ours.)

24 Wednesday: We began harassing fire about 8 p.m., when snow was begging to fall.

25 Thursday: About four inches of very fine flaky snow covered the ground this morning. We finished harassing fire at 3:30 a.m. with only nineteen rounds in all. Guns out of action about 1 p.m. and soon we moved back from Faenza Sarna, (the name of this parish,) to our old pits. An afternoon and evening around the fire. On picquet at night.

26 Friday: There must have been some rain during the night because the snow was slippery this morning. I went on a vino purchasing expedition to Cosina and Faenza this morning. The wine was used tonight for the birthday anniversaries of two of the boys. Dinner music tonight—my favorite "Enigma Variations" (Elgar), making me recall my frequent visits to the Music Room of the Wellington Public Library in those happy days of two years ago. To bed early—bad cold!

27 Saturday: Walked to Faenza this morning for a shower and to see Keith, but I ascertained that his unit had gone back to Forli. Bulldozers were busy cleaning up the rubble of former houses near the river. Civilians were beginning to return to the ruined town. Spent evening letter writing.

28 Sunday: Dull and miserable day. A little snow early this morning. Jerry active with Neberwerfers about 6 a.m.—not a great distance from here because the house rocked.

29 Monday: To Celle, or the remains of it, this morning to gather wood. Place deserted of Ities, thank goodness. While there, I had a good view of Castel Bolognese standing out in the distance the bright sunshine. Also, part of the Lombardy Plain. Air force active; also Jerry with shelling and airbursts, but not a great deal. Early this evening, about 9 p.m., Jerry put a "show" on above Faenza, with bombs dropped. To the Dorchester of

Forli for lunch. Spent the evening listening to the radio, in writing and in study.

30 Tuesday: A dull day, but not cold. Wood gathering expeditions to Celle this morning and afternoon. Also gun maintenance. Usual day of "base" sessions and radio listening. Hitler spoke tonight, but we did not wait up to hear the translation.

31 Wednesday: Fine and sunny. RAF on job early. Party at night for no particular reason. Much hilarity. To Faenza in the afternoon.

FEBRUARY

1 Thursday: Dull day. Many sore heads this morning. C.P. (*Command Post*) advised that the ammo restriction had been lifted and L.O.'s (*Lines of Sight?*) and the OP (*Observation Post*) were instructed to adopt an aggressive policy. As a result, we fired one round a gun this afternoon.

2 Friday: The war was stopped for an hour or so this morning, when we had a parade—battle dress, berets, clean boots and gaiters—at BHQ when the GO notified us that the replacement scheme had at last began. Peter, Wally, Jack and Doug were on the "Tongariro" list to ship out, while the remaining 5ths and 6ths would go as soon as replacements arrived. The boys left for 'B' Echelon after lunch. On Sunday, they will receive a "pep" talk from the G.O.C. at Forli and depart for the south.

3 Saturday: Rumor has it that the ammo restriction has been imposed again—2 RPGs *(rounds per gun)* a day. To Faenza this afternoon for a stroll and a haircut. To bed early—as usual. A dull and miserable day.

4 Sunday: Fine and sunny morning. To Holy Communion this morning at BHQ. Spent the afternoon writing letters in sunshine.

5 Monday: Fairly heavy mist all day. Rifle shooting cancelled. Two of the boys who went off to Faenza for the day returned a little worse for wear, their clothes soaked in mud! They did look a sorry picture.

6 Tuesday: Fine and sunny, thank goodness. The guns left for the sniping position this morning. Lot of activity at FDLs during the day, and during the night, both from Jerry and ourselves.

7 Wednesday: Misty this morning, but beautifully fine later. The guns did some shooting last night and today from the sniping position. F1 came back this afternoon and went up to the position. Members of the DAF (*Desert Air Force?*) were "entertained" at Battalion HQ today. When I asked Maria what were the most important things in the Italian mind, she replied: *"Prima la Vergine; secondo, il pane; terza la vino; il quartro, maiale; quinto, cioccolata."* (*"First, the Virgin; second, bread; third, wine; fourth, pork; fifth chocolate."*)

8 Thursday: A beautiful, fine sunny day. The guns moved out of the sniping position, and went off to Bellaria for calibration. They're going to straighten us up, they hope, in the following way: blankets have to be folded every morning, boots must not be worn indoors; standing gun drill (in action above all places!) The usual day's activities—nothing! But I forgot two things—lumping some boxes of charges for the calibration program, and digging drains to run off some of the water laying around here. The thaw, which set in more than a week ago, is well underway, and the snow is beginning to disappear rapidly from the face of the land. Evening around the fire, reading and listening to the radio.

9 Friday: This morning we started to fill in the tracks through the water and mud that were made by the vehicles, but I am afraid there wasn't enough rubble by any means. Rain, and fairly heavy too, during the day made things somewhat unpleasant.

10 Saturday: To Riccione al Mare this morning for four days at the Division Rest camp. Left about 9:30 a.m. and covered the sixty-odd kilometers in two hours. I could not help but notice en route how greatly things have improved in the last few months—wreckage cleared away, etc. After lunch, Phil and I walked along the marvelous beach and viewed many of the fine villa erected here during the heyday of Fascism. Riccione itself is a typical dirty little Italian village, but Riccione al Mare is vastly different. Spent the evening at the hostel reading Frida Uhl Strindberg's remarkable, "Marriage with Genius."

11 Sunday: Dull and miserable day. I went to a ruined and battered Rimini this morning principally to see the see the Temple of the Malatesta, now, unhappily, a ruin, a skeleton of its former self. This grand church is now without its roof; many of its precious marble slabs and monuments are broken. I saw some marvelous bas reliefs, which decorate the entrance to the chapels. The altar pieces and the altars have either been removed or smashed. This destruction of a very precious art monument reveals one of the many horrid sides of war. I also made a point of inspecting the Roman arch of Augustus and the bridge of Tiberius, the fountain in the Piazza Cavour, and the antique palace of a count whose name I cannot recall. Rimini has been most severely damaged. Spent the afternoon in this hostel. In the evening to the Grand Hotel to the film, "It Happened Tomorrow."

12 Monday: After lunch to the old gun position to the north end of the village. Our pits still remain, but they are filled with water now, as is also the drain in which some of us dug slitties. After dinner to the Grand to see a film—a dreadful old Western show it proved to be, but one couldn't help but laugh at it.

13 Tuesday: A really perfect day for this time of the year—sun shining brightly, and bracing air. I hitchhiked with Phil to Cattolica, and walked from the main road up to the Castle of Gradara. The hilltop is walled right around, and under the outer wall we found a quaint little village. This was the hill under which we camped overnight last September during our campaigning on the Adriatic coast. A couple of days before I went there I read an article in *The Crusader*, the 8th Army weekly, about the Castle and its 'Corporal King,' a Canadian corporal, who lives in the old pile and acts as guide to the numerous soldiers who visit the place. We climbed up the steep street, across the moat, rang the bell and waited the arrival of someone to let us in. Our 'Corporal King' arrived and conducted us through the courtyard to his chamber.

In the courtyard, we saw people carrying water from the well on their hips. Nothing was ever carried on their head in Gradara. The well is the only source of water in the area even though it is on the top of a hill.

The corporal took us from room to room—with many of their ancient treasures still remaining—and gave us a most realistic account of the castle in the days of the Malatesta and Sforza families. The Castle was the scene of the love and tragedy of Francesca and Paolo, immortalized by Dante in the 'Inferno,' and by Boccaccio, and our own Leigh Hunt in his 'Italian Poets.' I would like to tell their story now, but will leave it for another time.

Of considerable interest, however, was the use of Roman stone in the wall of the castle. The guard room was a magnificent place for it remained in much the same condition as it was in the 14th century. There we saw items used then: the wooden beds, the lamps, and cooking utensils, etc. We were then taken to the torture chamber, a dark and gruesome place with its scouring whips of nails, eye removers, and the dreadful lime pit. It was a glimpse into harsher times at this place. The judgment hall had another such symbol of 14th century justice. After his trial, the condemned man was pushed through a door into a tunnel studded with spears and spikes. If his death was not achieved by this novel device, the alert guards waiting at the bottom of the tunnel dispatched him and tossed his body into the lime pit. About thirty years ago, the present owner had the lime pit excavated. Eight cartloads of human bones were exhumed... Then the excavation was stopped.

It was not all gruesome. The chapel still holds beautiful frescoes by Perugino, although a number of the treasures are on loan to museums in

Rome, with several 'souvenired,' and some hidden. The chapel also has a superb piece of work, Andrea della Robbia's famous terra-cotta piece "Madonna and Child with Four Saints," as well as Perugino's fresco of the Crucifixion, much faded but still showing wonderful detail. What an intriguing job this Canadian corporal has, and I believe is writing a book about it called, "These were not nice people!" The visit proved to be one of the most enjoyable I have spent in this country. The view from the tower of the hills and the plain was superb. In the evening, we saw a film in the Hostel.

14 Wednesday: One or two things I must note. Before the war, a parent paid two thousand lire for the education of his child after the fifth class. Under the "*mezzadria*" system (*sharecropping*), the padrone is entitled to half of the milk produced while the *contadino*, although he does not own the cow, receives half the proceeds when it is sold. A girl working in a shop (a pharmacy) here gets eight hundred lire a month (about 10 shillings a week.)

Meantime, I whiled away the morning reading Churchill's, "Great Contemporaries:" Shaw, Morley, Haig, Asquith, Joe Chamberlain, a brilliant lively work to say the least of it. Left at 2:30. "Home" two hours later. Letters, letters, letters...

15 Thursday: To Forli after lunch to assist in cleaning up four buildings for the Regimental Rest Camp. Didn't do any work. Spent the evening at the "Dorchester" mainly in the gramophone room playing records and talking with the young and intelligent Italian girl in charge.

16 Friday: We worked all morning sweeping and then washing the many floors of the four buildings. Early in the afternoon to 'B' Echelon to interpret for the Battalion Captain in a theft case there—a bicycle, bolts of material, wool, etc. stolen in the night. Back to Forli, and then up to the guns. Apparently, we are to fire from here now. Letters, letters again including from ERS (*Education and Rehabilitation Services.*)

17 Saturday: Fine and dry. This afternoon played in the Troop "rugger" game—North vs South Island. South won 3-Nil. Most of us very stiff and tired later.

18 Sunday: On picquet 2:30 to 3:30 this morning. Imagine my surprise this morning when the door opened and in walked (*my brother-in-law,*) Vic! It is almost twelve months since I last saw him. To Faenza with him this afternoon.

19 Monday: A day of unusual activity. Jerry was fairly active during the night. I heard that the dummy attack launched by the Maoris, supported by D Troop to locate Jerry's DF's was a complete flop, because the wily

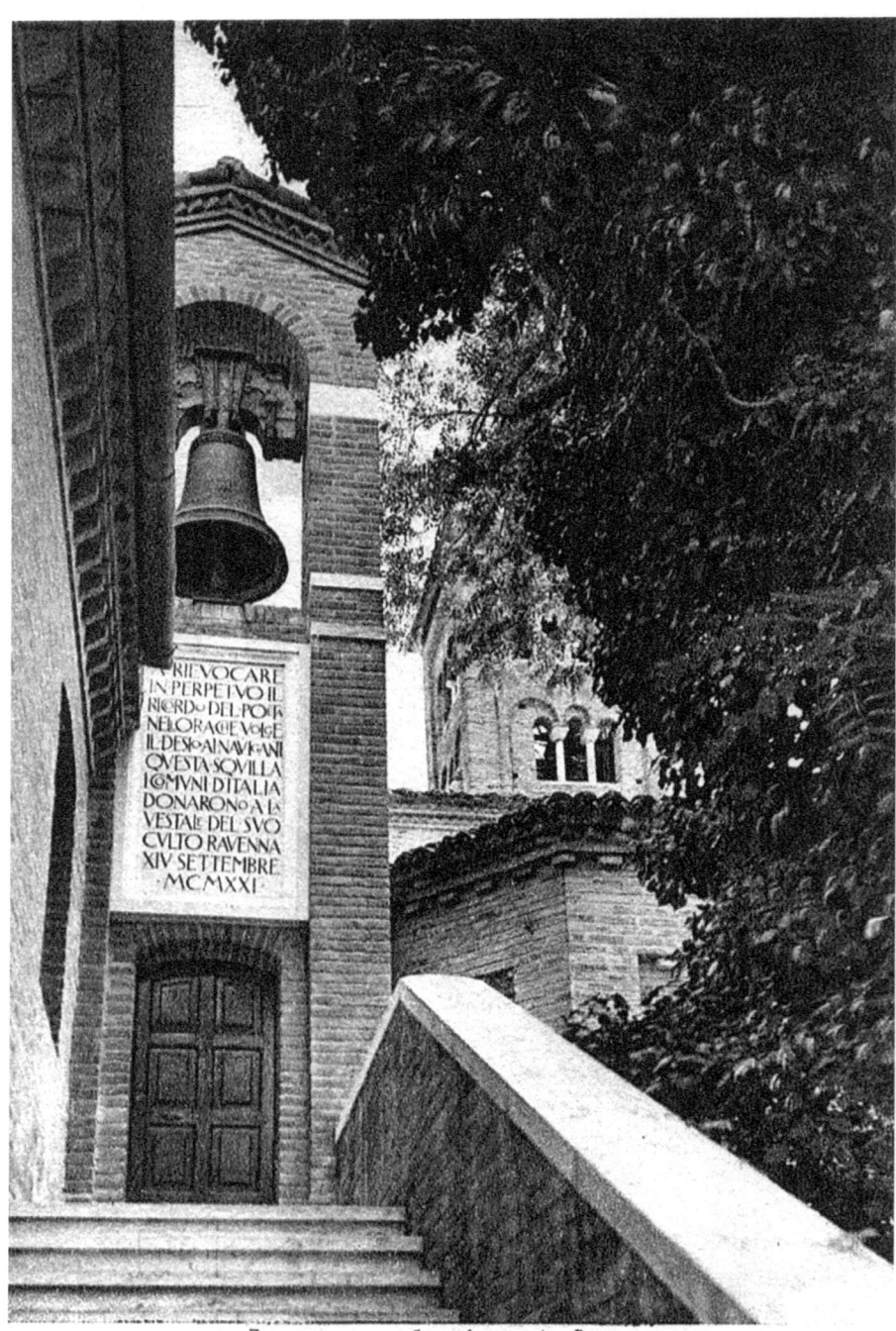

Ravenna - Sepolcro di Dante -
La campana offerta dai Comuni d'Italia.

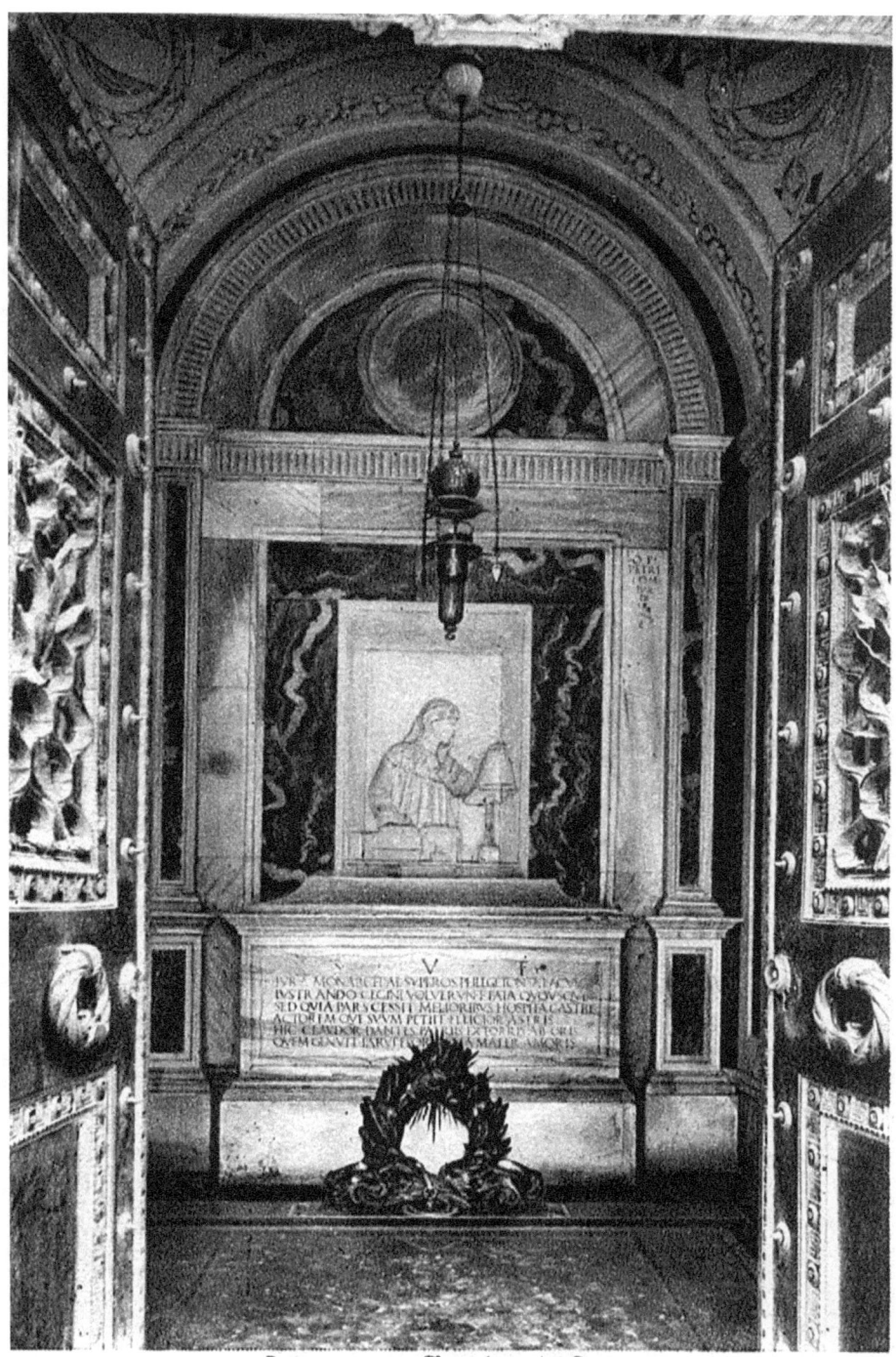

Ravenna - Tomba di Dante.

man did not take the bait.

20 Tuesday: To Forli this morning to the 4th Field's rest camp. To the cinema in the afternoon—"Song of Bernadette"—and a chat with an Italian family at night.

21 Wednesday: Beautifully fine and sunny, but cold. To Ravenna this morning. A beautiful town; not much damaged, thank goodness. Clean streets, clean and well-dressed people and some superb art. Visited the following places: The tomb of Dante, the Basilica of Sant'Apollinare Nuovo, the Baptistry of the Cathedral, San Vitale and its mausoleum, Byron's house (or where it used to be), Santa Agate Maggiore. I'll never forget those world-famous mosaics of the fifth and sixth centuries. Marvelous is the only word for them.

22 Thursday: Another fine sunny day. Jack and I went for a stroll, and visited an Italian household at night. They told us there was plenty of everything before the war. I wonder.

23 Friday: Perfect day. Said cheerio to Mick, Shorty, etc. on their way home. Back to the guns in the morning. Began harassing fire late in the afternoon, continuing through the night.

24 Saturday: Another perfect day. Harassing fire finished before breakfast. Over thirty RPG *(rounds per gun)* of harassing fire commenced again in the early evening. Jerry also very active with shelling. Played bridge at night. To H.C. in the morning.

25 Sunday: The weather still continues fine. The shift finished harassing fire about the same time as yesterday—about forty rounds per gun.

26 Monday: Beautiful again. "Training" started this morning with laying practice. Went to sniping position at Sarna to get the gear left there. A little harassing fire at night, with Jerry doing the same. Very heavy shelling and mortaring near Faenza.

27 Tuesday: Heavy mist this morning, but later a beautiful day. The Jerry shelling last night was in support of an attack on the Canadians. They penetrated six hundred yards into Canadian territory, but the status quo was restored by 4 this morning. A heavy mist last night. Very little activity. I must recall a visit we had here on Sunday afternoon. Three nuns, with about fifteen small girls (all neat and tidy and clean, and uniformly dressed) came along to our *casa*. The children sang "Tipperary" and several Italian songs. These were orphan children that were brought up and trained by the nuns until they are eighteen, when they are sent out to service and other duties.

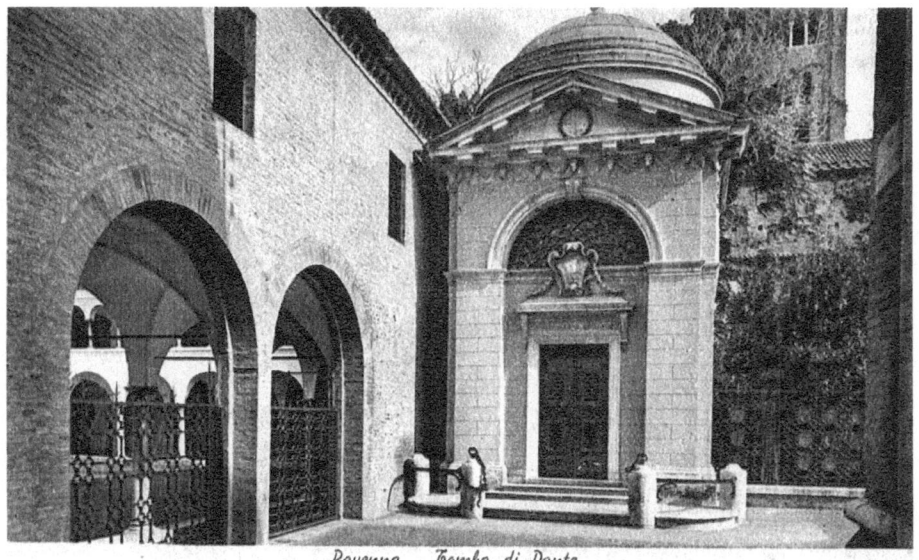

Ravenna - Tomba di Dante.

28 Wednesday: Nothing much to record, except very welcome arrival of parcels from home. Guns fired propaganda shells during the day, and did a little harassing fire at night.

MARCH, 1945
1 Thursday: Misty again this morning. Nothing to record.
2 Friday: We were told about the move to Castelraimondo this morning. I spent the whole day cleaning and oiling the gun and limber, and packing later. We fired a Chinese program for 23 Battalion between 7:30 and 8:30, only twenty rounds per gun. There were plenty of flares up yonder. Jerry got annoyed afterwards—probably 4th Parachute Division—and replied with mortars and shelling.
3 Saturday: Beautifully fine. This afternoon, I went to the Church of the Commenda, Faenza, which was at one time the Church of the Knights of St. John of Malta. Interesting because of its simplicity, and its two religious frescoes, but I felt the other ornamentation was rubbish. The cloister, of which two sides have been enclosed for habitation, has columns with Ionic capitals.
4 Sunday: A day in getting packed up for the trip. The locals all said goodbye, etc. to us. To bed early—necessary for what is to come.
5 Monday: Up at 2:30 and away at 4 a.m. Lunch south of Senigallia at 10 a.m. We reached Castelraimondo after 2 p.m. It had been a grand trip—in perfect conditions for traveling. No sign of the snow we had been told

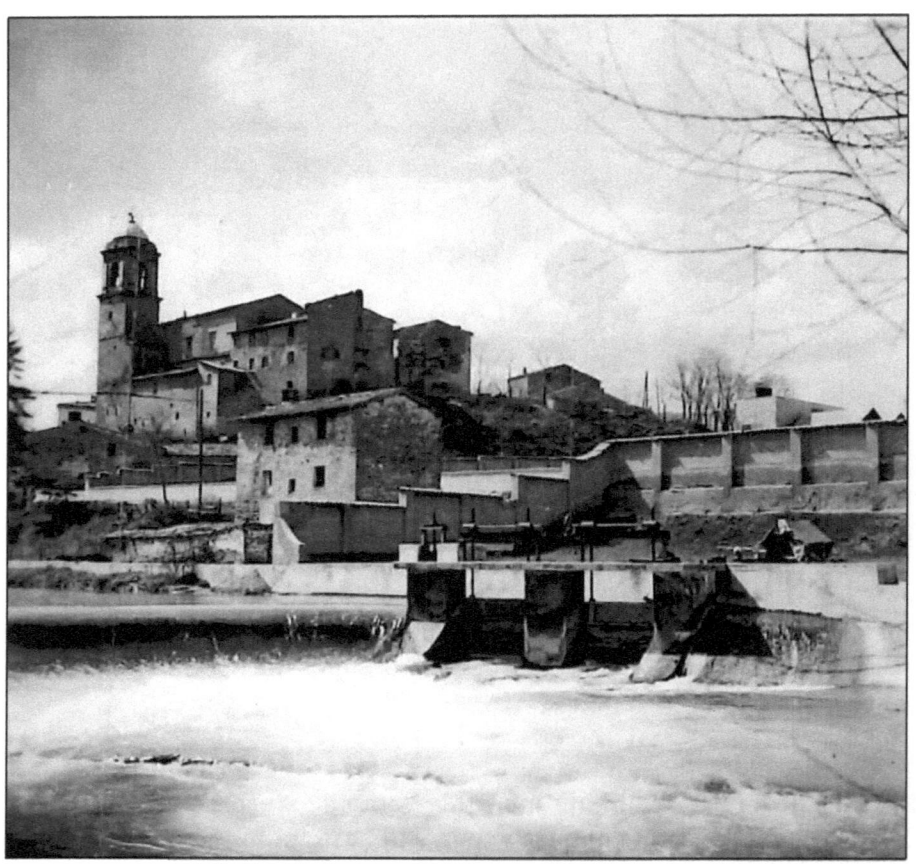

Castelraimondo

about over the last ten miles through the Apennines. Castelraimondo is a pretty little place lying in a valley of the Apennines. More anon on it. We messed about until our quarters were jacked up. Len and I were sent to one house—of which more anon—and the rest of the sub (*section*) to another—a charming family indeed. Some wine and discussion, and then to bed.

6 Tuesday: It is colder and fresher here than at Faenza. Parade this morning. After lunch, lumped ammo (at 1600 hrs) in the Regimental vehicle park. I think they'll try to be a little "regimental" here.

7 Wednesday: This morning, I worked as an interpreter for marching in, i.e. filling in billeting forms. Also, I was sent to the Mayor to elucidate if a certain house desired by RAP (*Regimental Aid Post*) had been "out of bounds" to the Canadians. Not so, it turned out. I did a little interpreting again in the afternoon, then worked on a gun. There was a party in the sub's *casa* in the evening. A light snow fell in the nearby hills at night.

8 Thursday: A perfect day. I was on the gun park this morning. The Battery played the Regiment in the afternoon. An observation: We are eating numerous eggs—twenty in exchange for a 5 lb. tin of marmalade; four for a little tin. The cost to civilians from a *contadino*—16 lire each. I walked up a hill to the farm of a *contadino* family, and sat in a chair outside the door and basked in the sun drinking two liters of light wine. It was a good night before the fire in the house.

9 Friday: Another fine day, although cold in the afternoon. On Regimental picquet—prowler and point duty. I saw Keith and others I hadn't seen for many a long day. Letter writing in the *caserma* (*barracks*) at night.

10 Saturday: Another bright day, although the wind was cold. After lunch, I took a walk up the hill where I found the *contadino* family in the *campo* (*field*) pruning trees of their vines, then tying the little branches up into bundles, which are used for the fire. Wood is very scarce in these parts. A few drinks at night.

11 Sunday: Perfect! There was a Regimental Parade this morning, followed by a hut picquet. Keith called, and I went to Camerino with him—ten kilometers to the south. Located on the top of a hill, Camerino is an ancient university town from around 1700. The view of the surrounding hills, mountains, of the valleys, farms and roads, etc. from the top is superb. We lunched at the home of the Professor of Zoology and his American wife. Our conversation was entirely in English. Lunch was whitebait, potato, spaghetti, and eggs, plus coffee and home again. I went for a walk to a section near the railway where I chatted with an English-speaking lady and her English-speaking daughters. More on them anon. Bridge at night.

12 Monday: On the gun park this morning, checking "1098" stores. It was so beautiful and warm today that I had sufficient courage to take a bathe in the swiftly flowing, clear Potenza. The water was frightfully cold, but I needed a clean up. Later I went to the section by the railway where I chatted with the Contessa, Libbia and Massimo. Libbia later took me to the home of Professoressa Garibaldi, who I arranged to visit on Wednesday. I took a long walk up hill nearby, and had a short chat with the *padrone* (who complimented me on my Italian), then I returned home to bed for a little study.

13 Tuesday: My 29th Birthday. A year ago today I passed an uncomfortable day on the "Batory," off Derna. A little translating for the Battalion Captain this morning in regard to inspection of quarters and an inquiry over stolen petrol. Late this afternoon I went to the house of the Contessa Piscicelli and her two daughters, Livia and Julia, two charming girls of seventeen and fifteen respectively. I helped the latter in translation of "Can I Forget You!" Julia played well by ear. I talked with the Contessa on religion and the system of inheritance in England, and with Livia for about two hours on Dante and education. A really interesting visit. I must record I have yet to meet New Zealand girls who compare in culture with the young Contessa.

14 Wednesday: A morning of letter writing. After lunch, I took a stroll to the river where I lay on the bank in the sun and swotted history. Later I was called up to settle the great petrol mystery. One of our chaps espied an Italian in a shed near the cookhouse syphoning petrol into the tank of his vehicle. The petrol came from one of the standard Jerry cans. The subject of my questioning: Had he stolen it? I accompanied the man and his escort to the Carabinieri, where he was questioned about the origin of the fuel. His documents were in order, and he was not perturbed, but regarded the situation in a humorous light. The Carabinieri could not commit themselves. The Battalion Captain came around. I told him the man had arrived that day from Rome to collect some refugees. He had brought his own petrol. We had lost petrol—about fifteen tins—the night before so I understand why Ities with Jerry cans of petrol were regarded suspiciously. After mess, I went to the Garibaldi Palace for a chat with the elderly Professoressa Garibaldi, a most charming, alert, intelligent gentlewoman. She spoke no English, but we got on excellently in her language. The Italians, she said, had the beliefs of an ancient race. On the subject of religion, she said they only went to church because it was obligatory. There was no religion of the spirit in them. Everything was purely superficial—they loved exterior things, processions, etc. Also, too many persons went to Varsity, with the result that the standards had been lowered too much. A beautiful signora.

15 Thursday: Early morning—foot drill, and on to the gun park. Later up the hill with the troop commander to investigate a disturbance of last night at a house of ill-repute. A difficult case, because it seems the woman had obliged four drunken soldiers to prevent her "dear" husband and herself from being assaulted. It was also difficult because the husband, an intelligent "Marco" (of French upbringing), whom the soldiers had come to the house to find but who had gone out to avoid them, did not present a very coherent story. At last, we got the tale. They alleged the soldiers threatened to draw a pistol, or belabor the husband if his wife was not agreeable. She gave in. The troops also were accused of stealing *roba* (*stuff*). (It was military stuff, the Italians confessed.) A statement was presented to us telling the sordid story. This Maria has without doubt been in practice since having an association with a German soldier, which resulted in her having a poor, delicate little child by him. The woman and her husband were keen that we should not proceed with our inquiries provided their place was put out of bounds. Later, I returned to the house with the Battalion Captain, who got the story again, and warned Maria that she would be run out of the village very rapidly if she continued her association with troops. A decision has not yet been made as to what to do about this disturbance. Bridge at night.

16 Friday: Kit inspection this morning. A free afternoon.

Letter No. 114, Friday, March 16, 1945

My sweetest beloved little girl,

It is twelve months today since I set foot on the shores of Italy for the first time. I remember the occasion well and my first impressions were not favorable. Taranto that day looked very drab and inhospitable. The morning was frightfully cold. In "celebration" of that day, I "shouted" the boys of the gun subsection a few drinks last Wednesday.

I would be delighted to hear that your dad has been confirmed in his professorship.

I can't but help notice the difference in my status from what it once was. I accept the status quo now, and am not much disconcerted about it. You may well imagine how I felt about it for some time, particularly when I thought of the qualifications of some of the chaps who obtained jobs.

Keith reveals a distinct interest in the art of this country. We have had the privilege to see much. My Italian is progressing well, so much so that I spent a good deal of my time interpreting. I only wish they were offering jobs for interpreters in the division. Unlike in the British army, there does not appear to be any official recognition of linguistic facility. The majority of chaps don't look upon interpreters as people who can, on numerous occasions, settle numerous problems for them, and get them out of trouble. It is natural, I suppose, in an organization which gives no recognition to academic achievement. No thought is given to the hours of study a person must give to the language to achieve a fair amount of fluency. It is my desire to complete my B.A. this year and then go all out for honors in history when I return home.

Your mother will be doing something very worthwhile in writing a biography of (*the New Zealand poet*) Jessie Mackay.

Keith suggested he might return home, and marry the girl next door!

Alex

DIARY ENTRY

17 Saturday: Up early, breakfast at 7 a.m. There were then troop, battalion and regimental parades before route-marching to a former POW barracks to do a Divisional artillery practice for the G.O.C's parade next week. On Regimental guard in the afternoon. Saw a few "shorts" at the cinema at night.

18 Sunday: On guard duty during heavy rain about 3 this morning. It finished at 4 p.m. when the change over was made. After mess, I went to the home of a retired schoolmaster where I dined with him—sausage, meat and vegetable pasties, a type of egg flip, wine and an orange. Then we chatted before the fire until 11 p.m. The guns went out into the country nearby for the officers' practice shoot.

19 Monday: A perfect day once again. The guns fired practice shots for the officers during the day. I took a walk along a country road to the village of Abosco (?) where I celebrated the festa of San Giuseppe right royally, so much so that on my return home, I wasted no time in getting to bed.

20 Tuesday: Another perfect day. I was on gun park duty for a time in the morning, then it was up to Terricoli to bring down a woman for questioning by the colonel. He reprimanded our men, the ones concerned, and placed the house out of bounds. Bars in the village have likewise been treated because of an affray a few nights ago. Had a swim and sunbathed in the afternoon.

21 Wednesday: After mess tonight, I took a long walk to San Severino. It was a beautiful evening. The peace and quiet was elevating. I chatted with peasants near the Gagliole Railway Station, and amused myself with a fourteen-month old baby of a little peasant woman.

22 Thursday: After several inspections and parades, we eventually got on the road to the barracks where Freyberg was to inspect us and present awards and decorations. A perfect morning for the parade. The usual ballyhoo, etc. I was very pleased when it was over. I did a little work on the gun park in the afternoon preparing for maneuvers. I then did some climbing—over the bridge and up the hill to Terricoli, then on to Crispiano, which I reached after an hour and a half climb at 4:45. I could not help but remember what I saw on the way—the hills, the valleys, the villages, *contadini* pruning the trees for their vines, the bundles of faggots collected from the pruning, the crops starting to show themselves, the odd ancient fort, the snow-covered mountains to the south, the leafless trees, the sheep, the mellowness...I very foolishly injured my ankle with a fast moving wooden wheel, so I went to a house where the woman massaged it for me. They offered me a meal—scrambled eggs, sausages, bread and wine. A talk with the woman, (Her husband is a POW in New York.), and her twelve-year old son; then home in a jeep with some infantry. The peasants are saving up their eggs now for *Pasqua*. Incidentally, people pay 15 lire (9 pence) for them. Another price: four hundred yards of ordinary black cotton thread—sixteen shillings!!!

23 Friday: The climate here is superb. We pulled out for the maneuvers after 7 p.m., and reached our destination on a flat in the Val di Chienti, just below the hamlet of Forcatura, about 20 kilos from Foligno about 10 p.m. After the platforms were down, I went to bed, sleeping in the open.

24 Saturday: With breakfast over, we prepared ammunition and messed about. I strolled up to the aforementioned hamlet. Entirely uninteresting. A few shots about 1 p.m., a divisional artillery barrage for the 9th Infantry Battalion. Each gun fired forty rounds. Five and 6 Field Force fired at 10 p.m., and 4 at midnight.

25 Sunday: Heavy mist and extremely cold temperatures early this morning. We were on the road early and back to Castelraimondo before 10 a.m.

Letter No. 115: Sunday, March 25, 1945

My sweetest beloved little girl,

Basil has written thanking me for the cards Alistair received.

I still do a lot of interpreting for the Battery. Several of the chaps have told me that I should say to the officers when they ask me to do such work for them, "I'm sorry, I'm a gunner, you know—not an interpreter." They contend that if I took up that attitude something would have to be done about the matter. On *no* account will I ever accept a position as an interpreter with non-commissioned rank. There are bound to be *officers* in the HQ doing this type of work, but I'm positive that they (at least most of them) cannot talk Italian as grammatically and as fluently as myself. But such is life.

I heard recently that we will earn an extra shilling per day. When I receive it, I will send home £25, which I want you to deposit in the Post Office Savings Bank for Alexander Paul Broughton. The interest on the money will be for our wee boy.

Alex

DIARY ENTRY

26 Monday: There was a battalion parade this morning. The B.C. (*Battalion Commander*) told us that when we go back to the front we'll have to dig in under camouflage nets and perhaps dig in a thousand rounds of ammunition as well. Every effort will be made to hide our intentions from the enemy. I was on Regimental picquet in the afternoon. Today, mainly this morning, the Easter fair was held here.

27 Tuesday: The guns left about 6 a.m. for an exercise near San Severino. They did not fire many rounds; off Regimental picquet at 4 p.m. An evening visiting several families.

Letter No. 63: Tuesday, March 27, 1945

My sweetest beloved little girl,

I want to record my impressions of the Easter Fair held in the village yesterday.

At an early hour the peasants began to arrive from the surrounding countryside in their bullock drawn carts, and on foot. All were dressed in their best clothes, as one would naturally expect on such an occasion. Soon a square at the bottom end of the village was a mass of white, working bullocks and cows, pigs and loud talking peasants.

Along the main street peasants with onions and lettuces, beans and seed to sell set up stalls. Also the pedlar was there with his wares: buttons, pens, pruning knives, material for clothing, buckets, pottery and various types of junk. Money changed hands quickly. In spite of their apparent poverty, the Italian peasant usually has a big wad of lire notes. He dug deeply into it that day at the cattle market. You would scarcely think it was possible that a man would be willing to pay two hundred thousand lire, (£500) for a big working bullock, £1-5/-for a kilo of pork, and so on. Such were the prices yesterday. I didn't see the animal fair but I gathered it was conducted this wise: the prospective seller and prospective buyer got together, took each other by the hand, and a disinterested third party held their hands together until the compact was made. One of the soldiers told me that hands were raised and lowered during the bidding.

A few more prices. Oranges went for 4 shillings a kilo (about 8-9 little oranges), spring onions at 1 shillings a bundle, and lettuce at 1 shillings and 4 pence a kilo. The prices of the material for suiting was between £1 and £10 a meter. Things went well until proceedings were temporarily halted by a heavy shower of rain. Covers were hastily thrown over the goods on the stalls, some of the stallholders moved to the shelter of the arcade in the municipal building, and young country lasses took shelter in the doorways, so that their best frocks would not be spoiled. About midday all and sundry began their journey home. You can imagine the conversation for many days to come. *Pasqua* is a great occasion here.

Apart from the religious significance, Easter means for the peasant the advent of new material life, because it heralds the spring. The people are preparing for the celebrations next week. They are saving up their eggs, which are now 20 lire each compared with 15 lire last week. With them, they make all sorts of special dishes and delicacies. They are also spring cleaning their homes. The little wayside chapels, usually in the honor of the Virgin, are being decorated with flowers and foliage. As they pass by, the men lift their hands, the women bow before their lady.

Alex

28 Wednesday: Another exercise today. I did not go but heard later that it was dreadful—no joking, no talking, no smoking on the guns in "action." I spent the day in the village.

Letter:

> 40455 Gnr. A. G. Protheroe
> 26 Battery
> 4 (NZ) Field Regt.
> NZEF   MEF
> Thursday, 28 March, 1945

My sweetest beloved little girl,

Enclosed please find two further British postal orders: Nos. 256042, 256043 for £1 each.

I have now sent you six, dearest, totaling in all £7, 10 shillings, which is enough for three terms for Judy at the kindergarten.

More will follow later,

Your ever loving,

Alex

29 Thursday: I went out on in R and O of two positions this morning. There was nothing doing in the afternoon because of football.

30 March: GOOD FRIDAY: A perfect day. Maintenance on guns this afternoon. We were told of the move in the near future and thus began a little premature packing. At 7:30 tonight was held the village's procession of witness. It is always held in Castelraimondo at night and every year it attracts inhabitants of nearby Camerino and other places in the locality. The facades of the houses on the route taken by the procession—the streets on the perimeter of the village—were festooned with Chinese lanterns, lamps and colored lights. First came two officers of the church followed by a large number of little boys in file. Then a girl dressed as a nun. Then, led by two men, a hooded man in white bearing a cross, and dragging chains. A little further back another, but in a red habit. Then chanting women and girls. Next, borne in a glass box on a bier, a reclining effigy of the 'dead' Christ, then, chanting clergy. Finally, a statue of the Madonna. The people crossed themselves and bowed. Church elders with staves kept the crowd from surging around the statue of the Madonna. A memorable procession—not to be forgotten.

Recce parties on the road last this afternoon.

Letter No. 116: March 30, 1945, GOOD FRIDAY

My sweetest beloved little girl,

The way things are going now we are becoming more expectant that Germany's end is near. On the Pacific front too, the Japanese are on the run. Thus it mightn't be long before we'll be home with our loved ones once again.

Keith called about an hour ago in his Jeep. He and I took a stroll along a road and up a hill where we sat down and had a chat. It was the first time I had seen him in about a fortnight. I hope to see him again in the near future.

A few days again I heard that there were some jobs going in the ERS (*Education and Rehabilitation Services*) for NCO's in the Division. Not being an NCO, I was not able to apply for them. I am still on the same job—on the guns, doing general work, but not special work.

Alex

DIARY ENTRY

31 March: EASTER SATURDAY: There was a parade this morning when the Battalion Captain gave us a talk on the war at large, and also our task here. I was kept busy going around the *case* filling in forms for "marching out." Deception (?)—we are going to Ancona for exercises and will be back here in a week. Actually, we are going back to the old front. This afternoon a priest went around the houses and blessed them. I noticed the preparation of the special *Pasqua* dishes—the iced cakes, the macaroni, the pigeons, pork, and so forth.

APRIL, 1945

1st April: EASTER SUNDAY Fine and sunny. A morning spent packing up for our departure. The *signora* of F1's *casa* presented us with a special tiered cake for Easter Day: pink meringue, sponge, filling, sponge, chocolate filling, sponge. Delicious. Jim, Len, Albie and I had dinner at the home of our hostess of the last month. First course: macaroni cooked in oil, with the flavoring of cheeses and organs of poultry. It was a big effort to make headway, although the dish was tasty. Second course: little pieces of lamb cooked in oil, a lettuce soaked in vinegar. Then two varieties of cake. The usual wine—but of a good quality. I visited various houses

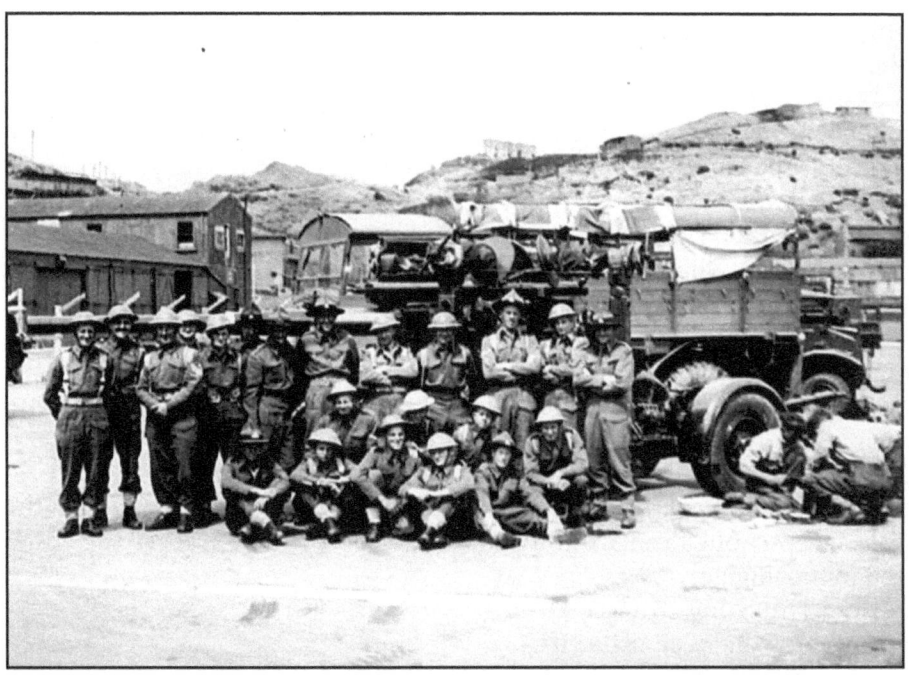

An informal group shot beside a transport. Alex is on the left. Perhaps taken while mechanics are effecting a repair (right).

where I was plied with the famous egg cake, wine and cognac. Somewhat heady when the time came to depart, Signora Fortunato and Pipo cried when I said "*arrivederci.*" We were away about 4:30. It was most uncomfortable in the back of the 3-tonner. Two points: All the Italians were dressed in their Sunday best for the great festa, and in every village we passed through, the streets and piazzas were packed with people taking the air.

2nd April: EASTER MONDAY We got detached from the rest of the convoy, and about 5 in the morning pulled into a farmyard at Faenza Fossolo. I walked about in the fresh morning air. Spring has come for the trees are in bloom. The old familiar sound heard from time to time. We had breakfast with 5 Field, and then set off to find the guns. Located at last—in an apple orchard (the trees are in flower) at Granarolo Faentino. Jerry is two thousand yards away on the stop bank of the Senio. Gun pits had been dug when we arrived, but we had to dig bivvy holes and place "camouflage." A very hard day, and all were very tired. I had a little sleep in the afternoon. The ammo arrived at 11:30 at night—four hundred rounds and charges for each gun. We were glad to get to bed finally.

Things are very active at night—*spandaus*, mortaring, shelling, Bofors, etc.

3 Tuesday: Another hot day. We unboxed the ammo in the morning, and made another bivvy hole in a dry place. I went to the village for a stroll in the afternoon and evening. Rain threatened at night. Jerry was active with *Spandaus*, mortaring and shelling.

4 Wednesday: There was an excursion this morning to buy eggs. I returned to the village in the afternoon where I watched Italian peasant women working hard on the washing—first, soaping and beating (in cold water), then into another tub, the top of which was covered over with a big cloth, ashes were poured on top, then boiling water. Jerry and our guns were very active with shelling and mortaring during the day and night.

5 Thursday: Awakened early this morning by Jerry's fire—possibly propaganda and what sounded like rocketed projectiles (similar to the *Neberwerfer*, but fired from a "packing case.") A day around the camp and in the village.

Letter: Thursday, April 5, 1945
My sweetest beloved little girl,

This is primarily a covering note for two British postal notes. They are for Judy's kindergarten education.

This country is replete with excellent material for short stories and the like, but a soldier in a job such as mine is not generally in the right frame of mind for finer writing.

Alex

Letter No 117: Thursday, April 5, 1945
My sweetest beloved little girl,

On <u>NO</u> account are you to spend one penny of the money I have sent home on me.

You might ask: "How did Alex spend Easter?" Well, the three of us on the gun living together in one *casa* were invited by the lady of the house to dine with her and her family that day. We sat down at the table at midday. A huge plate of macaroni was placed before us. It had been cooked in olive oil and was flavored with little pieces of poultry and cheese. It was a big commission indeed, but we struggled manfully with it until we couldn't eat any more. The Italians at the table devoured the macaroni rapidly. Not only have they acquired the dexterity to handle the stuff, but it is an integral part of their daily diet. Macaroni over, and having had two or three glasses of light red wine to wash it down, we began on little pieces of spiced lamb, cooked also in oil and lettuce. This proved easy to eat, and it was very tasty too. More wine, and then two varieties of cake with eggs in them—these had been saved up for Easter. But that was not the end of our eating. At every house where we knew people we were plied with cake (Huge slices of it!), with wine, and with Cognac. Easter in Italy: I'll never forget it!

A short time ago I was able to borrow from the ERS (*Education and Rehabilitation Services*) library a really fine book (*to study*) for History III, *(the final piece I need to complete my bachelor's degree.)* I am now busy taking notes for it.

We are all hoping so much that Germany will be finished, and then we will be able to join our loved ones soon after.

Alex

DIARY ENTRY

6 Friday: It remained fine throughout the day, although the skies were a little threatening. Bombers were on the job behind the Senio. I visited two Italian families at night. After I retired (although I went to sleep myself), Jerry opened up in a very big way. Hundreds of rounds whistled over the slitties…More of our tanks have arrived.

7 Saturday: I was awakened about 2:30 this morning by heavy *Neberwerfer* fire. The Spit-bombers bombed and strafed the stop bank and the area around it from 8 o'clock onwards this morning. I was told that Jerry had shelled the whole length of the front with intensity last night with a Mark-10 and its crew being hit. The Spit-bombers were active again almost until nightfall, while Jerry did some shelling and "*nebelwerfering*," not a great deal. I took a stroll in the village at night.

Letter No. 118: Saturday, April 7, 1945

My sweetest beloved little girl

I have applied for a job in the Education and Rehabilitation Services (ERS). There are two vacancies for journalists on the staff. It will be sometime before I hear whether I am 'successful' or 'unsuccessful'. Jim Sellar (the other ex-officer on the gun with me,) left today to take up a position in Ordnance Field Park. If I am successful with my application, I will leave with the knowledge that I have given twelve months field service.

Thank goodness your mother was not hurt in that unpleasant tram accident.

I am most keen to take an M.A. with Honors, and then get an academic appointment, if possible. Armed with such good qualifications and long personal association with Europe, I should be in the running for a good appointment overseas, either academic or journalistic. Oh, if I could have only completed my degree with honors before I came away! I would have then been in a position to make a big bid for a job in the History Department. Let us hope that such an opportunity is presented again in a year or two. I would be most happy to settle down in Christchurch for good if I had a position on the staff of Canterbury University College.

I know that a very good majority of the chaps who were interviewed on 18 November last have been given recommissioned positions.

Alex

DIARY ENTRY

8 Sunday: Mainly fine, and sunny, but a very cold wind blew nearly all day. Jerry dropped a number of *Neberwerfers* on the other side of the village this morning. Following Holy Communion, the padre held a service in the troop area this morning.

9 Monday: Today began a series of operations which the Army Commander hopes, (and we too, of course,) will end the war in Italy. Apparently, Jerry is very immobile here, only having sufficient transport to move one battalion at a time. The 8th Army show opened at 2:40 p.m. Box barrages were fired by the AA to indicate the FDLs and the bombers did their working—starting from the Poles on the left and working out towards the coast. What a tremendous rumble and cloud of dust! The fighters got on the job afterwards—bombing and strafing along the Senio and elsewhere. At least two heavy bombers took part. We started the barrage by three hundred and fifty odd guns at 3:20 p.m., and continued with various breaks until 7:30 p.m. when two of our battalions crossed the Senio covered by a smoke barrage and supported by flame throwers. The same barrage was fired about five times to 7:30 p.m. to deceive Jerry. Firing continued until 11 p.m. Meantime, the engineers were busy bridging the Senio as three battalions had to be across the river by midnight. Jerry did some firing near the river. Just after our show finished, we had three shells in our area, two being about thirty yards from our huts. Overall, each gun fired six hundred rounds. I saw a heavy bomber go down and three of the crew bailing out.

10 Tuesday: Many night fighters were on the job during the early hours for C/B (*counter-bomber?*) work. At 11 a.m., the AA put up a box barrage above us for the mediums. We had to don our tin hats because of the AA flak which almost rained down. We were ordered to move, and were away by 2 p.m., through the village and up to the famous stop back. We crossed over the stop bank and the Senio, a mere five or six yards wide. The reverse side of what was the German stop bank was pitted with mortar holes. All the houses nearby were ruined. Jerry had cut down all the trees to facilitate obstruction. We went on to Budrio di Cotignola—about 1 and a half kilometers past the stop bank—then dug-in in a lucerne (*alfalfa*) paddock. We were finished by 7:30 p.m. About eight POWs were escorted away from 5 Infantry Battalion HQ next to us. There was harassing fire during the night, but I was not on duty choosing instead to visit the *casa* next to the G.P. (*ground position?*) and talked with the Ities.

11 Wednesday: Our guns were engaged in a harassing fire program until about 4 a.m. It was hard to sleep. Early this morning about eighty Jerries were taken away from 5 Infantry Battalion. Tanks were going up the road for hours. RAF fighter-bombers were on the job all day. We fired a barrage of about ninety rounds at 2 p.m. to cover the crossing of the Santerno River, which was successful. Two Jerry Tiger tanks were knocked out, with four of our battalions across. What seemed to be a Jerry fighter strafed and bombed on our left front at night; also a lot of parachutes appeared in the direction of Lugo. The Poles pushed their way forward to the Santerno on the Faenza front where four hundred mediums "did over" the area yesterday. We fired a few tasks up to about 11:30 tonight. Jerry also did a lot of firing on the river line during the night.

12 Thursday: There was air cover over the area early—on the job in a big way. A barrage of about 100 rounds began at 2 p.m. to support the advance near Massa Lombarda—about three kilos north of the Santerno. We messed around, although there was a strong indication of a move. That came about at 7 p.m. Up the road we went past houses blasted to pieces by our bombers. We passed through Lugo and into a vineyard near Villa San Martino—about five hundred yards short of the Santerno, and had to dig-in in the darkness. The hand digging was grueling. Jerry was active with *Neberwerfers* and shelling. We finished at 11 p.m., when other crews did some harassing fire for an hour. (Via Pedergnano Superiore.)

Letter No. 119: Thursday, April 12, 1945
My sweetest beloved little girl,

Life has been hectic and grueling. Thank you for the parcel with the tobacco as, on the whole, the tobacco we get is very poor stuff.

I'm afraid there is nothing I can do with regard those jobs I applied for in November. Nothing seems to go right for me in regard to those jobs. I met Keith last night and he said, "It looks as though you will finish the war out on the guns." I don't dislike the guns by any means, but I look at things this way—I have been in action with the guns for twelve months, and yet have never been given the chance given to other ex-officers. Therefore isn't it natural that I should turn my eyes elsewhere. I am likely to see a good deal, with any luck. He commented that I wouldn't be able to do any swot these days, but I surprised him when I told him that I had been able to make a goodly number of notes that afternoon.

There must have been some pretty good jobs in the 3rd Division in the Islands. I've got my knife into the political powers at home for their policy in regard to officers. They demoted many of us, and we came over here a year and three quarters or a year and a quarter ago to serve in the ranks. Yet, men who went off to the Islands at the same time as we came here, have arrived home with their ranks confirmed in the 2nd Division. There are several in this battery—and in almost every unit of the Division. Very few have seen action, and yet they come here to take charge. It is grossly unjust.

I will let you know as soon as I hear the result of my application. They don't close until the 20th of this month.

We heard this morning that the Allies are only 70 miles from Berlin, and that they and the Russians are 100 miles apart. What grand news!

Alex

DIARY ENTRY

13 Friday: I slept like a log during the barrage at 2 a.m. to carry our forces south of Massa Lombarda. We were firing again about 9 a.m.—45 rounds per gun, both H.E (*high explosives?*) and smoke at 1100 yards. There was little rest for us. Firing, firing, firing. Apart from the barrage in the early morning, we engaged in fire orders with the observation post all morning and afternoon, in all about one hundred and thirty rounds. At about 5 pm, we moved to the west over the Santerno River to an orchard about three kilos from Massa Lombarda. It was hard digging the slitties. When they and the gun pits were completed and the tents pitched, we moved onto getting ready the ammo for the next barrage.

14 Saturday: The barrage that followed was to aid a crossing of the Sillaro River by our infantry with the intention of establishing a foothold over the stop bank. We (three of us) fired 274 rounds between 2 and 4:50 a.m. It was then to bed, but we were up at 6 a.m. for DF's and this we carried on until 8 o'clock. We then turned in for a much needed sleep. In the afternoon, I made my way to Massa Lombarda, which has been frightfully devastated by bombing and shelling. The scene of destruction is not to be forgotten. There was more harassing fire at night but by another crew. The infantry achieved their objective in the early morning.

15 Sunday: A beautifully hot day. There was some shooting during the day. In the afternoon, we prepared a pile of ammo for the barrage in support of the 9th Infantry Battalion, starting our firing at 9 p.m. and carrying on unto midnight. I noticed in the *"Crusader"* today that the Senio was the biggest show ever by the Eighth Army. On the day of the big bombardment, nine hundred and fifty heavies dropped four hundred and fifty tons of bombs; about two thousand planes in all took part, and the artillery barrage was bigger than El Alamein.

16 Monday: We were told just after the barrage that the infantry had reached all their objectives in positions about two thousand yards beyond the Sillaro, and intended to exploit their advantage for another two thousand. We thought: "Ah! Here's a good night's sleep for a change," but we were wrong because we were in and out of bed until 4 a.m. firing numerous DF's. Then at 5 a.m., we were up again, before returning to bed for a couple of hours. This was followed by a short barrage of fifteen rounds, but then we packed immediately afterwards, and took to the road, Soon we got tangled up with the Tommies and Poles on the left, and had to turn around and retrace our steps. At last, we struck the New Zealand sector again, found our G.P. *(Gun Position?)* and dug in as usual. We were able to have a much needed sleep in the afternoon, then across the Sillaro we went to the ruined—well and truly—village of Sesto Imolese, or Sesto d'Imola, all rubbish and dust and rubble, with Ities digging out their possessions from the ruins of their houses amidst the coming and going of hundreds of our vehicles, the movement of casualties to the RAPs *(Regimental Aid Posts)*, etc. Our guns fired at night, but only a few rounds. I saw a German woman soldier going out on a Jeep. These women, I gather, were "sigs," *(telephonists)* in German units.

17 Tuesday: Up at 6 a.m. and away by 7. We made our way via the Sillaro, and through Sesto Imolese up the highway to a position just out of Crocetta. We are some miles northeast of Castel San Pietro, the last decent-sized place on the Via Emilia before Bologna. We did not dig pits as we anticipated a move because of the continued advance. We sat around for the best part of a morning, and then started firing, our ranges set between nine thousand and eleven thousand yards to stop Jerry from digging in. All told, we fired two hundred rounds per gun before turning in early in anticipation of an early move. I took a stroll in Crocetta in the early evening and viewed the devastation. The Ities were busy sorting out their belongings from amongst the debris.

18 Wednesday: We did a little DF *(Defensive Fire)* firing in the early hours, but then at 6 a.m. we packed, pulling out after 8 a.m. and moving westward to the little town of Medicina, a town of fine spires that can be seen a long way off. We dug pits and bivvy holes and a few rounds were fired during the day. I went in Medicina where the inhabitants were do-

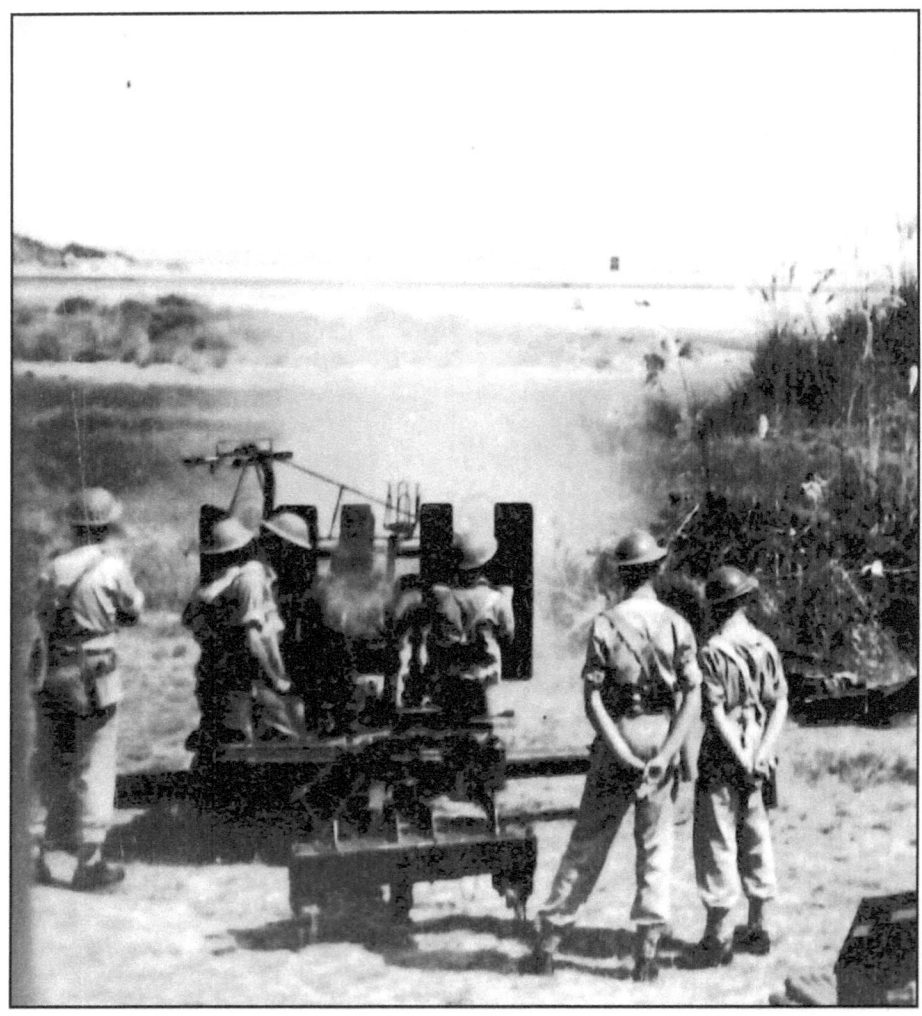

Gun in action, unknown location

ing the same as their compatriots in most of the places we have passed through of late. In the evening, we prepared the ammo for the long barrage which began at 9:30. An "I" (*intelligence*) report from captured Germans said they were to take all provisions off the land with them. Apparently, our 9th Infantry Battalion and the Gurkhas have had heavy casualties on the Canal along which the German 4th Parachute Division was dug in. Spities of the DAF (*Desert Air Force?*) have been on the job all day long today as they are every day. What a grand job they are doing. POWs—New Zealand Division in this present campaign: twelve hundred.

Letter No 120: Wednesday, April 18, 1945

My sweetest beloved little girl,

Conditions of life are so strenuous these days that one has little time for anything but work, and more work. What time we have spare we spend sleeping. However, I'm pleased to say I am in excellent health. The weather is constantly hot, and we are getting very tanned. The application for the ERS jobs close tomorrow. I wonder if I will be fortunate this time?

Of course, I have done no study during the last fortnight. I have seen Keith on a couple of occasions as of late. He too has been very busy as is to be expected. There is a dearth of news at the moment. There is of course plenty about the war, but that topic is 'verboten' for this type of letter.

Alex

DIARY ENTRY

19 Thursday: The weather continues to be beautiful, day after day. The boys fired about four hundred rounds in a barrage overnight. As usual we did a lot of firing during the day—almost two hundred rounds, but there was none at night, thank goodness.

20 Friday: We were up again at 5 a.m., and on the road again at 6. We bypassed Medicina, and took up a position in a field about two kilometers from the town. There we found the 25th Battalion, which was in reserve, getting a well-deserved sleep in their bivvies. We dug pits and put the guns in, but did not fire as our infantry were still advancing towards the Idice River. The DAF were active ahead of us, also a few bombers. We pulled out about midday, and drove through fairly open country towards the Idice, near Budrio. It was a scene of awful destruction—a dozen or so dead Jerries, burnt-out vehicles, houses, horses, mules, oxen...and fires still burning. We took up a position of a few yards in front of the 23rd Battalion's MG (*motorized gun?*) that had no sooner fired a few bursts than Jerry let us know he had received them. Then we fired our own, and then in came a stonk (*a coordinated artillery bombardment*) in the locality. We worked hard and fast on our slitties. Jerry pounded the areas in front of us with shells, *neberwerfers* and mortars, after we had fired a task to the area around us. One chap was bruised by shrapnel and went out. An F4 quad was ruined. One was killed and six wounded in 46 Battalion. The MG behind us fired spasmodically during the night. The reason for Jerry's hate was attributed to the occasion of Hitler's birthday.

The area we are in is one and a half kilometers from Budrio and 2 kilos from the Idice River.

21 Saturday: The barrage opened at midnight, and about two hundred rounds were fired. We were told that all our objectives had been reached, i.e., our infantry were well established across the Idice. We were told in the morning that a move was probable. We fired off and on—tasks running from five thousand to nine thousand yards. Then we were told the move was postponed. We fired forty rounds per gun of harassing fire between 9 and 10 at night.

22 Sunday: We were up at 6 a.m., and ready to move at 7:30, but no move was made until after 9, because of a lack of information as to the location of FDLs. We moved through Budrio, across the Idice to Granarolo dell'Emilia where we put the guns into action and awaited developments. I walked to the tiny village where all and sundry were beaming and smiling. I was invited to dine at two or three *casas*. The last Germans had passed through at 5 this morning, two of them were dressed in "civvies." We moved after 2 in Regimental formation, and there was a tremendous stream of traffic on the Divisional axis, mostly vehicles going "up." After nightfall, San Giorgio di Piano—some ten miles drive north of Bologna—was reached, and went into action about a half mile from the village of Argelato. A little harassing fire was done before midnight— about ten rounds per gun on a range of thirty-eight hundred yards. Two Jerry planes were over us after 10 p.m. They flew very low, bombing the north road and did some strafing as well. The AA was very active, but it did not stop them.

23 Monday: We moved again this morning. Every house displayed the flag of surrender, and we were cheered by the Ities as we drove past. The country is fairly open and exceptionally fertile with very fine crops of wheat, lucerne, etc. This Po Valley is very beautiful with its wonderful display of green. We put the guns down at Pieve di Cento, and dug slitties around them. In the evening, I went into the village. What a reception! We were really welcomed into the houses and bars for drinks; the happiness of the Ities at their liberation on full display with their "Vivas," etc., etc. I thoroughly enjoyed the visit.

24 Tuesday: We were on the road again this morning, up through Gualtieri, past cheering Ities and "partisans" (almost everyone) wearing armbands; and white sheets on poles outside the houses. We moved up and crossed the Reno River, which was bigger than the other rivers we had crossed. There were wrecked guns and vehicles in the water and along the roads. We passed through San Agostino to the 9th Infantry Battalion concentration area at Santa Bianca, located on the road between Finale Emilia and Bondeno—five kilometers from the Po. The boys pranced around on Jerry horses, which they had found in the area. The Americans have bridgeheads across the Po. There I saw some German POWs that were obviously Turkomen (*Turkmen*). We spent the night in Santa Bianca where a block of houses and several vehicles were burnt out by the Germans yesterday.

Letter No. 121: Tuesday, April 24, 1945

My sweetest beloved little girl,

It might be some time before I hear the result of my application for the ERS jobs. My swot is suspended. Life on the whole is extremely strenuous. Our efforts are more than justified by the results. The Italians are giving us 'grand' receptions for their 'liberation,' as they call it. Wine flows very freely, and one of our chaps was kissed by a man in a village last night.

We are all very heartened by the progress of the war. I see however that Churchill reminds the public that the war is not over when Germany is finished. There still remains Japan. However, let us hope that we don't have to take part in the Japanese war. The Division has given enough service in this beastly war already without having to answer other commitments.

Alex

DIARY ENTRY

25 Wednesday: This morning we moved early—only a few kilometers to a position near Ospitale di Bondeno where we dug pits and slitties. At 1 p.m., we went up on a hour's notice, but nothing eventuated owing to difficulties with bridging the Po. We were told that it was intended that with the 9th Infantry Battalion we would exploit the situation by aiming for the Adige river. Two of our Polish units are already across and are going ahead well. In the evening, we went into Ospitale, and on to Bondeno, largely deserted, which we found to be a quite clean little provincial town.

26 Thursday: We packed up ready for the road, and then waited for hours wondering when we would move. Eventually, we got on the road and reached the approaches to the Po Pontoon about 4 p.m. There was a good deal of Jerry equipment lying about. The river was very broad— about a hundred and fifty yards at the narrowest point, deep and with a fair current. We saw the wreckage of Jerry's bridges, and crossed at about 4:45 p.m. On the other side were numerous Jerry defensive positions, and a good deal of bridging material. There was little war damage for several kilometers. We had crossed the Po at the village of Ficarolo, passing through Trecenta, and over the Canale Bianco (very reminiscent of the Avon) through highly-developed country to within a few thousand yards of the River Adige. We dug pits in a crop of wheat near the village of Baruchella, about three kilometers from Badia. We found little evidence of war damage in these parts...With the pits and bivvy holes completed, I took a walk. We were told that our 5th and 6th Infantry Brigades had already crossed the Adige with very little opposition and were exploiting the situation. Meantime, each of our guns fired about sixty rounds of harassing fire.

27 Friday: There was heavy rain this morning, and some of the bivvies were affected. It is dull and threatening, but warm. B. and I walked to Baruchella, and roamed about where we saw about forty German POWs, who had been rounded up by the Tommy armor down the road this morning. We got a lift to Trecento, a rather pretty town on the south side of the Canal Bianco. Many houses had well-kept gardens and high walls, but the town was somewhat deserted. I saw many Kiwis, whose trucks and jeeps were laden with looted sugar, selling some in Trecenta and elsewhere. The countryside here is beautiful, the trees and the crops a mass of green. On the way home, we found a few families of Italian nationality who had been sent back here from Romania. In the afternoon, we set off again—passing through Badia Polesine, before reaching the Adige and its pontoon bridge. This big river, a hundred yards wide, is deep and fairly swift. We then moved along a road and up a slope being constructed by engineers, passing through the village of Masi, and up the road to a new position in a crop. There were hills in the distance. We had no pits, and had to dig slitties and bivvies in the dark before firing a round per gun at around thirty-five hundred yards, and turning into our bivvies for the night. It rained heavily during the night.

28 Saturday: It was dull at first but later the sun came out, although the weather is still threatening. We packed up before lunch, and were on the road by 2 p.m. What a tumultuous welcome we received everywhere along the road. The villagers and country people were lining the roads as we drove past—red flags, white flags, pink flags, streamers, toilet paper, lilacs, daisies, children with red bows...a banner of red streamers, eggs when we stopped...it was the best welcome we have had in Italy, and we saw no damage from war in this plain of trees, of vines, and crops. Jerry had left at 2 this morning. The Ities said he had demanded bicycles, chooks, (*chickens*), even cattle. A new gun position was set up at Santa Margherita d'Adige setting up in a wet cropped field in the rain. We all got very wet, however, we did not stay long, and moved again about 7 p.m. Once again, there was a wonderful reception for us everywhere! On and on we went through Este (at least the outskirts), an ancient city of towers, churches and ancient walls nestling at the foot of the beautiful Colli Euganei. Then, despite frequent stops, we continued up the main highway on through Monselice in the fading light into a well-kept flourishing *paese (countryside)*. Germans under partisan guard were marching back, and others were coming by themselves. We saw no signs of destruction—all the bridges, etc. were intact, although we saw much evidence of Jerry defensive fortifications. As darkness came we saw the ancient castle on the hill above Monselice, but this did not slow us. Into the night we went, still traveling.

29 Sunday: At last, we reached Padova (*Padua*), and went through the city to the outskirts where we camped on the road. It was about 3:30 a.m. We parked our trucks head-to-tail and placed a heavy picquet around them because elements of the 26 Panzer Grenadier Division were still at large on our right. I was having a wash and a shave, and was chatting and joking with the Ities, when suddenly there came a dramatic announcement. A column of enemy tanks was coming down the road which required the Regiment deploy in a hurry in defensive positions in the adjacent paddocks. We could hear tanks firing at no great distance. The guns went down on the platform—AP (*Armor Piercing*) and Hs (*high explosive*) were prepared, and slitties dug very quickly. A couple or so shells whistled over our heads, and we dug hard and fast. "Take Post—Change one for us," came the order with a range of 4050, but we did not fire. Then a new line was given; now the target was two thousand odd yards off. Small arms were held in readiness. Chaps were tense, but no-one got excited. Twenty-five battery hit a house in front and one man was killed and two wounded on the gun. All the Ities, with their streamers and arms disappeared, except for three partisans who helped the gun crews dig slitties. The Ghurkas went down the road to cover our flank. At last, the scare was over. Apparently, in the end, it was established there were four or five tanks that never came, and that they were either destroyed, captured, or escaped. We never found out what happened.

With the scare passed, we set out again about 1:30 p.m. on the road to Venice, passing through the city area of Padova—beautiful and clean with broad streets and fine buildings. The whole—or at least most of—the population was out to cheer us...all flowers, streamers, handshakes, and cries of "Ciao," and "Viva!" Wonderful! Then, it was the same all along the road—even deep into the countryside. We found Ponte di Brenta to be very badly battered by bombs and shells. A host of Jerry prisoners were there...Then, further up on the road to Venice was another column of Jerries escorted by partisans. We turned off near Stra, then made a deviation, and then got back onto the main highway in very open, low lying country where we saw more and more POWs. We struck Marghera, an industrial area near Venice about 5 p.m. A settlement of fine, clean-looking two-storied villas, Marghera was bombed in parts. We carried on up the coast road. I saw Venice's spires in the distance. A few miles up, we came to Mestre, another fine, well-kept and pretty town where again we were greeted wonderfully. We'll never forget the scene-—the happiness and joy of the Italians. What pretty girls! To the northwest, we could see the approaches to the Alps with snow on the highest peaks. About 8 p.m., we reached our destination, a little place called Croce di Piave, near Santa Dona di Piave, but on this side of the Piave river. We put the guns on line, and then cooked ourselves some tea because the cooks had not yet turned up. We pitched our bivvies, then it was to bed for a good sleep, which we all needed very badly. Meantime, we heard a 46 Battalion 3-tonner was strafed by a Mustang with two killed and others wounded.

30 Monday: We packed early but then sat about waiting to move. About 4:30, we were told three men from the troop could go to Venice for a few hours. We drew cards, and I was one of the lucky ones. We left at 5 and arrived in Venice at 6. It was a little wet and miserable. With the two other chaps, I set out immediately for the Piazza San Marco. Impressions en route—the canals, the bridges over them, the narrow, winding streets, the absolute absence of war damage, the beautifully-dressed women, the clean children, the well-dressed men. It seemed as if we had walked miles when at last we reached the famous Piazza. There were not the pigeons I had expected, and the facade of the San Marco's was covered as were several monuments in the interior, but we saw a great deal. We made our way to the top of the Campanile for a wonderful panorama before making our way back through the winding streets, over bridges, and back to the station. The visit was only two hours, yet it was thoroughly enjoyable. While we were away, the guns had crossed the Piave and had taken up positions near Santa Dona di Piave. At 11 p.m., we arrived back at our positions to the news that Jerry had counterattacked...

THIS IS THE LAST DIARY ENTRY

Venice, 1945

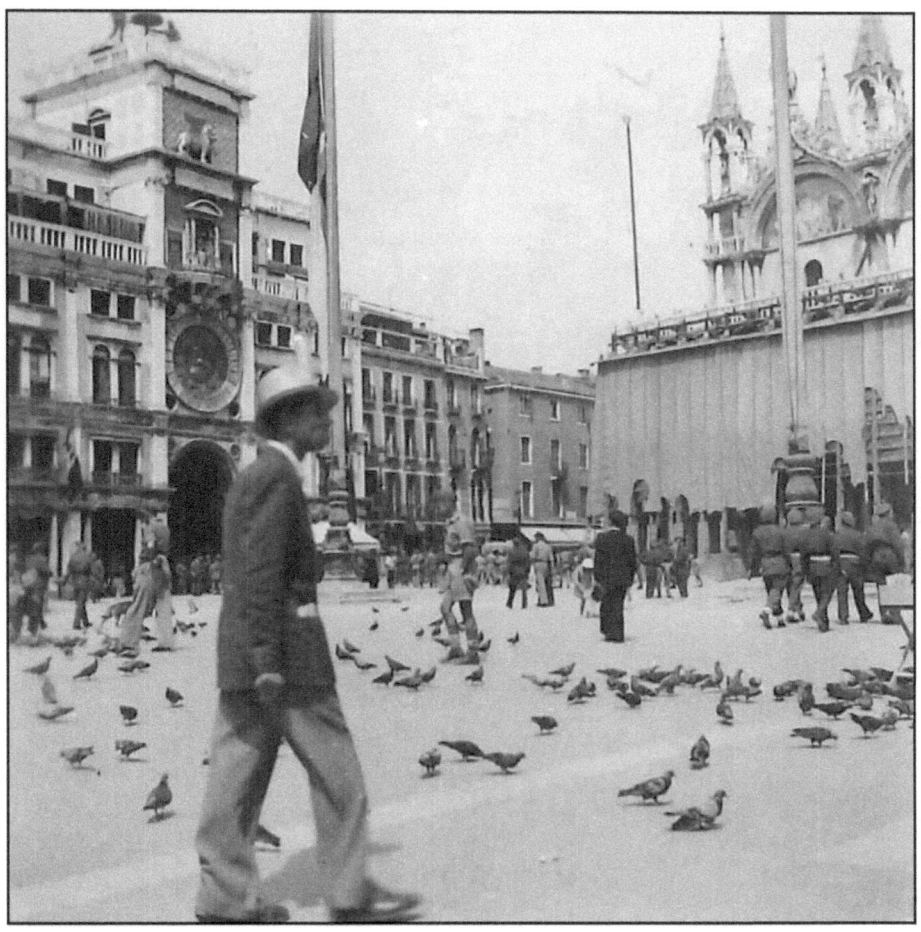

Piazza San Marco with the front of the Basilica covered and the square still showing a military presence, 1945.

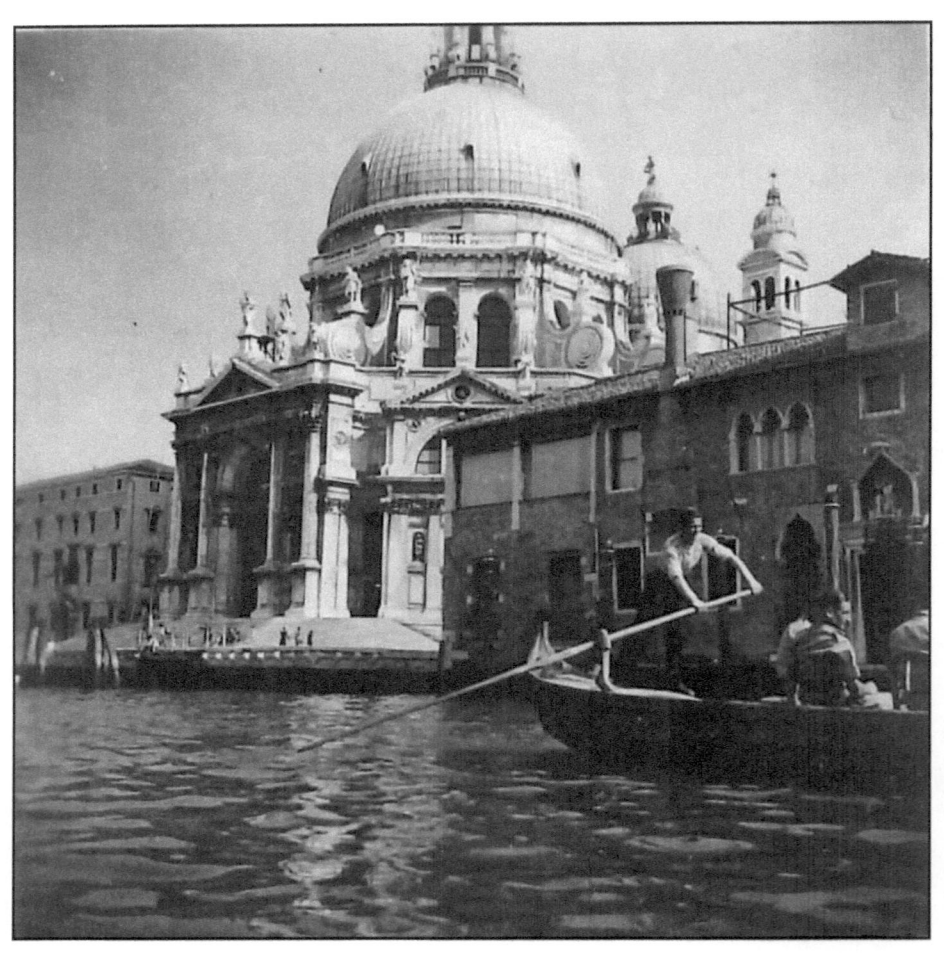

Grand Canal and Santa Maria della Salute

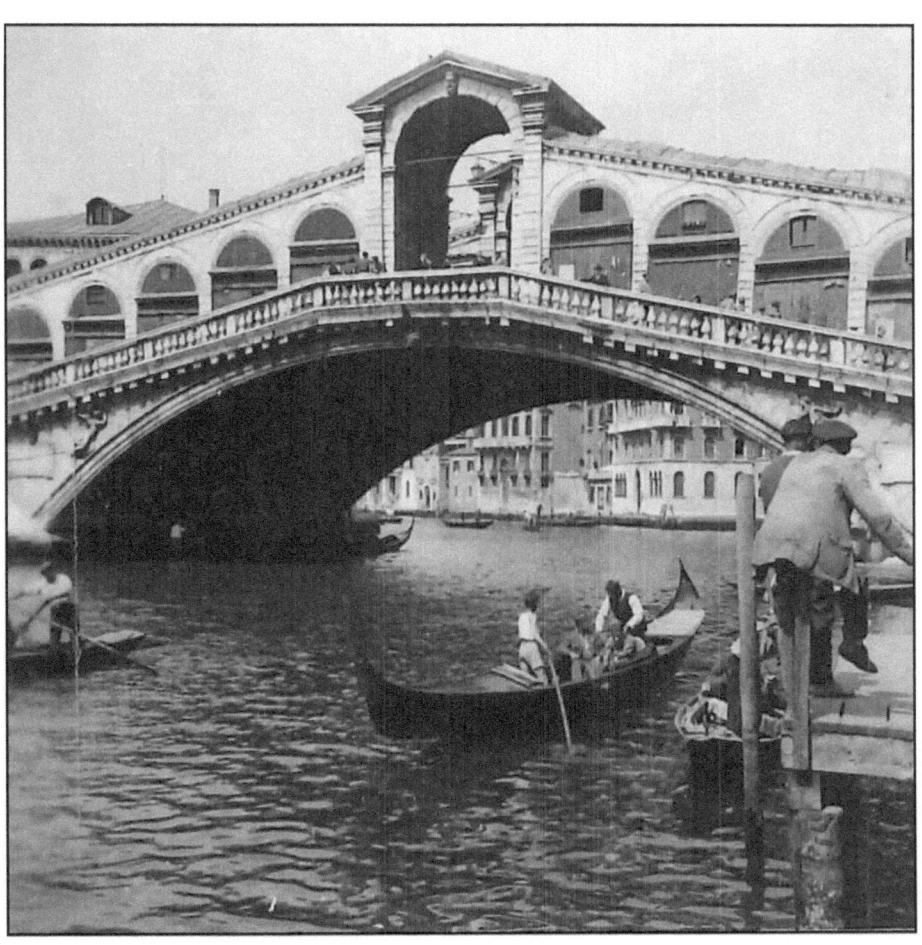

Rialto Bridge, Venice with soldiers on the bridge

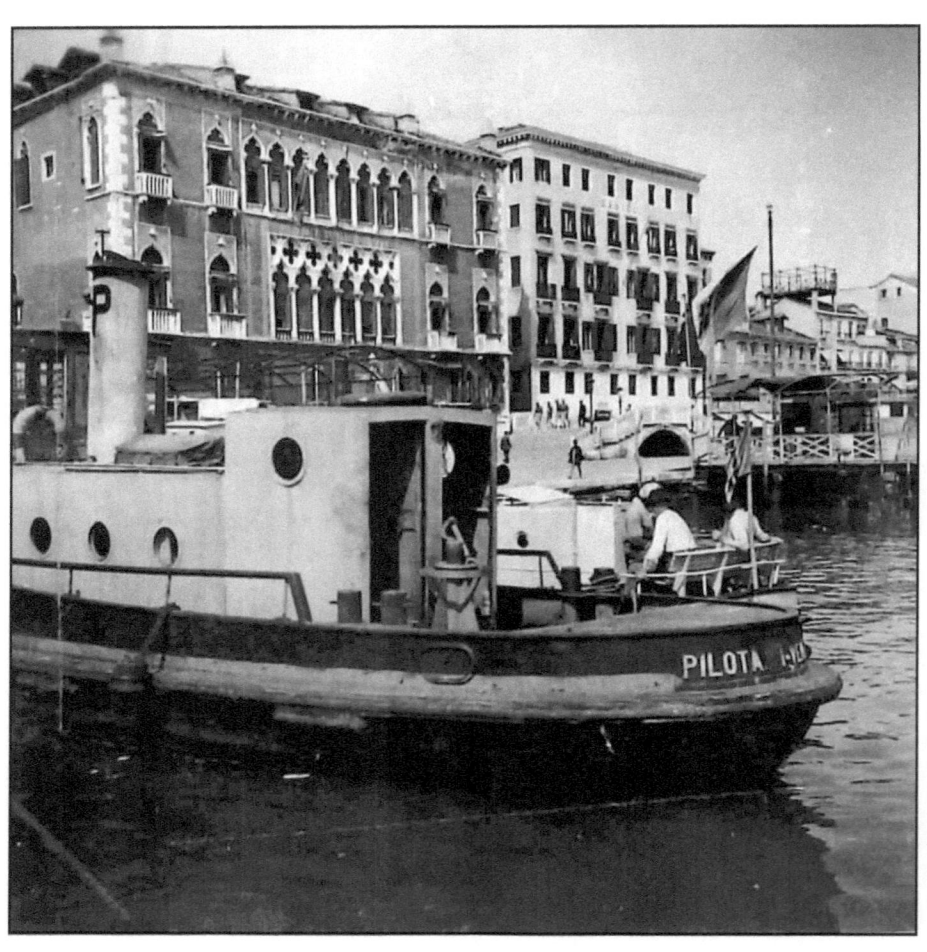

Albergo Danieli, Venice, 1945. New Zealand Forces Club

The End of Hostilities

Letter No. 122: Monday, April 30, 1945

My sweetest beloved little girl,

We don't expect to receive a lot of mail these days as we are always on the move.

Still no word about the ERS job. If I am fortunate enough to receive the appointment, it will take several days traveling to get there.

I don't think of Paul as Roger any more. Paul comes instantaneously.

Germany indeed is on her last legs. The number of prisoners our Division has taken alone is remarkable. I was talking to some of them yesterday morning. They have real horror—a fear of Russia, particularly in the political sense. One chap who spoke quite good English was just nineteen, and another I saw in the afternoon was very worn out and aged at forty-four.

Keith has told me about his friendship with a cultivated Italian while we were in the rest area.

The Po valley is a very rich area. The houses of the people are much cleaner than those down below, and the people themselves are a far better type than their southern compatriots.

Alex

Letter No. 123: Friday, 4 May, 1945

My sweetest beloved little girl,

It is 5 o'clock at night and I have just heard what the BBC correspondent, Michael Reynolds, has to say about the situation in Trieste, which you will have heard was conquered partly by our Division and partly by Marshall Tito. Trieste's layout is somewhat reminiscent of Wellington with its port, its surrounding hills covered with houses and its harbor. I think the panorama from the top of Trieste's hills is a little more beautiful than that of Wellington.

We were more than delighted to hear the dramatic announcement that Germany had unconditionally surrendered in that part of Italy to the south of the river a little below Monfalcone (to the west of Trieste.) Germany is finished here too, and will be elsewhere very soon. When that has been accomplished let us pray that we will be shipped home forthwith. That will be a wonderful day!

I have been to Venice, that lovely jewel on the Adriatic. About 4:30 a ballot was held for three men from the troop to go there for a couple of hours. I was one of the lucky ones. We set out a 5 a.m. and arrived there in the rain at 6. We took a long winding walk, over canals and under archways to the famous piazza, San Marco. The church was open and we inspected it. The edifice is Byzantium in architecture. Probably copied from some church in Constantinople. The decoration is considered the richest and most splendid in the world. The principal facade, glittering with gold and gorgeous mosaics was unfortunately covered. Inside is a collection of mosaics, different kinds of marble and precious stones, bas reliefs and inlaid wood which presents a never to be forgotten sight. Next door is the Ducal palace, the most famous monument of the city. The style of painted arches predominates. It was a grand spectacle.

We took the lift to the top of the Campanile from which we saw all of Venice. The gondolas are not decked up at the moment.

War has not touched Venice. The people were excellently clad, clean and neat, the shops also. It would be a grand place for a holiday. It is a distinct city with an air of its own.

No news about the ERS job.

Alex

Letter No. 124: Friday, 11 May, 1945

My sweetest beloved little girl,

I am doing quite a lot of work (*study*) now. Providing I can get all the books I should be able to pass (*History III*) alright.

I saw Keith last night for the first time in a fortnight. He is living in a very fine house next to the beach. Life for him and me is now very pleasant. Trieste is a big place. It reminds me of Wellington more than any other city I have seen. But it has big, wide streets with more modern shops than those in Wellington. It also has a most beautiful marine drive, the best I have ever seen. Before the war it had a population of two hundred and eighty thousand.

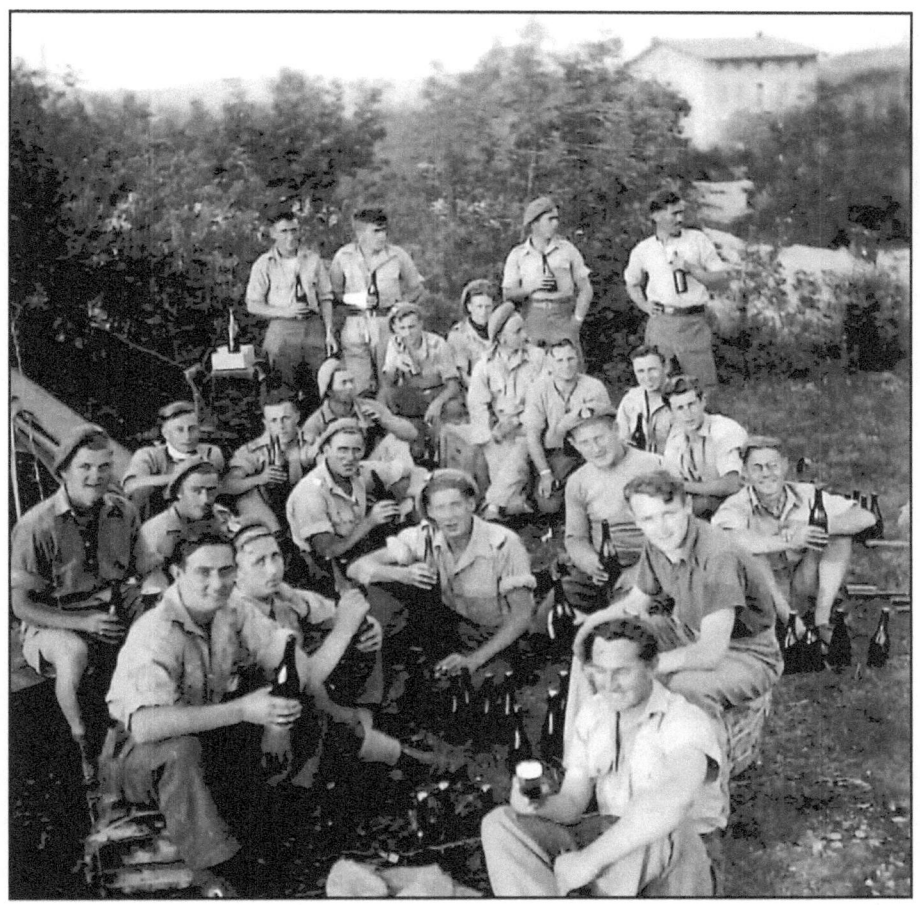

V. E. Day celebration, Sistiana, near Trieste, May 8, 1945

As the sun pours down on us every day, how brown and tanned, we are becoming, and I have bought a snappy summer parasol and a nice pair of blue beads for you. I'll buy other things before prices begin to soar.

It is a great wish that the 14th Army and the Americans are sufficiently powerful to crush the Japanese without further aid.

Alex

Letter No. 125: Tuesday, 15 May, 1945

My sweetest beloved little girl,

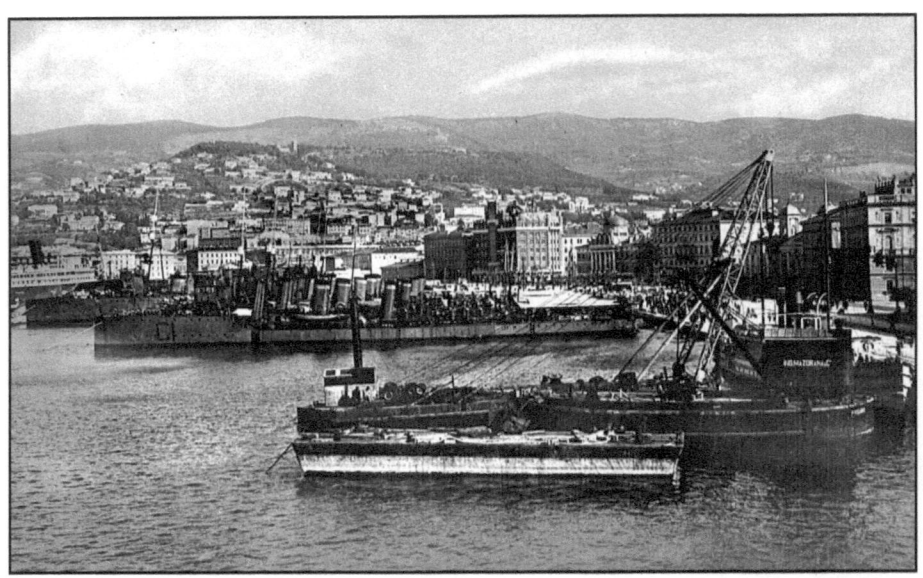

Trieste, Il Porto

Today has been a day of study and taking history notes. The weather continues to be very hot, so much so we get around clad only in shorts. Bathing in the Adriatic is to be had nearby.

I have made the acquaintance of a hospitable Trieste family consisting of a middle-aged Italian businessman and his wife, (He has a very fine shoe store.), his widowed sister-in-law, and her 13 year-old daughter. It goes without saying that discussing politics there is *verboten* for me. The apartment is much better than 999 of a thousand of our homes. These people have a sense of taste in house decoration which we have yet to acquire. The furniture is expensive. There are a few tasteful modern pictures and extremely artistic ornaments (not showy but blending with the room perfectly) and a magnificent cut glass ashtray. The floor is of inlaid wood. All very tasteful. This style of decoration is to be found in numerous other flats, apartments and houses in the city. I have been made to feel very welcome by the family. They have given me coffee and tea. Last night I had two eggs for tea. (They cost 3 shillings each!)

On ANZAC day, we crossed the Po River on a pontoon bridge. Jerry shelled us for the last time on 2 May. That evening we entered Trieste. What a terrible night that was too—trying to work in pitch blackness to erect our bivvies in heavy rain. I think this is the only comment I have ever made to you about the war. I have given up thinking about the job I applied for last month.

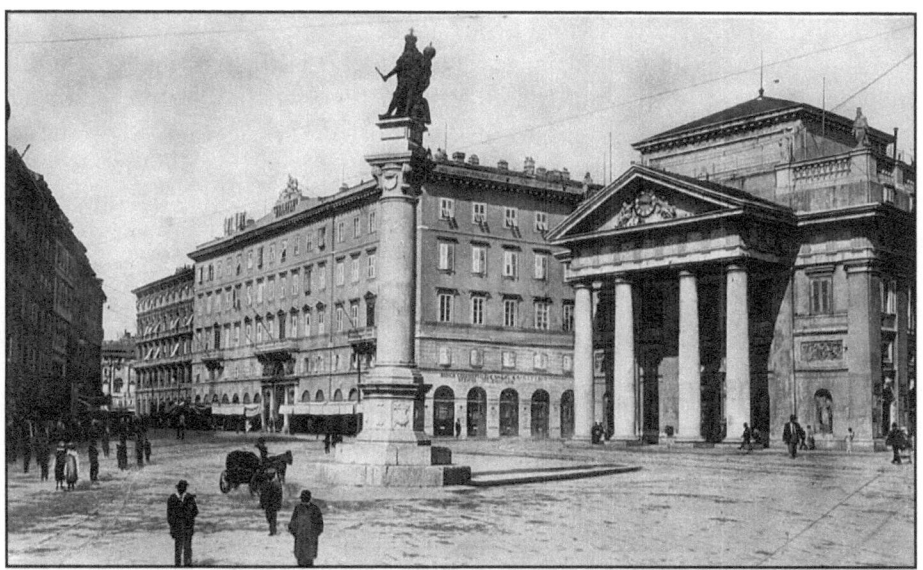

Trieste, Il Borso

Alex
Letter No. 126: Monday, 21 May, 1945
My sweetest beloved little girl,

I must confess that this is being written in hospital—in that section of 2GH attached to No. 1 CCS (*Casualty Clearing Station*). I developed a spot of bladder trouble following an attack of diarrhea. I reported to the M.O., who gave me some tablets and powders with various instructions, and then told me that he would take me to the Div. Rest camp at Grado to which the whole troop was going that day. I don't think you will find Grado on the map unless it is a very detailed one. It is situated amongst that cluster of islands and lagoons to the west of Trieste at the head of the Gulf of Trieste. The beach is magnificent, and near the foreshore are a large number of hotels, pensions, etc., that are three or four stories high standing in nicely wooded sections next to the tree-lined avenues—a really delightful spot. But all of Grado is not like the aforementioned beach area. As in most other places, there is a poor quarter. Grado's depressed area is one of the worst I have ever seen. Narrow, high walled alleyways, crowded with a host of dirty fisher folk and children likewise dirty, suffering from sores and other skin infections. Oh! the smells! I did not feel as well as I might have done while I was at the camp, and I spent most of the time lying around. However, I could not miss the Welsh choir. The average ENSA show is not very good, but this one was a refreshing exception. There were about twenty-four in the choir, an equal number of women and men, under a very good conductor. The women all wore tall black top hats. One half had red coats and the other half green. The program lasted two hours—delightful songs—English, Welsh, Scottish, Irish, and religious. I was very sorry when it was all over. The following night I saw, "Thousands Cheer," an American variety film, which I enjoyed in patches. At the hostel, we had an orchestra each evening. We returned to camp the next day.

The bladder trouble caused an inflammation and I had to go out. I should be out in a few days. I am feeling very good other than a little sore. Yesterday, I read an informative book, "The Reawakening of Italy," which gave me a host of information about the country. You will be listening to the news about Trieste and how things will end up there. Let's hope the dispute can be solved without warfare. But the question paramount in your mind is: 'Will the Division go home, or will it go to the Far East?' We are all awaiting the decision. Need I say which we hope it will be!   Alex

Letter No. 127: Tuesday, 29 May, 1945

My sweetest beloved little girl,

About midday on Friday, with about twenty other chaps, I was taken into an aerodrome well in the north of Italy. We were given a cup of tea and something to eat by the Tommies there. When everyone had been loaded onto the transport plane, we set off for the south. We reached the aerodrome near No. 1 General Hospital about one and a quarter hours later. What a wonderful saving of time compared with road and rail! Another cup of tea and sandwiches, and an orange, and then off to No. 1 GH. I started on a treatment of sulfa drugs the day before yesterday. Late yesterday, I was told not to eat or drink anything. At the theatre, the doctor told me he was going to drain an abscess inside my right testicle. I went to sleep around 4:30 and woke up again in my bed at 9 p.m. at night. I feel perfectly alright in myself, although it will probably take a fairly long course of treatment to cure my affliction.

Early yesterday afternoon, the ERS chap attached to the hospital was around, and I asked him if he had any history books touching the period which I am studying. Imagine my surprise and pleasure at finding an excellent book on colonial policy by Egerton in my locker this morning.

Of course, I miss the Trieste area very much—the almost perpetual sunshine, the swimming, the sunbathing, the outings, the easy time. But one must grin and bear it.

I see in the *NZ Times* that there have been floods in Canterbury.

I posted to you the other day the fine summer parasol which I bought in Trieste.   Alex

Letter No. 128: Wednesday, 30 May, 1945

My sweetest beloved little girl,

There's been a lot of talk around here today following the broadcast of New Zealand news from London last night. I didn't hear it personally, but apparently Nash said in Hamilton that those in units up to the 10th Battalion would be going home. I pray earnestly that it will be the whole Division. I was not surprised that *The Press* produced something special for VE Day. It is a newspaper of which New Zealand should be proud. Let us hope that its standard does not fall.

                                        Alex

Letter No. 129: Wednesday, 6 June, 1945

My sweetest beloved little girl,

As soon as I leave hospital I intend to buy some more postcards for our Judy.

I was intrigued with your suggestion about the Rehabilitation Scholarship at one of the English Universities. For years, I have had the ambition to study at Oxford. I would be able to equip myself with a degree which carries so much weight in the academic world. A person with a degree from the University of New Zealand, and certain other specified universities, is permitted to take a shortened course at Oxford, or Cambridge for a degree from those ancient institutions of learning.

On 18 July last year, I was interviewed by Col. Thornton, and others, about the British Army in India. I wonder now if I was wise in turning down the opportunity of going there with the rank of Lieutenant?

If a malicious fate decrees that the 10th go to the Far East, I will go as a gunner, not an officer. But let us hope and pray that we all go home. Better to be an 'acting private' on a ship taking me back to civilian life than an officer in India.

What, you may ask, is Alex doing all day long in a hospital bed? Well, there is an ERS chap here, and he has lent me Hugh Edward Egerton's "British Colonial Policy." I spend hours note taking. I have also read, "While Rome Burns," by Alexander Woollcott—excellent amongst many books.

The patient is getting along well. Following the draining of the abscess the swelling has been going down steadily. I am patiently waiting the order that I can get up.

                                        Alex

Letter No. 130: Monday, 11 June, 1945
My sweetest beloved little girl,

I have been back on my feet for several days. I am feeling very well indeed. The colonel expressed pleasure at the way the swelling was going down. I'll be here for another week, I think, and then probably on the road again. I can candidly say that I have done more study than at Varsity. Some really excellent books are coming into my hands: Egerton's "Colonial Policy," a book by two Americans on the U.S.A., a book on the effect of the French Revolution on England and others.

Alex

Letter No. 131: Monday, 18 June, 1945
My sweetest beloved little girl,

A couple of days ago, I received a card from the University saying I would be granted a B.A. provided I passed in History III or English III only. Excellent news, particularly in it coming at a time when I am deep in study, doing several hours a day. I am still in hospital, but have been up and around for about ten days now. I feel very well and am getting tanned once again though swimming in the sea. The sea this morning was calm as a millpond and delightfully warm. I am still here as the swelling has not completely disappeared. However, it doesn't affect me in any way. A few nights ago, I went to a concert by the Ancona Symphony Orchestra, which presented a grand program of Offenbach, Hayden, Elgar, Nicolai ("Merry Widows of Windsor") Novello, Berlioz, and another. I notice that the gratuities have been announced: £3 for every month overseas, and £1 for home service. That will bring in a tidy little sum for me.

If rumors are correct, those of us after the 10th will be going out to the Far East. If that unpleasant prospect does materialize I should be due for a base job, because I'll be a 'veteran' in the Division there.

I heard last night that the ex-officers were to be offered the opportunity of re-commissioning. If true that will be good news for me because that extra money will enable us to do so much in regards to Judy's and Paul's education. No advice on the ERS journalistic jobs. It will be wonderful if I can complete my degree before I leave Italy. Then I would be in a position for a rehabilitation scholarship at Oxford, or Cambridge.

Alex

Letter No. 132: Saturday, 23 June, 1945
My sweetest beloved little girl,

The doctor told me a couple of days ago that the ERS had called inquiring when I would be discharged because they wanted me for a job! That news was a bolt out of the blue! I went to the hospital officer to find out if there were any details, but they had none. I wonder if it will be an educational or journalistic appointment. When the colonel was doing his rounds a couple of days ago, I mentioned the matter to him, and he said I could go. However, the ward doctor has gone on leave for a few days, and to avoid missing out, I mentioned the question of my discharge to the doctor who has taken over his patients. I'll let you know the developments.

I have exhausted all the history books in the ERS library and am thus having a day or two off from study. The sea is my attraction. Everyday, I put a delightful hour or two in a boat and in swimming. I am feeling very fit and well.

I think New Zealand will be represented by only a token force in the Far East. There is no information confirming this, but I think if personnel from the 11th to the 16th Battalions go, I should not entertain any great hopes of returning home soon. Let us hope and pray that events will make it unnecessary to dispatch New Zealand troops out to the East.

I recall the insatiable appetite I had for books when I was just a little older than Judy. I am sure Judy is filling her mind with a host of thoughts and pictures.   Alex

Letter No. 133: Friday, 29 June, 1945

My sweetest beloved little girl,

I am now in the Reinforcement Transit Unit (RTU), where I arrived on Tuesday from hospital. Before I left, I spoke to the sergeant on the hospital ward to inform the ERS that I had been discharged. As far as the RTU is concerned, all I will say is that it is a most depressing place, a barrack with an atmosphere of a morgue. What a contrast with the hospital in every way! At the hospital, there was comfort; here there is only a tiled floor on which to sleep, exceedingly poor meals (in fact the worst I have ever had), no spoon with which to eat, just a fork, and no mug. A draft of ex-hospital personnel was collected for the return to unit, and my name was on the list. In view of the circumstances, I thought it was wise to see the O.C. about the matter. What was the point in traveling several hundred miles, and then come back again in two or three day's time? The officer agreed with my point. I am anxiously awaiting the instruction to report for duty.

In regard to my health, I have to report to a surgeon every three months for an examination of the epididymis.

I began guard duty at a supply depot last night. In the morning, an effort was made to get me to wait upon those dining in the officers' or sergeants' mess. Although I am an ex-officer, I am only too willing to do my bit, but I shall never do the duties of a waiter in a mess. That would be strictly against principle. That is one thing I will say in favor of those in charge of the unit; they would never think of asking me to undertake such duties.   Alex

Letter No. 134: Saturday, 30 June, 1945

My sweetest beloved little girl,

Last night, I had a chat with a soldier who came over with me eighteen months ago. He told me what had happened to the ex-officers who were with me on the troopship. I must admit I was stricken with pangs of envy. It is only natural, I suppose, when I and two others are the only ones who have not been recommissioned. Some of these chaps have received appointments which I could fill equally as ably as they would, but such is life for me here committed for more than a year to hard manual labor and the fortunes of war in the field, and now filling in time doing guard duty at night. But I must thank God that I was not maimed in battle. I must endeavor to bear my lot of being clay in the hands of lesser men. Perhaps the opportunity may come when I can use my talents. It was a sorry day when I severed my connection with the Air Force for there I had status which I think I am entitled now, and if I had made a strong endeavor to have transferred to that Service and had been successful, I would have been very happy.

                    Alex

Letter No. 135: Wednesday, 4 July, 1945

My sweetest beloved little girl,

I am writing this just before I head for the south of Italy. Today, our Judy is three years old. This day three years, ago I was O.C on the docks in Wellington. You can imagine my state of mind then, waiting for the big news (*of Judy's birth*) from Christchurch. To think that I would go to the Wellington Post Office, and meet Hilary to hear the news that our little daughter had arrived.

In regard to troops coming home, I can only hope that there will be shortages in the quota up to the 10th on the troopship and then—as I am married with two children—I should stand a good chance of inclusion.

When I next write I shall be telling you all about my new job. I wonder if I will be fortunate to regain my old status? Wouldn't that be grand!

                    Alex

Letter No. 136: Friday, 6 July, 1945

My sweetest beloved little girl,

I have now joined the staff of the ERS. I left the RTU (*Reinforcement Transit Unit*) on Wednesday in a 3-ton truck with about a dozen other chaps, the majority of whom are going home on compassionate leave. We stopped the night at an isolated and largely deserted camp near the Sangro River. Leaving at 8 a.m. yesterday, we made Foggia for lunch and then went onto Bari (which I had not seen for thirteen months). Afternoon tea and dinner at the Club, I was taken onto Mola di Bari, a small town some fifteen miles down the coast. Wasn't I tired after a journey of 350 miles! I was completely in the dark about the job. Was it to be journalism, or teaching?

I found that both sections wanted to have me! However they went to the journalism first. The officer in charge said I would be needed for article writing for *Cue,* an informative little booklet published by the ERS twice monthly. The articles are on a host of subjects (history, geography, sport, music literature, science, agriculture, etc.) and are very ably illustrated. At first, I was inclined to return to my old profession, and then I thought of that oft-repeated saying: "Stick up for yourself!" Thus I made enquiry with regards to promotion and advancement. I explained that I was an ex-officer, married with two children, and that I desired to regain my commission, if that were possible. The officer said that the highest rank to which I could *aspire* was staff sergeant. I felt very disappointed. The *Cue* has no connection with war correspondents, unlike the *NZ Times*, which is controlled by Public Relations. Accordingly, I broached the subject of my posting to the tutorial staff, and I was told that opportunity was better there. I was interviewed by the 2 I.C., Major Sinclair, (who was a signals officer at C.M.D. while I was liaison officer for the Air Force,) and I told him I was keen to regain my commission so that I would be better able to support my family. I said I had never been given a chance while I was in the field. He said he had no objection to my going over to the education section. Well, I spent the morning learning something about the machinery of the job. I am to do tutoring in history, and I know I am going to be happy in this work.

Apparently almost everyone here has had leave to Rome during the last six months. It would be a shame if I have left this country without having become acquainted with that city. As you know, I have only had seven days leave in the last 18 months.

Today is the anniversary of our marriage at St. James's five years ago. How little of that time I have spent with you. Oh! the beastly war!

Alex

Letter No. 137: Wednesday, 11 July, 1945
My sweetest beloved little girl,

It is eighteen months ago since I boarded the troopship in Wellington.

I have settled down very well. As yet, I have not taken on the marking of history papers. There is another chap doing that, but I will be fully occupied when some other chaps go home. The ERS is a congenial place. Writing will enable me to rehabilitate myself mentally. The long time I spent in the field has not been beneficial to me mentally (at least from the point of view of study.) Thus I am in a position to recapture my old powers of concentration, and when I arrive home I should be able to carry on my study and thinking of old.

Alex

Letter No. 138: Monday, 16 July, 1945
My sweetest beloved little girl,

The ERS has been elevated to the status of a Corps, and all ranks are now compelled to adopt infantry ranks. Therefore, I am really just a 'Private.' Fancy isn't it, that one who is engaged in higher education work—now marking History and English papers—should have such a lowly status! No doubt something will be done about it as I am the *only* private, there is one corporal and two sergeants. I have never been given a chance to regain my commission. I cannot understand it. Many of my old contemporaries at Burnham Camp have expressed surprise that I have not been recommissioned.

Alex

Letter No. 139: Wednesday, 18 July, 1945
My sweetest beloved little girl,

Today, Paul is one year-old.

Let us hope that I am able to secure a scholarship for myself next year and also go to England with you.

Other news: I hear that Vic was left behind when GH (*General Headquarters?*) was moved to Egypt. He is a patient in the No 2 British Gen. (*Hospital*) with an infection of the middle ear. Keith is getting browned off by his life of inactivity.

I am very happy in this job. I feel that a last I have found my real calling in life, either tutoring or lecturing. Let us hope I can realize this wish in civilian life. The weather continues to be hot with lots of swimming. Last night, we went to Bari to see "Rigoletto." Thoroughly enjoyable in every way. I hope to get to Rome soon.

Alex

Letter No. 140: Tuesday, 24 July, 1944
My sweetest beloved little girl,

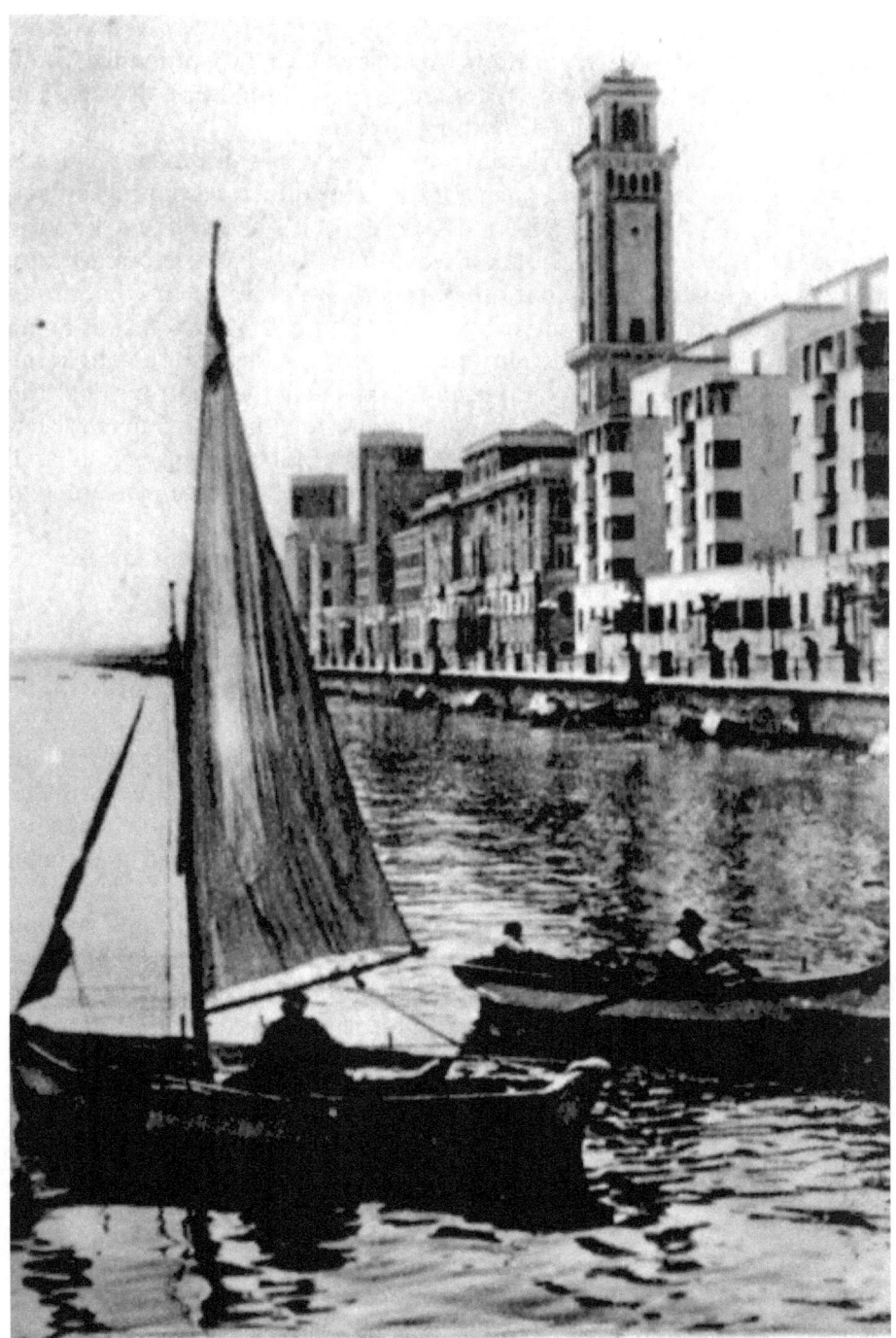

Bari - Marina al L'ungomare Nazario Sauro

It seems I am fated to remain in this lowly rank. I received a letter from my former troop; Ray said if I had stayed there I probably would have had the chance of being recommissioned. I am still a private, and there is no indication I will be anything else.

There is a marked differentiation in rank here: an officer's mess, a sergeant's mess and a men's mess. Of the eight tutors, all but myself and a corporal are in the sergeant's mess. So be it. If I had gone back to the unit and had been commissioned I would not have had the opportunity for study, or mental rehabilitation. But there are other points that are of great importance to me—the extra money, the better standard of living and social life when not in action, and the fact I am likely to remain in the army for many a long day yet. I read in the news this morning that the New Zealanders have been in action alongside the Australians. That would seem to indicate that the Division will not be going home, and, before long, will be in the Pacific. Also in regards the recommissioning of ex-officers, the ERS will not be considered. So be it.

Swimming has been forbidden as of late as we are in quarantine.

Alex

Letter No. 141: Friday, 27 July, 1945

My sweetest beloved little girl,

I had a chat with an officer yesterday and he suggested I write to the Regiment inquiring about the OCTU business. He said I would have to chose as to whether I would go back to the guns as an officer, or remain here as a NCO. He said that the establishment of officers in this unit was full. Most officers were new and therefore there would be no chance for me. Several other chaps recommissioning in this unit had also been knocked back. There appears to be no chance.

Two years at Oxford pursuing philosophy is my ambition. As you know, I have the chance of securing that Diploma in Public Administration course, but I shudder at the thought of passing all my life in one Government department or another subject to its regulations, grading, small salary, and obsequiousness. Never that for me. A post as an adviser, or lecturer, or tutor or foreign correspondent—certainly! But never, never a Government department.

Alex

Letter No 143: Wednesday, 8 August, 1945

My sweetest beloved little girl,

I am still a private, but I believe something has been done to give some slight recognition of the work I am doing here. The 8th Battalion left yesterday—very suddenly—leaving only five of us in the Arts department. The 9th and 10th are now going on leave either to Venice, or Florence and Rome, and thus I have been set back. But I have resolved to get leave by hook, or by crook. If anyone should get leave, none is more entitled to it than me because there are few here who can compare with me in continuous combatant service. I have no desire to leave Italy until I have seen the art of Rome.

Vic is now back in Egypt. He left Italy on the 3rd of August.

As for work, I have now taken on English, languages, and history.

There is still no news about our future, but I'm positive myself that the balance of the Division is destined for the Far East, provided, of course, there are any Japanese left after the truly devastating Atomic Bomb raids.

Alex

Letter No. 144: Monday, 13 August, 1945
My sweetest beloved little girl,

It may be not so long before I am home seeing that Japan has put out very strong peace feelers. We are to hold a big VJ day when it arrives: a race meeting and other activities are on the program.

I shall be going on leave on Friday and yesterday I spent several hours browsing guide books on Rome.

Today I have been very busy marking Italian papers. Yes, I am quite convinced this is my calling in life. The history I am marking is Stage 1 and 2.

In regard to your query on the results of the British election, I think that the new government will do so much more for the working classes than its predecessor, and will also avoid being involved too closely in "other countries'" businesses. However, the ordinary Tommy here, when asked what he thinks of the new government he greatly helped to place in power almost invariably replies, "I don't know what to think yet."

Let's hope I will be home for Christmas!

Alex

Letter No. 145: Wednesday, 15 August, 1945
My sweetest beloved little girl,

About 5.15 this morning, I was awakened by the pealing of the bells of several churches here. Did I need to enquire why they were being rung? I arose, and went to the window. It was still a little dark. The piazza was empty. My constant thought was thanks to God for this goodness. I hoped so much that I would be reunited with you all a little earlier than I had expected previously. But I did not become excited as many others did during the day. I was in the field too long for excitement to affect me.

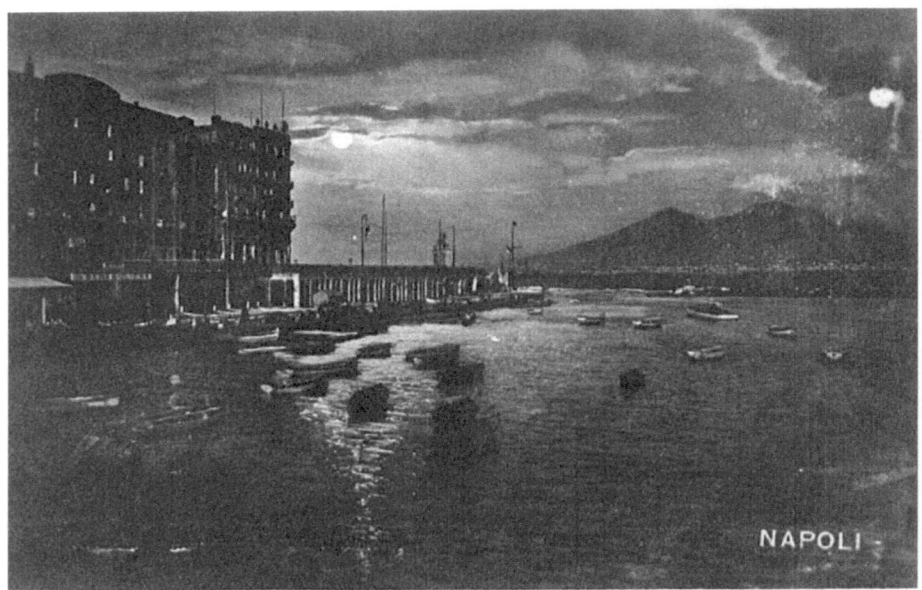

There we took things as they came, whether good or bad. The job of killing and the prospect of being killed turns one into a figurative block of ice. And then, later, the thought came to me that I would be most happy when I doffed my uniform and donned civilian clothes. The treatment I have received in this Division made me think that thought. The fact that I have seen so much service is a questionable honor which I would not offer to any man if I had the position to do so. Thank goodness that the bonds of discipline which have bound me for so long to many whom I despise will soon be loosened.

I shall open the floodgates and release my long stored up thoughts on the aforementioned to you when I return.

I had a swim this afternoon. Tomorrow there is horse racing (without the horses) and a big dinner, which should prove to be a very pleasant function. I leave for Rome early on Friday morning. How keen am I to see that remarkable city.

Alex

Letter No. 146: Tuesday, 21 August, 1945
My sweetest beloved little girl,

We held a big day of celebrations last Thursday the 16th, in honor of the end of the war. There was no program of interest in the morning, but in the afternoon we held a race meeting (without horses, of course, but with dice) in the courtyard of palazzo of Mola di Bari. While there, I thought I might as well start my leave that day.

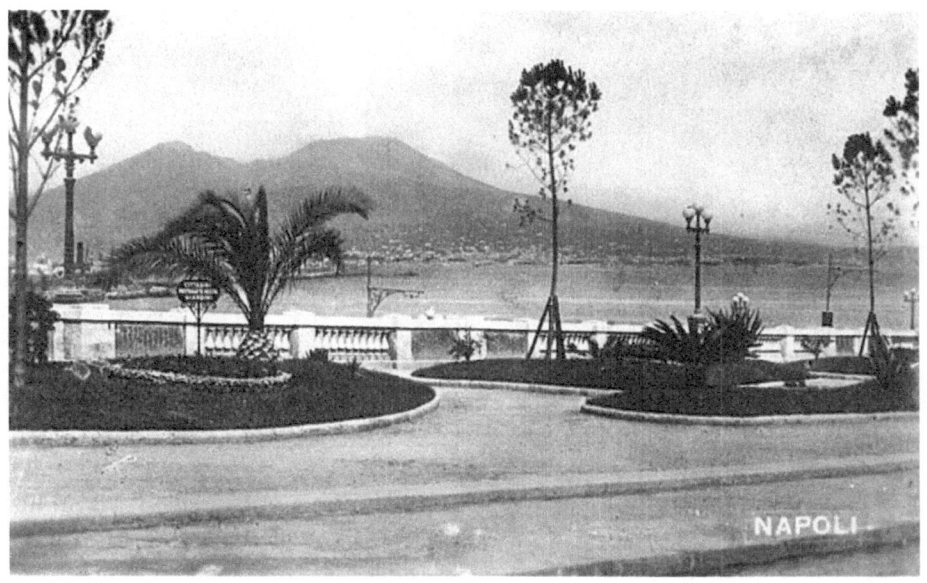

I arrived in Bari in the middle of the afternoon. Some English airmen told me that a truck of theirs would be leaving in the morning for Rome, via Naples. I could go in it. They gave me a bed (and the following morning a breakfast of eggs and bacon). In the evening we went to Monofoli when I saw for a second time, "The Stars Looked Down," a fine film of life set in a mining district in England. It is harvest time for fruit now. The little stalls in the street were loaded with grapes, apples and peaches and outside numerous houses the folk are engaged in removing almonds from their kernels. What patience and perseverance there must be as the piles were large.

The truck was a 3-tonner, and the only passengers were a student and myself. This girl was born in Rome, and spent most of her life there. She spoke good English. We lunched at Foggia, and there we were joined by RAF men going to Rome, and South Africans to Naples, which is about 140 miles west of Foggia.

In Naples, we drove along beautiful tree-lined highways, but what a contrast when we arrived in the port area! It was the nearest resemblance to the backstreets of Cairo I seen since being here. The filthy roads, people, and general atmosphere. Once we had passed these depressing sights, however, there was a big improvement. The Marine Parade around the bay was superb. It stretches for several miles, and is a sight not to be forgotten. I stayed with the Air Force men in the Malcolm Club. You can imagine how tired and dirty I was as we had been on the

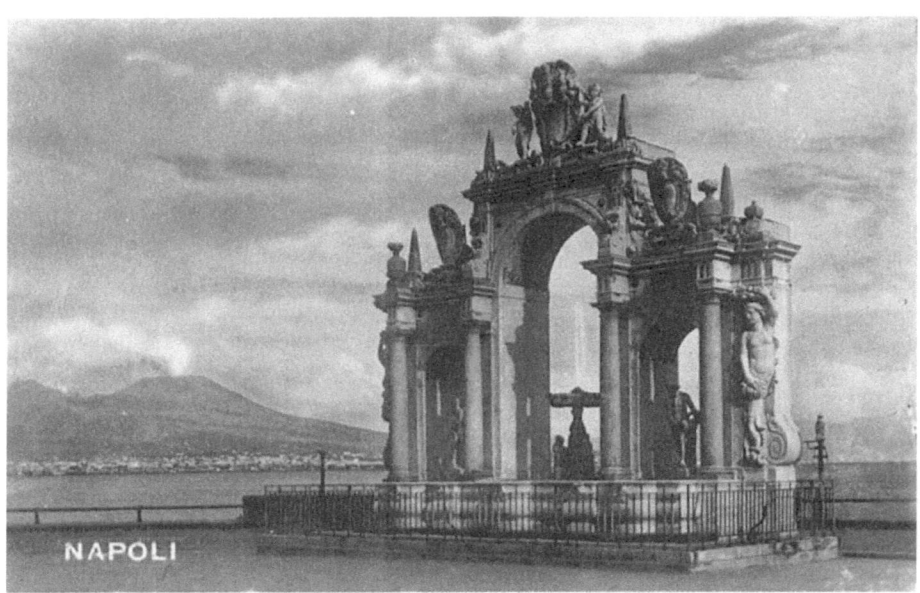

road for the best part of eight hours. However, I was determined to see a little of the city before our departure. Therefore, after dinner, I took a stroll around the Marine Parade into the city. In the distance was Capri, to the left, Vesuvius that billowed forth just enough smoke to show that it was an active volcano. Jutting out into the harbor near the city is Castel del' Ova (of the Egg,) an ancient Norman structure. In the centre of the city, I glanced at the ugly Cathedral, San Francesco di Paola, with an interior design copied from the Pantheon in Rome. The nearby Royal Palace has been turned into a military club. Its facade is uninteresting but for the statues of eight Neapolitan kings. Its interior is really striking. A big double staircase leads up to the apartments. There is a good deal of ornamentation, but I am pleased to say it is not of the glaring type. It was also in this palace that Nelson conducted his famous love affair with Lady Emma Hamilton. There is a really lovely terrace in front of the apartments. An opera was on in the Teatro di San Carlo, but I was told it was not a good one, and thus I did not go. I made enquires with an art dealer in Naples. He told me that much of the good work was still away. Was it necessary for me to stay another day?

Alex

Letter No. 147: Wednesday, 29 August, 1945
My sweetest beloved little girl,

A fortnight has passed since I left for vacation. Here I am back in Mola di Bari once again. When I set off for Rome on the 17th, I had full intention of writing full accounts of the places I had seen while I was there. That good intention came to nought. The letters on Rome will be written as soon as opportunity arises. As expected, I had a large file of papers needing to be marked on my return. The holiday in Rome cost me approximately £20, but that is not a great sum for nine full days in the present conditions with the price of everything so exorbitant.

Now that the war has ended I have no ambitions in regard to the Army provided I am not so placed as to be subject to an annoying type of discipline for any length of time. When are we going home? I wish I could give you some news, but there is none. Let us hope and pray that sufficient ships will be available soon to take us all home. Patience is indeed a virtue, as what is to be gained by one who becomes impatient with the Army?

Keith has written to me and says he hopes to do Assisi and Perugia thoroughly from the art point of view.

Alex

Letter No. 148: Wednesday, 29 August, 1945

My sweetest beloved little girl,

If I had adopted the policy of self advancement, which has brought so much success to many, I would probably have regained my commission long before now. I did not do so as self advertisement is repugnant to my nature. How well do I remember the driving force that came from you when I successfully competed for those open University prizes! My successes then were in great measure due to your constant encouragement. To bring you happiness in every way is my greatest desire.

"Man is born free, but is everywhere in chains."* The truth of this depends entirely on the subject discussed.

Alex

(*from Jean-Jacques Rousseau*)

Letter No. 150: Monday, 3 September, 1945

My sweetest beloved little girl,

I am carrying heavy cases from one part of the ERS to the school. I would prefer to live in Christchurch depending on obtaining a congenial position in the city. If I cannot find a suitable academic post in New Zealand, I would go back to Italy for a year or two, taking the children with me. I would obtain a position as a teacher of English. By living there you would learn the language. So Judy went on a merry-go-round! I agree there is no point in sending more parcels. I keenly await the arrival of tobacco, which is a problem in this unit. I wrote to Vic more than a month ago, but so far I have not received a reply. It should not be long before he is on the way back. Apparently young Ian is a bit of a scamp; Joyce *(Macleod, née Kidd)* is kept busy watching him. I wonder how stern a father is Jock? I learnt from Hilary that your Aunt Clara has lost her power of speech. I should be interested to learn how Bee *(MacCaughan, née Muff)* is progressing with her study of the difficult Russian language. I recall that Harold Williams, a famous linguist, found Russian very diffi-cult even though he lived in Russia and was married to a Russian woman.

I must confess that the people of our country are frightfully parochial. New Zealand has many excellent qualities—the climate is healthy, life is good and simple, and has more equality than in most coun-tries. The big fault is undoubtedly the educational system. I can never be convinced that a person can call himself well educated by spending three to four years at a secondary school, and perhaps a further two or three years at university. A person can still come out dreadfully parochial, see-ing little good in other people's way of life; such a person lacks the poise and accomplishment of an educated foreigner. The air of the old world is catching. In the old world, however, the conditions of the lower orders is appalling, but it is obvious that the middle and upper classes get much more from life than we do.

I won't find it hard to settle down because you, Judy and Paul will be dominating influences. Nor would I find it hard to settle down in Rome or Florence as a lecturer, teacher or newspaper correspondent, but con-ditions of life may be difficult there for some years to come. I had intend-ed answering your mother's letters, but instead I shall type another let-ter about my trip to Rome from Naples. Tell me what Dr Milligan has to say about little Paul, beloved.

Alex

Rome

Letter No. 151: Monday, 3 September, 1945
My sweetest beloved little girl,
Saturday, 18 August 1945.

Yesterday, we made the long, tiring trip from Giovinazzi, north of Bari on the Adriatic to Naples on the Tyrrhenian Sea. The journey in the back of a 3-ton truck was not comfortable. To the west of Foggia is barren land, an area sparsely inhabited. All the farms are the same design; each bearing a number, part of an agriculture scheme introduced by Mussolini. In Naples, I took a stroll around the wonderful Marine Drive, gazed on Vesuvius and Capri in the distance, saw inside the royal palace, now a club for British other ranks. This morning, we set out and took Route 6 for Rome. This road passes through country I know—battered towns of Capua, the mountains of Cassino, through Arce, Frosinone, Valmontone to Rome. At Cassino, the ruins are being demolished, and building has begun. To the right of the monastery is a monument erected by the Poles in honor of their numbers who fell in the grim and bloody assault. We lunched at Arce, Frosinone and Valmontone, which still bear the scars of war. On reaching Rome, I obtained a room in a pension near the Albergo Quirinale (the New Zealand Forces Club).

Sunday, 19 August 1945.

I began my tour at the Quattro Fontane (the Four Fountains). In conjunction with the art division of the Italian Government, the Americans had an excellent idea of placing information boards outside places of historical and art interest. We first passed the Barberini Palace that is entered from the Piazza Barberini. It was completed by the great Bernini

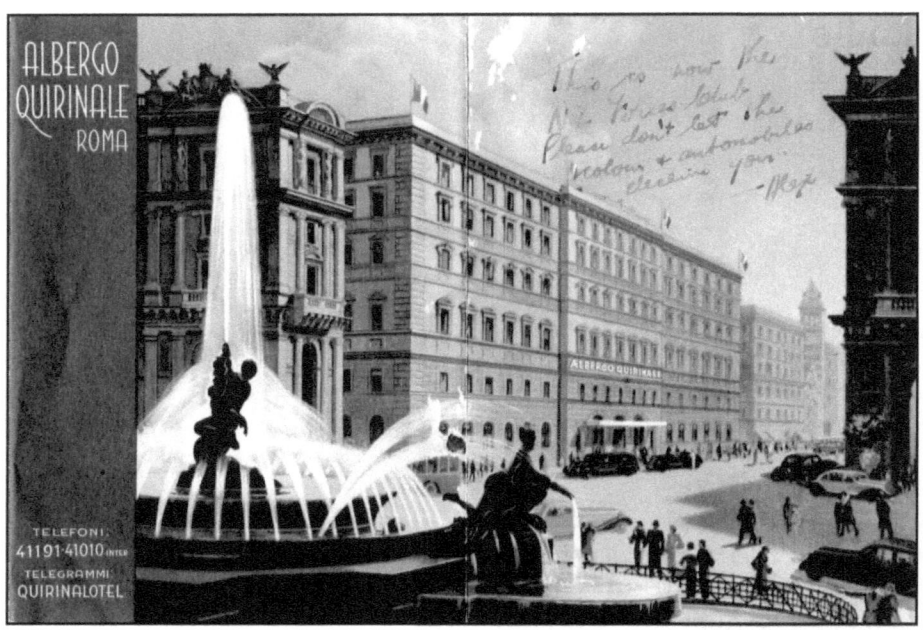

but was not open to the public. It has huge suites, the smallest containing forty rooms and formerly a collection of paintings of Raphael, and others.

Finally, I reached the top of the hill (above the Spanish Steps) on which stands the Church of Trinita dei Monti (Of the Hills). There was a fine Egyptian obelisk in red granite in front of the Church. At the bottom is the Keats-Shelley Memorial House, where Keats died in February, 1821. Fascinating place! It contains a priceless collection of works, mementoes, busts and paintings of the poets. I left the Memorial House and glanced at the Piazza itself. In bygone days, it was the most important square in old Papal Rome. The name "di Spagna" was given to the Steps because the palace of the Spanish ambassador is there.

Alex

Letter No. 152: Tuesday, 4 September, 1945
My sweetest beloved little girl,
Sunday, 19 August 1945.

Before I went on holiday, I planned a visit to the Caffe Greco in Rome. Based on a pamphlet I read in the *caffe* and written in many European languages I learned it was where "Byron, Shelley, Goethe, Keats, Thackeray, Twain, Canova, Bizet, Berlioz, Wagner, Leopardi were "constant habitués." The interior decorations of the *caffe* are hideous by modern standards.

Alex

Letter No. 153: Thursday, 6 September, 1945
My sweetest beloved little girl,
Sunday, 19 August 1945.

This evening I went to hear Verdi's "Aida" at the Baths of Caracalla, a tremendous stage show. The cast is huge, but the music did not have a great appeal to me. I thought there was far too much pomp.

Monday, 20 August 1945.

We arrived at the Vatican, and when the party went off to inspect the Museums, I made my way to the entrance of the picture gallery. The doors were closed. I saw a custodian and told him in Italian that I would be leaving Italy forever and had only come to Rome for one purpose—to see the priceless collection of paintings. My tale of woe was successful, and after glancing around to see that no one observed him, he opened the door and locked me inside. I was alone with all those wonderful paintings.

The gallery itself has been excellently conceived. There is the natural light from above. Also the pictures are arranged in chronological order so that the visitor can study the gradual evolution and progress of art. From the first hall—that of the Byzantines and Primitives—one passes to the Hall of Giotto, where I saw some remarkable 13th and early 14th century paintings of religious subjects by Giotto and others. Hall No.3 is dedicated to Fra Angelico, the greatest of the religious painters. I was particularly interested in the early works of Benozzo Gozzoli there, because I possess four reproductions of his frescoes I found in the Medici-Riccardi Palace in Florence. I moved on from this point to works from the second half of the 15th century—the Hall of Melozzo de Forli. There I saw the series of "Musical Angels," some of them are of truly marvelous beauty. The angels are what angels should look like.

One wall is occupied by a tremendous tapestry from the town of Tournai in Belgium. In the Hall No. 7, I was delighted with the works of Pinturicchio whose freshness and color in the frescoes in the library of the Cathedral of Siena I shall always remember. Then I came to the Hall of Raphael. I felt a thrill of pride to be alone there since before me were some of the most celebrated pictures in the world, all of which you will have seen in prints.

"The Coronation of the Madonna" was the first of these great compositions, which Raphael painted in 1502 when he was just nineteen while he still under the influence of his master, Perugino. In the lower part of the painting, that is, on Earth, you see the Apostles finding the coffin of the Virgin empty of Her body and full of flowers; above the Apostles, the

TEATRO REALE DELL'OPERA

TERME DI CARACALLA

Alexander Brotherton

AIDA
DI
GIUSEPPE VERDI

at Rome Sunday 19th August 1945

ESTATE MUSICALE ROMANA
LUGLIO - AGOSTO 1945

Virgin is being crowned in Heaven among the glory of cherubs and angels. Raphael's "The Madonna of Foligno" was a commission by a count who had it painted to fulfill a vow he made following a narrow escape from the explosion of a bomb during the siege of Foligno. In this picture, we observe the new conception of religious painting. The Virgin is no longer on the earth familiarly seated among the saints, but instead has come down from on high in a glory of angels on a throne of clouds while below the saints contemplate and worship. Between these two paintings is his "Transfiguration." It was his last work and was left uncompleted when he died in 1520. What can I say about it? I must quote here: "In the upper part, the great painter has represented "The Transfiguration of our Lord on Mount Tabor in the presence of the Three Apostles." High up in the centre the Savior is seen ascending to Heaven. From his face and garments emanates a brilliant radiance of celestial light which also envelops Moses and Elias and dazzling the Three Apostles who are sheltering their eyes from the unbearable brilliance. The lower part represents the power of Christ over the infernal spirits.

Alex

Letter No. 154: Thursday, 6 September, 1945
My sweetest beloved little girl,
Monday, 20 August 1945.

At this stage of the tour, I had reached Raphael's "The Transfiguration." As I said previously, the lower part of this great picture represents the power of Christ over the infernal spirits. I could not pull myself from it. Along with the paintings, the hall also contains the tapestries of Raphael, which were originally created for the lower walls of the Sistine Chapel. The cartoons were designed by Raphael and then transformed into textiles in Flanders by Willem Van Aelst, the most celebrated Flemish artist in this kind of work. I must go through again, I said to myself. I shall go there again if there is an opportunity as I had not seen much of the Vatican. I have still to see hundreds of its wonderful pieces—superb Greek and Roman sculptures, and paintings too. Again I am at a loss for words. Will I ever forget the Crouching Aphrodite, Laocoon and his Sons, the Apollo Belvedere, the Aphrodite of Knidos, and the Apoxyomenos? Then I came to the four Raphael Rooms (In Italian: *Stanze di Raffaello*), with work after work of the master on religious and historical subjects.

I had heard so much about the Sistine Chapel. When in was in Rome for a day in August 1944, this wonderful place was closed. It is noted that Pope Sixtus and his successors did all they could to obtain works of the most renowned Italian painters. The chapel thus became a kind of arena for the display of pictorial art where the greatest masters of Italy competed for the palm of victory—Signorelli, Botticelli, Ghirlandaio, Pinturicchio, Rosselli, Perugino, plus we can add two princes of art, Michelangelo and Raphael. We can assert that no other building in the world has had so many men of genius working together on its decoration.

There was not much of the afternoon left for visiting, but there is San Pietro in Vincoli (in Chains), a church renowned for one truly great treasure, Michelangelo's "Moses." I went there, and again, I am at a loss for words. Nearby is the Mamertime Prison, the earliest and best preserved monument in Rome.

Finally, for the day, I went to the Palace of the Conservators to which some of most famous sculptures of the Capitoline Museums have been removed. There I saw "The Dying Gaul," "The Venus of the Capitol," and some great Greek pieces. Reading of the great works and seeing prints of them are colorless compared with the actual seeing of them. No true conception of their greatness, their genius, can be gained by any other means. One feels so puny in the company of the work of the masters—such inspiration, such beauty.

Alex

Letter No. 155: Friday, 7 September, 1945
My sweetest beloved little girl,
Tuesday, 21st August.
My first stop this morning was at two of the four patriarchal churches of Rome—Santa Maria Maggiore, and San Giovanni in Laterano. Santa Maria is a lovely church. Competent critics assert that it offers all the characteristics of a pure classic Roman building. Both walls of the nave are decorated with a series of mosaics illustrating biblical history and the development of Christianity. Here is an expert opinion: "They surpass all the other mosaics of Rome for grace of composition and perfection of execution and are a wonderful monument of the splendor of the Roman art of mosaic." Then I saw the ceiling, gilded with the first gold brought to Europe by Columbus. One would have thought that the mortal remains of the great Bernini—sculptor, architect, painter, musician, actor, writer of comedies—would rest in a magnificent tomb. But not so. He lies beneath a slab on the floor bearing the simple inscription—"Familia Bernini." His works are his monument—imperishable. I walked along the tree-lined street to St John's Square (*Piazza San Giovanni*.) In its centre is another of those Egyptian obelisks—this one famous for it is the largest and most ancient in the world. It was originally erected at Thebes by Ramses six-

teen centuries before Christ and brought to Rome by the son of Constantine. First, I saw the Baptistery at St John's."Urbis et Orbis" is the title given to St John's for it is said to be the first Christian church opened to the public and the first consecrated to Christ, then I saw the cloister. I have visited many cloisters in various churches in various parts of this fair country. Although it does not compare with those wonderful ones in Florence and Ravenna, the cloister of St John's is still among the very best.

Finally, I viewed Antonio Montauti's masterpiece in marble, "The Descent from the Cross," or "La Pieta" in the crypt of the Corsini Chapel. The church also houses an interesting picture, Giotto's, "Pope Boniface VIII between Two Cardinals, announcing the Jubilee of 1300." Although these early works do not possess the wonderful, captivating charm of the later Renaissance work, one must remember that Giotto and other early masters sowed the seed of that beautiful flower—the Renaissance. I crossed the square to the Scala Santa (*Holy Steps*)—one of the types of religious shrines which do not appeal to me.

There was a trip planned for the afternoon to the Colosseum, the Catacomb of Callixtus, and to St Paul's Church. I decided to go. I dislike guided tours. I much prefer to go to a place either by myself, or with a friend, and take time to see the art thoroughly. In a guided tour, one is rushed from one place to another, and thus one's impressions become more jumbled. But in this case, there was no option. I had no desire to walk to the Catacombs and to St Paul's as they are many miles from the city, and I had no intention of paying a taxi man 5 or £6 to transport me there and back.

Alex

Letter No. 156: 7 September, 1945
My sweetest beloved little girl,
Tuesday, 21 August1945
After lunch, we set off in a 3-ton truck for the Coliseum. Our guide was good, and took us to the spot from which we could view all that was worth viewing. Historically and architecturally, the Coliseum is of great interest, but I myself see little beauty in the huge mass of brick and mortar. When I visited the Roman ruins a year ago, my enthusiasm was great, but since then my views have changed. In that period, I have seen so much of beauty—in Florence, in Ravenna, in Venice, and in Siena. Thus, I could not warm to the Coliseum. We came to the Catacomb of St Callixtus. Like many places, the Catacomb has been much commercialized. There are books, pamphlets in several languages, souvenirs for sale, and also a photographer who takes a photograph before one goes in.

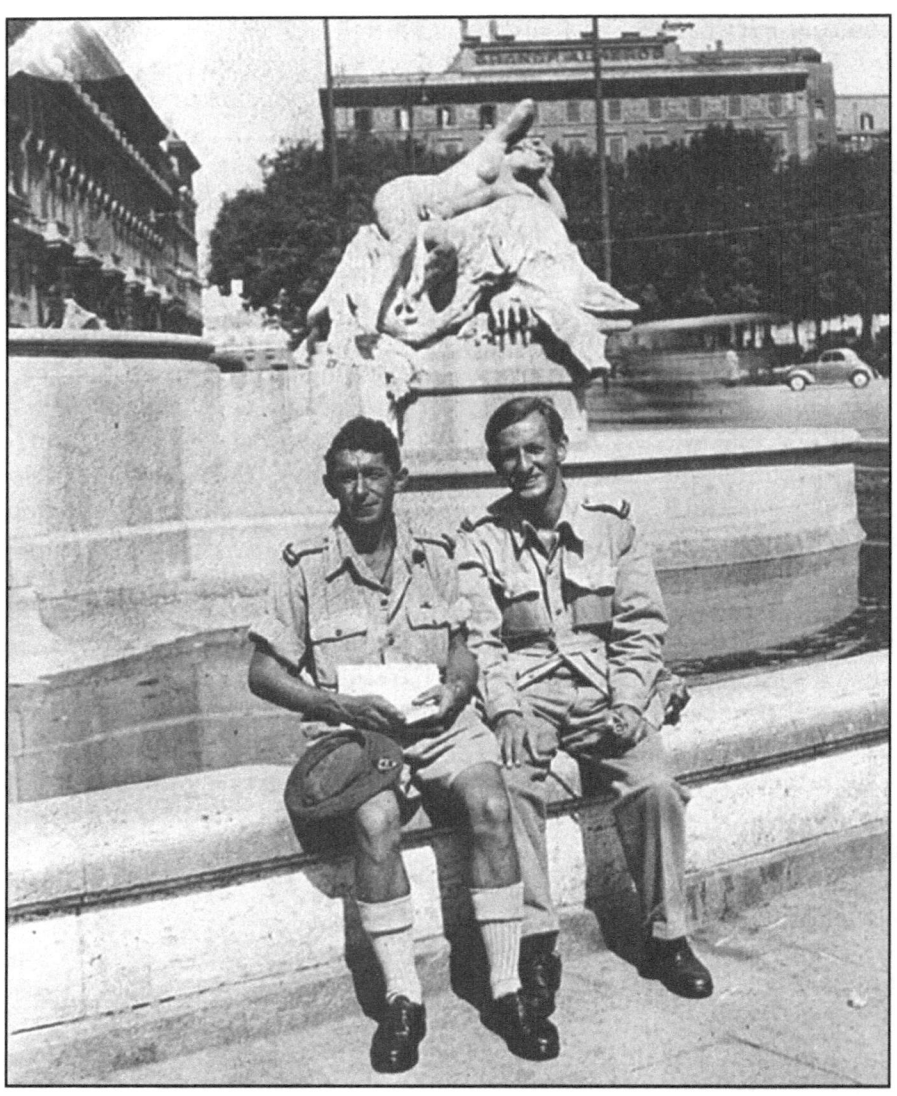

On leave, presumably in Rome, with an unknown companion

From the Catacomb, we went to the lovely modern church of St Paul (*San Paolo fuori le Mura, St. Pauls Outside the Wall*) I say "modern" because the original church was destroyed by fire about 120 years ago. In its place was erected the present lovely edifice. The marble work to be found in the church is a never-to-be-forgotten sight. It is so rich, so harmonious, stately and serene. All around the nave and the transept are portraits of the popes. We passed to the cloister, similar to that of St John's, but not so beautiful because it has less shrubbery. What a pity that commercialization has penetrated even this beautiful place.

I saw my second opera that night. Again, it was performed at the Baths of Caracalla. What a treat it was for me to hear Beniamino Gigli, and other leading opera stars sing in Amilcare Ponchielli's lovely work, "La Gioconda." It has great appeal.

Alex

Letter No. 157: Friday, 7 September, 1945
My sweetest beloved little girl,
Wednesday, 22nd August, 1945.

I felt tired when I awoke because, again, the opera finished very late. An Australian friend and I went for a stroll. We decided to first visit the Church of the Capuchins, noted principally for its cemetery. This cemetery is gruesomely decorated with the skulls and skeletons of the four thousand monks from the monastery who died there, beginning in the 17th century down to 1870. Beginning from that year, burial inside the city was prohibited and discontinued also in this cemetery. A more hideous sight, I have never seen.

We then went to Il Gesù, the principal church of the Jesuit Order. The church is literally one mass of rare marble, and its chapel of San Ignazio (*St Ignatius)* perhaps the richest that I have ever seen. We then went and saw an exhibition of Venetian art at the Palazzo Venezia. The exhibition was divided into two parts: firstly, pictures of the Venetian School drawn from State Galleries in Venice, Naples, Milan, Ancona, Viterbo, Florence, Padua and Lazio; and secondly, works of art drawn from private collections. In this exhibition, the paintings were also arranged chronologically—the only reasonable method, in my opinion. Since we found it impossible to complete our inspection before lunch, I returned alone in the afternoon and began all over again. It was a wonderful collection, but I shall mention one picture only, the "Fantastic Roman Landscape" by Bernardo Bellotto (1720-1780), belonging to the Albertini collection in Rome. It will be always vivid in my mind. I would pay several pounds to possess a good reproduction of it. So natural, so fresh, so vivacious. On the right of the painting are fantastic ruins the shadows of which fall onto the home of the Italian peasant. There is the ever-so-typical scene of life—the peasant women, the children, the animals in the yard, the rubbish. It is delightful.

In the evening, another Kiwi and I went to an open-air performance of Wagner's music in the Basilica di Massenzio. The Basilica itself is just another ruin, but an ideal spot for such a gathering. After the performance had begun, I discovered I had lost my wallet containing about £35 in Italian, English, Egyptian and Australian money. I went into a cold sweat. I did not hear the sublime strains of Wagner. Instead, I went to the Italian police. They were very sympathetic. I did not lose hope. The intermission came. A plain-clothed detective accompanied me to the parts of the theatre where I had trod previously. He started a whispering campaign among the audience in those areas. The performance started again. But still no wallet. I went to the police again. They had found it near one of the walls! How fortunate I was! I will never forget the Wagnerian concert at the Basilica di Massenzio—never!

Alex

Letter No. 158: Friday, 7 September, 1945
My sweetest beloved little girl,
Thursday, 23rd August 1945

This morning another chap in the club asked if I would care to accompany him with two Italian university students, Anna and Maria, on a visit to the Castel Sant'Angelo. We took one of the *circolare* trams that run round the city to the river Tiber. We entered the famous castle. The castle was built by the Emperor Hadrian (130-135 AD) after his return from his travels throughout the empire. In the course of about eighteen centuries, the castle has been the tomb of emperors, the place for the execution of popes, eminent personages and lately a barracks and museum. About the beginning of the 14th century, the papal residence was removed from the Lateran to the Vatican. There is a host of things to be seen in the castle, among many other things, a most interesting armory, with the weapons being arranged in chronological order to reveal to the visitor the "development" of weapons of war.

Friday, 24 August 1945

Our university friends were again our guides today. We started at St Mary of theAngels (*Santa Maria degli Angeli e dei Martiri,*) which is very close to the club. This church is, in fact, the best preserved hall of Diocletian's Baths, that was converted into a church by Michelangelo. This was the last of the many great works of his long and glorious career. He was then 88 years of age. The church contains pictures formerly in St Peter's. From a scientific point of view the church of interest as it contains the meridian line that fixes the date of Easter, a date that was routinely miscalculated. The meridian line was traced by Francesco Bianchini, the famous mathematician and astronomer, by order of Pope Clement XI in 1701.

We then went to view the exhibition at the Borghese Gallery, which I had seen previously, but my friends had not. In the evening, I went to "Mayerling," with Charles Boyer and Danielle Darrieux, which I first saw in New Zealand some years ago. Then the sound was in French, but this time it was Italian. Following the film was a variety show I greatly enjoyed. The peculiar aspect of the entertainment was this; I could easily follow the living word, as in the variety show, but found it extremely difficult to follow a great deal of the dialogue in the film. The more Italian films I see, the more attuned my ear will become to the voice of the screen.

Alex

Letter No. 159: Friday, 7 September, 1945
My sweetest beloved little girl,
Saturday, 25th August 1945
This is my second-to-last day in Rome for I was due to leave on my return journey to the south early on Monday morning. I went carefully through my guide book. I knew, of course, that there were still a hundred and one places I could see, but I could at least congratulate myself that I had seen the most important. Therefore, I had an easy day. There is a firm in Rome named "Parasio," which turns out most artistic reproductions in oils of the great masterpieces. I went there. It was a very happy visit. I bought one for myself and one for another soldier who was unable to go there. Reproductions of the pictures I desired most were not procurable, unfortunately.

Sunday, 26th August 1945.
I resolved that I must see St Peter's today. What more fitting place could one visit for one's final day in Rome! First, I went to the Piazza del Popolo, which is the most important square in Rome. The centre is decorated with four fountains with four Egyptian lions throwing water into basins. Above the fountains arise one of the largest obelisks in the world (118 feet high). It was originally erected at Heliopolis in ancient Egypt fourteen centuries before Christ and was brought to Rome by Augustus (23 BC) to decorate the Circus Maximus. Before I took the *circolare* tram to St Peter's, I inspected Santa Maria del Popolo, a church not listed in my guide book, but well worth the visit for in it I found some of Pinturicchio's colorful works along with paintings by other masters.

Once again, I was at St Peter's. It was my first visit for a year, but my memory of its grandeur and beauty did not fail me. You have received the books—illustrated and others—which I posted to you a year ago. If you glance through them, you will see in illustration what I saw in reality. "La

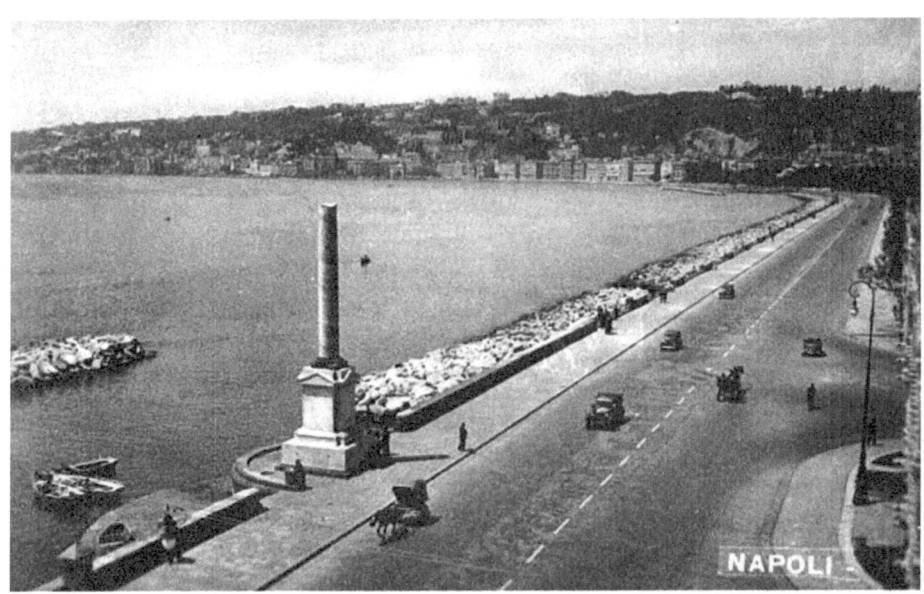

Pieta" of Michelangelo was so wonderful that I lingered before it. No illustration of it—no matter how finely executed—conveys anything of its sublime beauty. My feelings were very mixed. I was at once proud that I had the honor to see this wonderful achievement, yet I had to go away from it and from all those other wonderful works which will remain indelible in my memory. Later on, I shall write another letter on Rome, not of historical art, but on the Rome of everyday things. That will interest you, I am sure.

Monday, 27 August, 1945.

The journey home was uneventful. We reached Naples in the early evening, and stayed overnight at a British Army Transit Camp in a park above the city called Capodimonte (Top of the Mountain). I went to town for an hour or two, but was pleased to get to bed after our hundred and fifty mile trip that day. The following morning, we set off for Foggia, and were in Bari—dirty and uninteresting Bari—once again in the mid-afternoon. So ended my holiday.

Rome enchanted me as did Florence, but it is not possible to compare the two cities. Florence's beauty is Florence's; Rome's is Rome's. This is the fairest comparison. Have I bored you with detail? I have made my letters full because I desire to have a complete record of my visit. In view of that will you please forgive me!

Alex

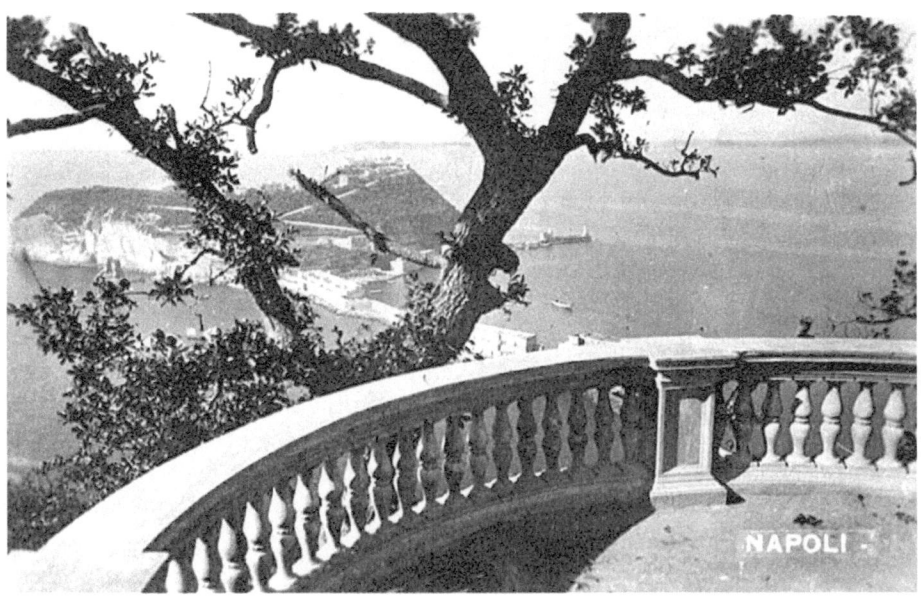

Letter No. 160: Wednesday, 12 September, 1945

My sweetest beloved little girl,

Keith wrote to me a few days ago and tells me he went to Siena recently, and thoroughly enjoyed the visit. That was my experience when I went there more than a year ago. There is little news from here. Freyberg has given us a message that he hopes to be able to tell us something about the future very soon.

The staff of ERS grows. About eighty chaps have joined in the last fortnight.

I had a letter from Vic a few days ago. He described how he got to see Algiers and Athens on the way to Egypt. It shouldn't be long before he is on his way home. I doubt if I will be home for Xmas.

Alex

Letter No. 163:

40455 Cpl. A.G. Protheroe
Div. Attachment
ERS   2NZEF
CMF (*Central Mediterranean Force*)
Monday, 1st October, 1945

My sweetest beloved little girl,

This is the promised letter on Chianciano. It is a famous little place— famous because of its healing waters for sufferers from *fegato* (liver) trouble and heart ailments. It lies in the beautiful hills of Tuscany. From my window facing towards the west, my eye takes in the deep blue hills bordering Lake Trasimeno, the numerous clumps of oaks, the great variety of trees, which give this rolling land so gentle and undisturbed air. From here I can see the haystacks, the farmhouses, the towers of distant villages, the now dry pasture; and just in front of me—about two kilometers away—is the *paese* (*village*) of Chianciano, a drab, red-brown cluster of houses, standing on its little hill. To the southwest, and away in the distance behind the hills, I catch the white tops of the Apennine peaks; I see those little strips of blue-white water, and above the sky is, to quote Dante, the "dolce color d'oriental *zaffiro*." I am in a land of tranquility, of calm, of quiet.

Chianciano (pronounced Kiahn-shahno) is an Italian spa of most ancient repute. It has been famous since the ninth century B.C. as one of the attractions of King Porsenna's country—the country of Etruria. "What is it actually like?" you might ask. It is well for me to differentiate between Chianciano—the *paese*—which can be seen in a thousand other places in Italy, and the Bagni (or the baths) di Chianciano, the spa. The latter is exclusive. Here one does not find the dirty little stone homes of the peasants, the pigs, the cats and the dogs, and the fowls running all over the place, the narrow cobbled streets...and all those other things characteristic of an Italian village. Instead one finds a large number of luxurious hotels and pensions (there are about sixty all told) to which the wealthy of Italy come, (and before the war) those of France and Germany came to take the cure. I cannot believe that all who come are here for the cure. Perhaps it is the prospect of a quiet holiday—a rest—that has been the motive of some? There are many Milanese, Romans, Florentines, Venetians, Neapolitans...counts and countesses, barons and baronesses, wealthy landowners, business people—the professional classes. Where they stay is governed by their means, for the cost of living is high, very high. I have been told that a stay of three weeks at the best hotel, with a generous admixture of social life, might cost up to sixty thousand lire (£150)! The visitors have meat every day—a luxury these days—but there is no butter. Those from the south do not miss butter, but the Milanese do. I will not dwell on the properties of the waters, but must say something on the Terme Sillene spring. I have been there twice for a bath. One is conducted to a beautiful, clean bathroom of shining white tiles. The bath is half sunk in the floor. There are numerous towels, a chair and a footrest, a bed on which one can receive a massage...in fact, it is a perfect bathroom. The naturally-heated water, at 101.3° Fahrenheit, gushes in and flows continuously as provision has been made for overflow holes at the top of the bath. What a most pleasant sensation I experienced as I lay for the best part of a half an hour! And when I pressed the bell, an attendant came immediately with a big hot towel in which he swathed me. For the pleasure of such a bath I paid 3 shillings and 9 pence (3/9). (For civilians, 7/6.)

For the last three weeks there has been a dance every evening in the festival hall. It is a magnificent place—a big domed building with a paved floor. The last dance was held last night. The orchestra came from Rome —a really good orchestra of professionals. Some nights one had to pay to enter (50 lire, or 2/6), but on others it was free. The dancers and the watchers arrived between 9 and 10 p.m., and the dance ended at midnight or soon after. One had to pay an exorbitant price for drinks—four shillings for Vermouth, and five shillings for a nip of anything else. I attended these dances on several occasions. I was very fortunate to meet there a party of people who had come from the Viterbi-Lake Bolsena area to take the cure. (To be continued).

Alex

The Two Letters of Celeste Cussoni

Grotte di Castro
10 October, 1945

Alessandro,

This morning I received your letter. You can't imagine how much pleasure I felt knowing that Alessandro still remembers Celeste.

As soon as it arrived here at Grotte, I felt the desire to write to you, also because I wanted to explain to you our sudden departure; but I found myself without your address. Therefore, you can imagine how thrilled I was this morning to receive your letter with your address.

I returned home (as you say) to my children who were waiting for me. However, I think often, and with great nostalgia, of the lovely hours spent together, of the evenings at the dances, and of the walks back after the dance.

Do you remember all this too? You tell me that now around seventy student/soldiers have arrived who are preparing for exams, therefore you'll have a lot of work to do teaching them. However, this is what you really like doing.

Have you heard from the young lady in Rome? Must you always reply to all her letters? When will you return to Rome?

I still don't know when I'll get to Rome. However, if you were able to come, I'd l always be happy for you to visit. Even if you visit close to Grotte, it would be such a pleasure for me to see you again.

I'll leave you now because my children are calling me, but if you have a free moment please drop me a line again.

My very best wishes,
Celeste Cussoni

Grotte di Castro
31 December, 1945

Dearest Alex,

Please excuse me for not having replied sooner, but when your letter arrived I was in Rome. I have just returned over these past days to spend Christmas with my dear ones. This morning I received your postcard with your greetings, and you won't believe how thrilled I was to know that Alessandro still remembers Celeste. I'm immensely sorry, however, that you must return to New Zealand because we'll be unable to see each other and I would have loved to do so.

You say that you'll return. Is this true? If it were possible, don't forget my address because I really would love to see you again.

I too remember the six days that we spent together at Chianciano. The dances and the walks we took in the moonlight, days that will never ever return again. In another year, I must return to Chianciano, with who knows how much nostalgia thinking of you and of the lovely hours we spent together.

When you'll have returned to your homeland will you still think of me? Will you write sometimes? I shall so appreciate your letters. You will tell me everything new that has happened (in your absence) and you'll tell me about your children.

My children are well and they are growing up strong and healthy; this for me is a great satisfaction and joy, but I feel so alone. I feel so much the need for a person who loves me and shares with me their joys and sorrows.

How sad it is to lose a person for whom one feels so much affection and to whom one is connected by children. But let's not speak of such sad things! I send you in return my best and most affectionate wishes for the New Year and a happy return to your homeland and for everything you wish to do there.

I will always appreciate receiving your letters.

Best wishes and I wish you every good thing.

Celeste

Letter No 186: Saturday, 12 January, 1946
Onboard HMT "Orion" Sergeant A.G. Protheroe

My sweetest beloved little girl,

We expect to arrive at Port Said tomorrow morning and thus I am taking this opportunity to type this letter to you before we reach port.

The forty-six hundred of us left Taranto at 4 p.m. on Thursday. Keith and I, and the rest of the personnel of Group 1 at Advance Base, embarked on Wednesday and the remaining groups the following day. The day was perfect for our departure; I'll never forget the calmness of the sea, the distant prospect of Taranto as we steamed away, and the wonderful sunset over Calabria. The sea hasn't played any pranks to date.

The sergeants and staff sergeants are quartered with and dine with the ORS in the very, very crowded mess decks. But this time, unlike the voyage on the 'Mooltan,' the port holes are open, and there are none of those dreadful blackouts which kept out the air and prevented one smoking.

I am on the editorial staff of the *Orion Oracle* being produced by Les Hobbs and myself, with the help of artists and other chaps.

We are attached to ERS, which is running an excellent library service and other forms of entertainment for the troops. Soon we shall come to the tropics and then I trust I will be able to rid myself of a beastly cold, which I contracted soon after I came onboard.

I won't ask you any questions, my dear. There is no point in my doing so, as I would be home before any letter of yours could reach me. Today is the second anniversary of my departure from New Zealand. The time seems longer. Now, God be thanked, I am on my way home to you, our July and our little boy Paul. I wonder if he will be walking by the time I see him for the first time?

I am sending the three of you my dear devotion and deepest love

Ever your loving, Alex

P.S. Tell Mother I am on the way home.

THIS IS THE LAST EXISTING LETTER

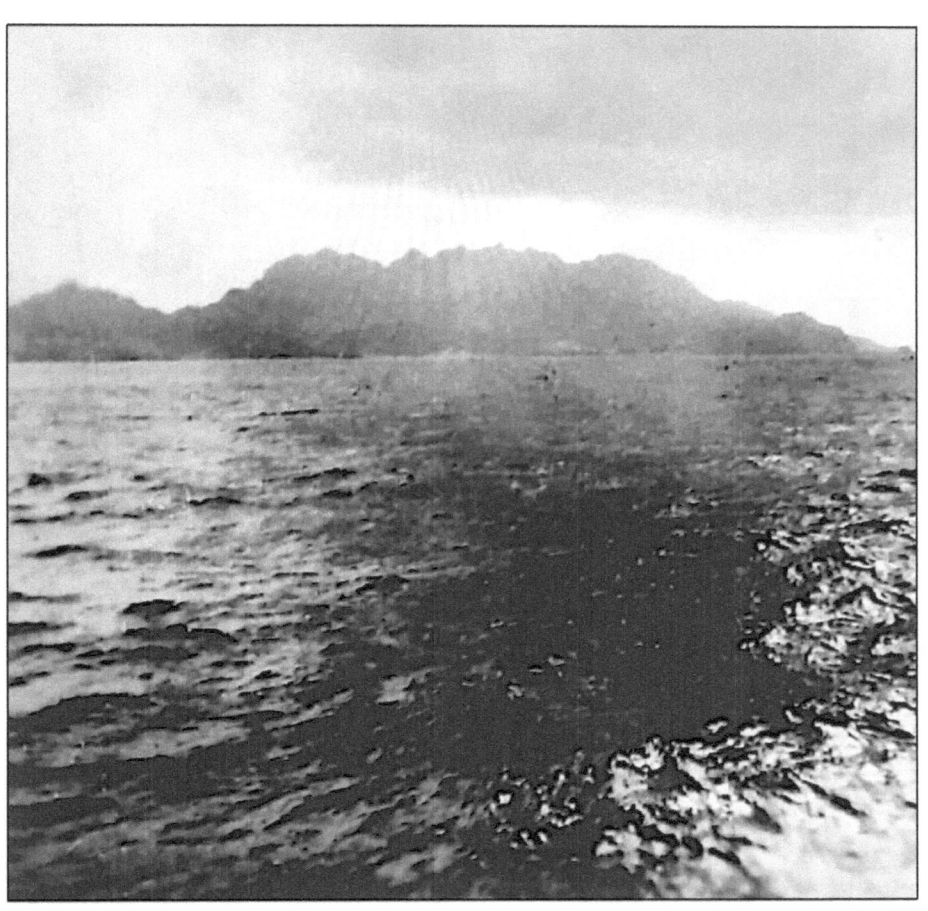

Going home

Afterword

F inally, after the long delay in Italy, Alex reached New Zealand shores early in 1946. It took until 20 April for him to be officially demobilized. At first, while they were finding their feet, the now expanded family—Alex, Margaret, Judy and Paul—stayed with his in-laws, Don and Nellie Macleod, at their Whareora Terrace residence in the Cashmere Hills of Christchurch. Since he had been awarded a pass in English II by the War Concessions Committee of the University in 1940, and while still in Italy in 1945 had, by passing History III, completed his BA, he was able to reenter Canterbury University College for his Master's degree immediately upon returning. By the end of the year, with his course work done, his finals completed and his thesis on the history of the New Zealand Broadcasting Service submitted, he had done enough to graduate, and so only a year after returning from war—in February, 1947 —he was ready to move forward with a Master's in History with Second-Class Honors under his belt.

Meantime, on 30 October, 1946, while he was still working on his degree, an ad in the paper caught his eye. It must have jumped out at him, for it seemed perfectly suited to his skills and interests. We still have the letter from the War History Branch in which they offered him a researcher's position, dated December 24, 1946. At first, there was a mix-up. It was lucky for Alex that the letter with the offer arrived when it did, as initially it was sent to their Christchurch address after the family had already moved north to 75 Epuni Street, Wellington. But arrive it did, just in time it seems—on 15 January—so that by 20 January, 1947, having accepted the terms of employment, he was ready to start, even though he

WAR HISTORY BRANCH, Internal Affairs Dept., Wellington.—Sub-Editor: Successful applicant will be required to carry out sub-editorial duties connected with the publication of unit histories and a popular war history. Applicants should have served with the armed forces, and have experience in journalism or publishing. Commencing salary from £485 to £560 according to qualifications and experience. Appointment to permanent staff. RESEARCH ASSISTANTS: Successful applicants will be required to undertake research work for either service or civilian sections of the war history. Applicants for the service positions should have had considerable experience in the armed forces, at home and overseas. Academic qualifications in history desirable, though not essential. Salary up to £610 p.a., according to qualifications and experience, and the responsibility of duties to which successful applicants are assigned. Appointments to permanent staff. 4922

considered the starting salary of £435 p.a. subpar, which led him to apply for a review almost immediately after his degree was conferred—on February 26—although it is unclear whether he was ever awarded a raise.

Wellington was a different place then. It was a humbler, more parochial city, its vitality squeezed by postwar scarcities, and by an atmosphere stifled by a pervasive cultural conservatism. It had none of the cosmopolitan atmosphere he seen in Rome, Florence, and even in Trieste, and that must have been a shock at first. Still, Alex must have taken to the new job with relish, and being home with his family in a safe and orderly city must have more than compensated for being deprived of Italy's artistic and cultural patrimony. Luckily, the offices of the War History Branch, located just off Courtenay Place, were close to their Epuni Street flat—just a short tram ride away—and you could imagine him on the tram (Sadly, they are gone now!) hanging onto a strap as it rattled down the windy streets to his office. How he must have enjoyed working with the other veterans on a subject so fresh in his mind, seeing the job as a just reward for all his years of intellectual self-discipline, this despite him being involved in an unfortunate fall onto a closed window that resulted in severe lacerations and broken glass in his hand.

During its tenure, the War History Branch published some fifty volumes encompassing all aspects of New Zealand's war effort. We grew up with many of them, their red spines occupying pride of place on the family bookshelves. And there were other reminders of his service. The Renaissance prints he brought back decorated our walls. I particularly remember the framed prints taken from a Benozzo Gozzoli fresco he spoke of in his letters from Rome. My wife Deborah, and I were fortunate enough to accidentally discover the originals in Florence in the Medici-Riccardi Palace a few years back. And then there was his second lieutenant's hat that we boys would sport around the house for fun. Recently, I learned that the old kit bags filled with gear that he stowed away were possibly being held just in case he was called up in an emergency. We had no idea that he was not officially freed from all military obligations until 1958.

But then, he knew from the beginning that the war histories job, by its very nature, would be temporary. It would end when all the histories were completed. Even during his first year there, he pondered over what Plan B might be. At first, he resurrected his dream from Italy—that of studying in England. In July, 1947, he applied for a bursary from the War Concessions Committee to attend the Honour School of Modern History at Oxford University to study the constitutional relationship between Britain and the Commonwealth, hoping to parlay that particular knowledge set in a government job, or in academia. Again, it was a bridge too far, so in March, 1949, he chose instead to apply for law school. This brings us back to the letter he sent to the Registrar of Victoria University that was a part of his application where he asked for an exemption from the Latin prerequisite.

He began attending Victoria University part-time. His entry into law school coincided with the move to 24 Milne Crescent, Taita, a state house located on the outer edge of the Hutt Valley, and a train ride from the city center and the University campus. Financially, these years must have been hard, especially with an extra mouth to feed after a third child, Simon, was born in December, 1950. Around 1952, the family moved back into Wellington to yet another state house—107 Sunshine Avenue, Karori—where Guy was born in 1960.

Alex officially graduated with his LLB in May, 1955, and it was then that he began the career that occupied him for the rest of his working life. His first position was as a partner in a two-man firm with legal offices in an old industrial suburb, the seaside town of Petone on the north shore of Wellington Harbour. In those days, I remember visiting his gloomy office at the back of a single-story Victorian storefront, and him using the crank to start the old Morris 8 on frosty mornings to make it to the office in time.

From there, he decided to branch out on his own, and for most of his career, he was a sole practitioner—A.G. Protheroe, Barrister and Solicitor—with offices in Lower Hutt in a more modern high-rise. In the late 1960s, the family moved to Wadestown, a more mature inner city suburb with harbor views. After a long, successful career, and shortly before retirement, he brought in a partner, but then the partnership was dissolved when he sold his business prior to retirement. He was appointed Coroner for the City of Wellington, which in New Zealand is a legal position, not a medical one. He held this position until his final retirement.

But it was not all smooth sailing. Sadly, in 1957, tragedy struck. After a long illness, Judith died. She was only fourteen. It was a blow from which Alex and Margaret never fully recovered. Sadly, Alex himself died in August 1988, and Margaret the following year. Two sons, Paul and Guy, live in New Zealand, while Simon lives in the United States.

Recollections about Alex as a father are complex, and this is not the place to tackle such a subject in depth. Suffice to say, like many of his generation, he was loyal and dedicated family man, a man of integrity who worked hard for his family and took his responsibilities seriously. How often do we remember him pounding out correspondence on the old Remington late at night working some case or another. As a barrister, he was often in the Magistrate's court defending a wide range of clients. Only once do I recall seeing him in his wig before a judge, although he often appeared in the higher court. Those cases must have challenged him.

But then, we boys mostly remember him in his roles outside the office. We particularly remember him leaving for his masonic lodge meetings (with their "secret handshakes!") toting his Masonic apron. (I remember with fondness the annual Jack Frost parties they put on!) And how could we not feel pride in him in his role as the chairman of the Christ Church Preservation Society with its mission to restore and main-

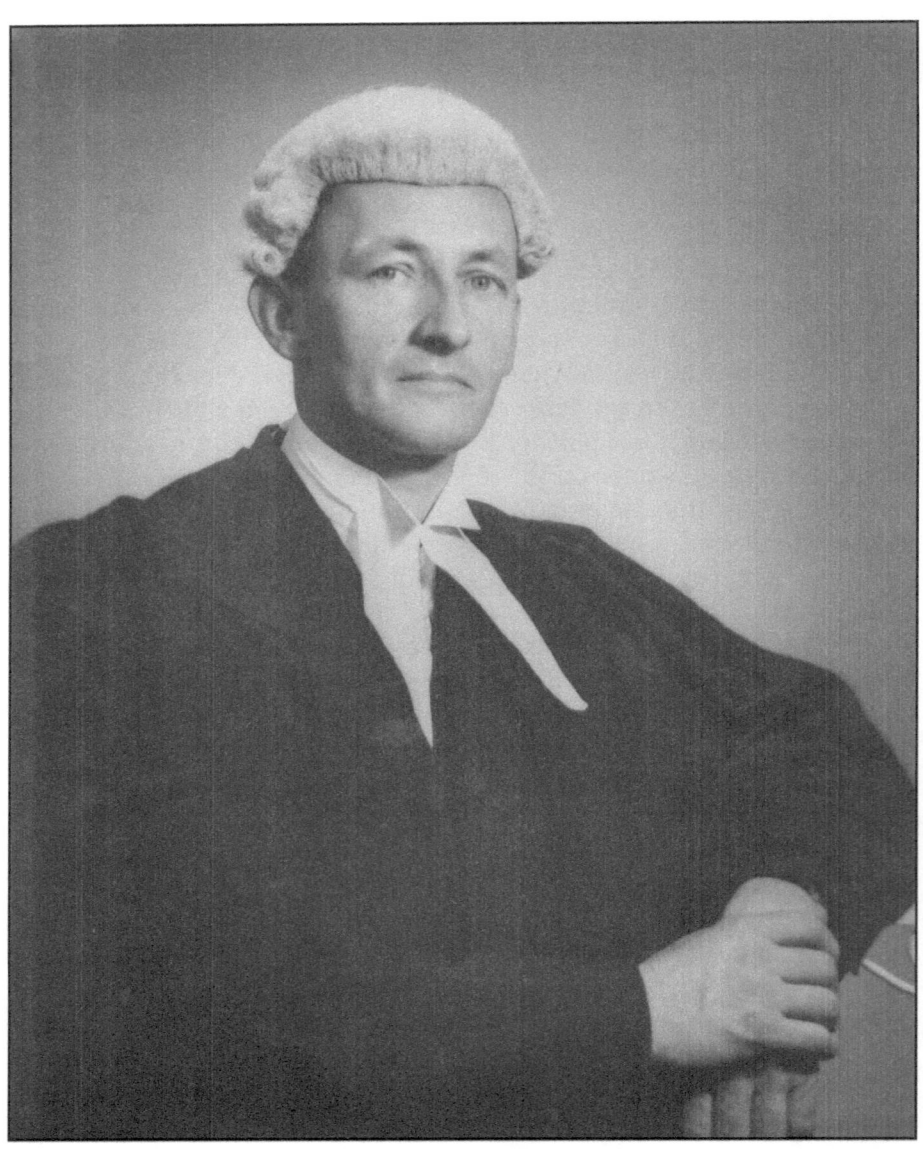

Alex's formal portrait as a young barrister.

tain the historic church and its grounds in Taita where, he, Margaret and Judith were all ultimately interred? Of course, just when we three boys assumed his wartime memories were buried, we all remember when he would come home late on ANZAC Day after a day with his wartime "cobbers" a "little merry." At those times, he could be an extreme extrovert. Conversely, we also remember him in more reflexive moments sitting contentedly with a book—a biography, or a military history—while on vacation at our Raumati beach cottage. He seemed happy then, as happy as he seemed when he was cutting the dry grass with a sickle under the summer sun, or running a lawn mower dressed only in his old army shorts and his best shoes. And will we boys ever forget the sight of his head bobbing above the surf as we dragged our net along the shoreline hoping to snag a flounder or a sole for breakfast, or how he could spontaneously open himself up in conversation with total strangers without a trace of embarrassment! But that was how he was; that is how we want to remember him. Our world is a poorer place without him.

Simon Protheroe

excerpt from
**New Zealand in the
Second World War, 1939-1945
EPISODES and STUDIES, VOLUME 2**

Panzer Grenadiers in the Senio Bridgehead

Major General Dr. Fritz Polack,[1] commander of 29 Panzer Grenadier Division, [2] felt certain by the evening of 19 December 1944 that a New Zealand attack was imminent on his Senio bridgehead near Faenza. During the previous three days the New Zealanders had been probing his defenses north-west of the town in the vicinity of the Via Emilia (Route 9) and the high railway embankment with strong fighting patrols, mostly platoons, but in some cases of company strength. That afternoon there had been an increase in traffic up the highway from the town, but his troops were unable to report its destination. Again, the enemy's artillery had not engaged in any noticeable ranging activity that day. Air reconnaissance planes had not been over the sector since the 17th. Finally, the enemy's searchlights, previously trained towards the north–west—towards Castel Bolognese—were now directed more to the north, which seemed to indicate the direction of the expected attack.

General Polack's division had been on this part of the front for only three days. The Panzer Grenadiers had recently come out of action in the Bologna sector for a rest, but the acting Army Group commander, Colonel-General Heinrich-Gottfried von Vietinghoff, [3] had found it necessary to commit them again earlier than he had intended. The British 5th Corps divisions—the 10th Indian Infantry Division and the 2nd New Zealand Division—had made substantial gains south of the Via Emilia. Only by throwing in every available man had von Vietinghoff been able to form a continuous line north-west of Faenza. The situation in the Faenza area had become grave.

Polack's division took over the front formed by 26 Panzer Division in the course of its withdrawal. His sector jutted out from the Senio River roughly in the shape of a wedge pointing at Faenza. One side of the wedge was the boundary with 278 Infantry Division, whose front ran across the ground to the immediate north of the town. On the other side were the railway embankment and the Via Emilia. The ground in the narrow bridgehead was typical Romagna country—an area of cultivated flat ground, with irrigation ditches, rows of trellised vines, trees, and groups of farm buildings. The weather at this time was distinctly

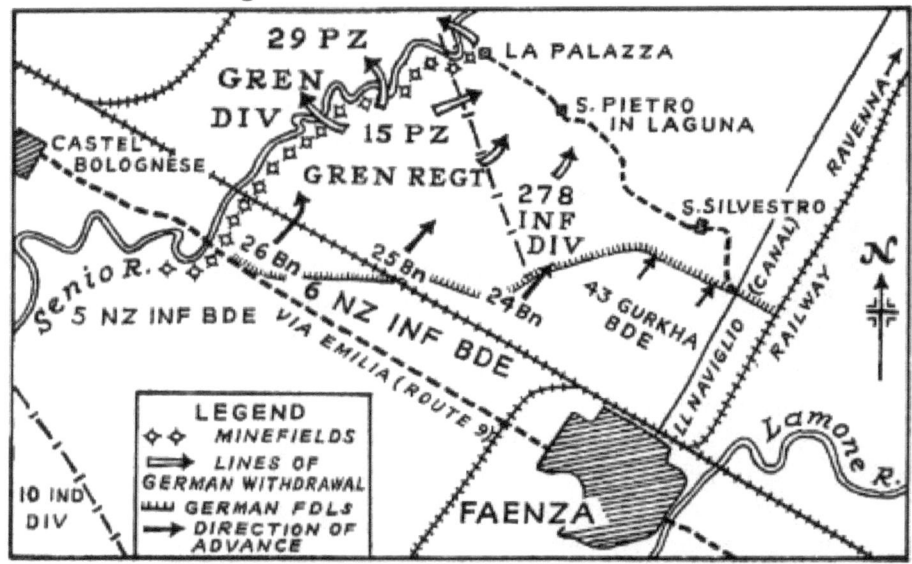

wintry. On some days there were hard frosts and weak sunshine, but mostly the days were raw and grey. There were occasional showers.

To the defense of this ground General Polack committed his 15th Panzer Grenadier Regiment, one of his three regiments of infantry. This regiment had fought the 6th NZ Infantry Brigade once before—in the heavy actions for the control of the hilltop village of San Michele in the New Zealand drive to Florence in July. The Panzer Grenadiers established their defenses in the main in and around the farm houses and buildings. Digging was carried out only to a limited extent because water was close to the surface of the heavy ground. The western bank of the Senio had already been heavily mined to protect the Irmgard defense line along the river-front. Small minefields were laid in the bridgehead.

From the outset the Panzer Grenadier Regiment put into operation a policy of aggressive defense. The thrusts of 6 NZ Brigade's 24th and 25th Battalions up the Via Emilia and to and beyond the railway embankment, and of 5 NZ Brigade's 23rd Battalion and 28th (Maori) Battalion nearer the Via Emilia crossing of the Senio, were countered by carefully planned concentrations by guns, mortars and *spandaus*, and on occasions by Panzer Grenadier counter-thrusts, assisted by Tiger tanks. These measures made conditions difficult and unpleasant for the New Zealand battalions, and at the same time cost them casualties.

The policy of aggressive defense created—as Polack intended—an impression in the minds of the New Zealand troops that the bridgehead was strongly held. This was certainly not the case. About 700 men, including supporting tanks and guns, had been put into the bridgehead at first, but on the night of the 18th, Polack, on orders from 76 Panzer Corps headquarters, withdrew about two-thirds of his troops to the western side of the Senio. The bridgehead defense was left in the charge of battle outposts only, totaling in all about one battalion of Panzer Grenadiers and supporting arms (about 200 men).[4] Polack ordered the battle outposts to cover and screen the adoption of the new positions of the regiment, to keep up plenty of activity and vigorous fire so as to deceive the enemy into thinking that the ground was held in strength, and to make a fighting withdrawal by groups over the Senio if attacked by a superior force.

Most of the men withdrawn were in their new positions on the west bank of the river by the morning of the 19th. The battle outposts left behind in the bridgehead reported a quiet day. Sixth Brigade patrols which tried to test the forward positions found the Panzer Grenadiers very much alert, and were immediately brought under well-directed *spandau* fire. Guns and mortars supporting the outpost defense lent a hand with effective bombardments of the New Zealand positions, particularly those of 25 Battalion. The New Zealanders retained the impression that the Panzer Grenadiers were still in strength on the ground beyond the embankment.

The attack Polack had been expecting opened at nine o'clock on the night of the 19th with a heavy artillery barrage. The New Zealand Division was making a full-scale set-piece assault from the Via Emilia and the railway embankment with about 1600 infantrymen—three battalions of 6 Brigade and two of the 43rd Gurkha Lorried Infantry Brigade. The fire came down on most of the 6000-yard-wide stretch of ground between the Senio and the Faenza-Ravenna railway.

The attack overlapped both the Panzer Grenadier and 278 Divisions' sectors. Eight regiments of field artillery laid down the line of creeping fire. Other field guns and about 100 medium guns sought out the bridgehead gun, mortar and headquarters positions. Heavy mortars, machine guns, and tanks assisted with diversionary and other tasks. Searchlight beams gave artificial moonlight. Red tracer shells of Bofors guns fired above the heads of the attacking infantry marked the lanes and directions of advance. The New Zealanders expected that their full-scale effort would surprise the defense. They thought it would be the cheapest way of winning the ground they wanted north of the Via Emilia and the railway embankment.

Polack's divisional artillery and mortars and the 76th Panzer Corps artillery acted with great promptitude. As no fire came down on them in the early stages of the attack, they were free to bring down the whole weight of their own fire on the New Zealanders. Heavy and accurate concentrations of shells and mortar bombs fell on the 6th Brigade's forming-up areas on the Via Emilia and the railway embankment, and on battalion areas south of the highway. The mortars caught 26 and 25 Battalions on the left and centre of the 6th Brigade front. Several men were killed; many more were wounded. Farther east, a Panzer Grenadier minefield took toll of one company of 24 Battalion, inflicting 15 casualties in one platoon. The New Zealanders' counter-battery fire against two of Polack's batteries fell on empty ground. The batteries had taken up alternative positions only an hour before the bombardment began. Even later in the night the New Zealanders' guns did not pay methodical attention to the German artillery. A thick curtain of fire came down, however, along the river line, between the new FDLs[5] and the outpost positions. It was concluded that the New Zealanders had laid this curtain to prevent Panzer Grenadier divisional reserves from moving into the bridgehead and to prevent the battle outposts withdrawing over the Senio.

For two hours the wide and deep barrage moved forward from the vicinity of the railway embankment. The guns then turned their attention to the sectors where the attack was to be made. About 11.30 p.m. the second phase began. The wall of fire crept towards the la Palazza-San Pietro-San Silvestro road. The attackers came straight ahead, following close behind the advancing line of shells. To Polack's troops it seemed that certain batteries in the barrage were firing shells with no shrapnel effect, creating safe lanes in which the New Zealand infantry could come forward immediately behind the falling shells. The terrific noise made it impossible to distinguish these shells from shrapnel.[6] The night was so pitch black that the New Zealand rifle companies were able to penetrate the battle outpost line, closing on Panzer Grenadier company and battalion headquarters while the forward outposts were still reporting 'No sign of the enemy yet'. The heavy shellfire soon cut all the telephone lines; about midnight wireless communication also failed. From 1 a.m. it became completely impossible to co-ordinate the operations of the outposts. Each outpost group was forced to act on its own initiative in accordance with the order previously given: to make a fighting withdrawal over the Senio if attacked by a superior force.

For the Panzer Grenadiers it became a matter of getting back. Old soldiers, taking their weapons with them, showed remarkable skill in making their way across the enemy-held ground, through the curtain of fire along the river and the minefields to the security of the new line on the western bank. Most of these men were back in the new line by midday on the 20th. The new soldiers—recent reinforcements—did not give so good a performance. Houses and slit trenches had given good protection even against the tremendous bombardment. Losses from shellfire had not been heavy. But the morale of many of the new men had been smashed. These were the men who did not return. General Polack thought they should have done better:

"If the enemy penetrates the positions or breaks through, there are always opportunities for men to get back from enemy-occupied territory the next day or next night. In the daylight a situation is never so hopeless as it seems at night."

About 2 a.m. the New Zealanders had closed up to their objectives towards the east bank of the Senio and along the road running southeast from la Palazza. The Gurkhas were further down the road in the San Silvestro area. The barrage ended. The attack was over. The New Zealand casualties totaled 120, most of which had been suffered when the battalions had been caught by Polack's mortars on their start lines. German prisoners totaled 180, but of this number only 86 were recorded by the New Zealanders as belonging to 15 Panzer Grenadier Regiment. The rest, it would appear, came from the neighboring 278 Infantry Division.

To Polack the whole operation was a most satisfactory success for his 15th Panzer Grenadiers. Their aggressive defense had deceived the New Zealanders into making a major attack,[7] using strong forces of infantry and wasting an enormous amount of ammunition–about 100,000 rounds.[8] Yet only about one battalion of Panzer Grenadiers was engaged. Taken by and large, the New Zealand thrust was wasted. On the morning of 20 December Polack found that his casualties and losses were fewer than ever before, and that his regiment—and the division—remained largely intact. Above all, valuable time had been gained by his division to perfect the plans for its further defense.

The Senio line remained secure until Eighth Army's final offensive in April 1945

Alex Protheroe

[1] This officer joined the German Army as an officer cadet in 1911, fought on the Western Front, and on Gallipoli with the Turkish Army. Discharged from the Army in 1920, he gained a doctorate in political economy and finally became a partner in a printing firm. In 1934 he rejoined the Army as a supplementary officer, transferring to the active list about two years later. In 1943 he was awarded the Knight's Cross as leader of a battle group in Sicily. He was promoted lieutenant-general in March 1945. His superiors' reports stated he was an excellent leader and an outstanding artilleryman.

[2] The division took part in the campaigns in Poland and France, and in 1941 went to Russia where it was virtually destroyed at Stalingrad in January 1943. It was reformed and then went to the Italian theatre, where it fought in various operations until the surrender on 2 May 1945. Its full strength was 12,000 men, and it ended the war with a strength of 5400. The division was known as the 'Falken'(Falcon) Division, and was cited three times for distinguished action.

[3] Acting in the place of Field Marshal Kesselring, who had been seriously injured when his car was involved in an accident on 23 October. Subsequently, as German Commander-in-Chief, von Vietinghoff negotiated the surrender of all German forces in Italy.

[4] When interviewed in August 1945 Polack said there were 120 men of the Division on the south bank of the Senio after the withdrawal. [This number probably does not include supporting arms.]

[5] Forward Defended Localities.

[6] As far as can be ascertained only ordinary HE shells were used in the barrage. The second phase actually followed an arranged pause.

[7] The New Zealanders knew that there had been a withdrawal by troops of 278 Infantry Division from the northern outskirts of Faenza, but up to the moment of the attack they did not really know whether 15 Panzer Grenadier Regiment 'was falling back now or not, but at any rate it was too late to do anything'.

[8] 'We counted 94,000 shells in three and a half hours', Polack later told a New Zealand officer. In point of fact, the Allied artillery could ill afford to expend large quantities of ammunition at this time.
The German sources used are:

- '29 Panzer Grenadier Division Report on Fighting on the Italian Front, 16-20 December 1944', incorporated in a pamphlet entitled 'Preparations for Defensive Campaign in 1945' issued by the Commander-in-Chief, South-West.
- Daily reports of Commander-in-Chief, South-West, to OKH (High Command of the German Army), December 1944.
- (29 Panzer Grenadier Division in Italy—GOC's reminiscences.' (Recorded by a New Zealand Archives officer.)
- War diary of 10th Army.
- Personal reports on German officers.

Timeline: 1944-46

Location	Date	Event
Taranto	16 March, Thursday	Arrival
Bari	12 April, Monday	Moving north
Cassino	17 April, Wednesday	Arrival at front, first experience of action
Cassino	30 April, Sunday	Medical evacuation from front
Bari	9 May, Tuesday	Begins recuperation
Riardo/Arce	15 June, Thursday	Heading north again
Arezzo	12 July, Wednesday	Heading for back to action
Castiglion Fiorentino, near Arezzo, Tuscany	14 July, Friday	Begin shelling German positions
near Siena	21 July, Friday	New positions taken further up the line
Rome	22-24 July Saturday-Monday	Weekend R & R
Florence area	25 July, Tuesday	Action on and around Gothic Line west of Florence
Castellana, near Siena	15 August, Tuesday	Begin move across to Adriatic front
Follonica	22 August, Tuesday	Weekend R & R on the coast
Iesi, Fano, & Adriatic front	26 August, Saturday	Strategic relocation completed on east, resumes action against enemy
Rastia, Fabriano	25 October, Wednesday	Regrouping behind the lines in Le Marche region
Forli/Faenza area, Emilio Romagna	19 November, Sunday	Return to line and action
Florence	8-15 January, 1945, Monday-Monday	R&R along the Arno

Timeline: 1944-46

Location	Date	Event
Faenza	16 January, Tuesday	Resumes duties on line
Castelraimondo	5 March, Monday	Return to Le Marche for training/maintenance
Faenza	1 April, Easter Sunday	Return to action at Faenza
Senio River	9 April, Monday	Major offensive begins
Padova	29 April, Sunday	Collapse of German forces
Venice	30 April, Monday	Daylight excursion to the city
Trieste	2 May, Wednesday	Germany forces in Italy surrender
Grado, Gulf of Trieste	21 May, Monday	Hospitalized with infection
Location unknown	29 May, Friday	Airlifted to British Army hospital for surgery
Mola di Bari	6 July, Friday	Moved to southern Italy, begins at ERS (Education and Rehabilitation Services) first in journalism, then teaching history
Rome	18-26 August, Saturday to Sunday	R & R in the Eternal City
Chianciano	1 October, Monday	R & R at spa in Tuscany
Port Said, Egypt	13 January, 1946, Sunday	Returning home